Anonymous

The Leading business men of Dover, Rochester, Farmington, Great Falls and Berwick

Anonymous

The Leading business men of Dover, Rochester, Farmington, Great Falls and Berwick

ISBN/EAN: 9783337713287

Printed in Europe, USA, Canada, Australia, Japan

Cover: Foto ©ninafisch / pixelio.de

More available books at **www.hansebooks.com**

LEADING BUSINESS MEN

OF

DOVER, ROCHESTER,

FARMINGTON,

GREAT FALLS AND BERWICK.

ILLUSTRATED.

BOSTON :

MERCANTILE PUBLISHING COMPANY,

No. 258 Purchase Street.

1890.

[*See last pages for Index to Business Notices.*]

DOVER

AND ITS POINTS OF INTEREST

INTRODUCTORY.

Nearly three centuries have elapsed since the territory now included within Dover's limits was first visited by white men ; and this vast period of time has been so crowded with incident, has witnessed so many stirring and decisive events and has brought about so great a number of radical changes in modes of government, manners of living, habits of thought, and methods employed in manufacturing and in commerce, that even were this brief sketch to be so extended that it would fill a goodly volume it would still be but an incomplete record of the doings which have transformed a howling wilderness into one of the most important, flourishing and beautiful cities in New Hampshire. The Seventeenth Century had but barely opened when the expedition, which was to number among its results the first visitation by civilized man of this region, left England, for it was the tenth day of April, 1603, that two tiny vessels sailed from the port of Bristol, sent out by the enterprising merchants of that place on a voyage of discovery and exploration. Tiny indeed were these vessels—so tiny in fact that both of them could easily be stored in a corner of the hold of one of the great steamships now so common, for the larger vessel was of but fifty tons burden while her companion was only half that capacity. But, small as they were, they reached the shore of the new world in safety under the skillful captain-ship of Martin Pring, and from them a boat expedition was sent up the Pascataqua River for a distance of twelve miles or so. "Very goodly groves and woods and sundry sorts of beasts" were seen by the little band of explorers, but no attempt to found a settlement was made, the purpose of their errand being merely to gain an idea of "the lay of the land."

Eleven years later, or March 3, 1614, no less a personage than Capt. John Smith, of Pocahontas fame embarked from London and reached Monhegan on the thirtieth day of the following month. After arriving at this point he built seven boats, and in one of these, accompanied by eight men, he entered the Pascataqua. At this time there was not, so far as is known, a single European residing at any point on the long coast line extending from Plymouth to the French settlement on the island of Mount Desert, although scattered along it at sparse intervals were places temporarily visited by fishermen. This state of affairs continued for nearly a decade after Smith's visit, the time and manner of its termination being stated in Hubbard's " History of New England " thus :

THE FIRST SETTLEMENT.

"Some merchants and other gentlemen in the west of England, belonging to the cities of Exeter, Bristol, Shrewsbury, and the towns of Plymouth, Dorchester, etc., . . . having obtained patents for several parts of the country of New England, . . . made some attempts at beginning a plantation in some place about the Pascataqua River about the year 1623. . . . They sent over

RESIDENCE OF EX-GOVERNOR SAWYER.

that year one Mr. David Thompson, with Mr. Edward Hilton and his brother, Mr. William Hilton, who had been fishmongers in London, with some others that came along with them, furnished with necessaries for carrying on a plantation there. Possibly some others might be sent after them in the years following, 1624 and 1625, some of whom first, in probability, seized on a place called the Little Harbour, on the west side of Pascataqua River, towards or at the mouth thereof ; the Hiltons in the meanwhile setting up their stages higher up the river towards the north-west, at or about a place since called Dover."

The accuracy of the above statement has been questioned, particularly that portion of it which gives the year of settlement as 1623, but the author was certainly in a position to gather and preserve authentic information relative to the history of those times for he was the Reverend William Hubbard, a graduate of Harvard in 1642, and a learned and careful historian, who not only made free use of all available records but also of the abundant opportunities he possessed for consulting the early settlers, and in this latter connection it is worthy of note that when Mr. Hubbard was officiating as a minister in Ipswich, in 1658, Dover's original settler, Edward Hilton, was living near Exeter, less than a day's journey distant. But happily it is no longer necessary to depend upon mere probabilities to establish the date of Dover's settlement, for a few years ago there was discovered among the files of Suffolk Court, an original document which determines it beyond a reasonable doubt. This paper is in the form of a petition for a confirmation of a sale of territory made by Tahanto, Sagamore of Penacook, in 1636, to William Hilton, Sr., and his son, William Hilton, Jr., the petitioner. The petition was presented in 1660, and fully covers the point at issue as will be seen by the following extract :

" *Whereas*, your petitioner's father, William Hilton, came over into New England about the yeare Anno : Dom : 1621, & yor petitioner came about one yeare & an halfe after, and in a little tyme following settld ourselves upon the River of Pascataq with Mr. Edw. Hilton, who were the first English planters there—"

The petitioner was a nephew of Edward Hilton and bore a high reputation for integrity. It is known that his father came to Plymouth in the ship *Fortune*, November 11, 1621, and that his wife and children followed in July or August, 1623, or in other words after an interval of about a year and a half, as stated in the petition. Thus the evidence is conclusive that Edward Hilton settled at Dover in 1623, and as such is the fact Dover is entitled to the honor of being the first settled town in New Hampshire, and Hilton to the distinction of having been the first permanent settler in the State.

The exact locality of the original settlement is not positively known, that is to say it is not established by record, but tradition places it at the extreme southern point of Dover, and authorities very generally agree that this tradition is worthy of credence. Certainly a more advantageous spot could not have been selected, for it was easy of access by waterways, which always form the chief and often the only means of communication in a virgin and wooded country ; the broad expanse of water on all sides but one rendered it practically impossible for the savages to approach in any considerable force unseen, and the great abundance of fish, so easily available at certain seasons, afforded an unlimited and invaluable food-supply which insured the settlers against that famine which was a by no means uncommon experience of New England pioneers less fortunately located. From an æsthetic point of view, also, the choice was a wise one, for the scenery is beautiful and varied in this region which is now a popular summer resort.

ST. THOMAS' CHURCH AND LAFAYETTE'S HEADQUARTERS.

Despite these advantages of location the work of settlement proceeded very slowly, Hubbard stating that in 1631 "there were but three houses in all that part of the country adjoining the Pascataqua River. There had also been some expense about salt works."

The title under which Edward Hilton and his associates in England held their lands was somewhat vague and unsatisfactory so they made application to have it more specifically defined. All the territory on this continent between the fortieth and the forty-eighth degrees of north latitude was controlled by an organization generally called the "Plymouth Council," which held and disposed of the lands within these limits by virtue of letters patent received from the King, November 3, 1606, and it was this body which made the grant desired by the Dover settlers and those associated with them. It was issued March 12, 1630, and as all the land titles in Dover and several neighboring towns proceed from it it is of sufficient interest to warrant our giving it almost verbatim :

" Now know yee that the said President & Councell by Virtue & Authority of his Majties said Letters Patents, and for and in consideracon that Edward Hilton & his Associates hath already at his and their owne proper costs and charges transported sundry servants to plant in New England aforesaid at a place there called by the natives Wecanacohunt otherwise Hiltons' point lying som two leagues from the mouth of the River Pascataquack in New England aforesaid where they have already Built som houses, and planted Corne, And for that he doth further intend by God's Divine Assistance, to transport thither more people and cattle, to the good increase and advancement & for the better settling and strengthing of their plantacon as also that they may be better encouraged to proceed in soe pious a work which may Especially tend to the propagacon of Religion and to the Great Increase of Trade to his Majties Realmes and Dominions, and to the advancement of publique plantacon, Have given granted Enfeoffed and Confirmed, and by this their p'sent writing doe fully clearly and absolutely give grant enfeoffe and confirm unto the said Edward Hilton his heires and assignes for ever, all that part of the River Pascataquack called or known by the name of Wecanacohunt or Hiltons' Point with the south side of the said River, up to the ffall of the River, and three miles into the Maine Land by all the breadth aforesaid. Together with all the Shoares, Creeks, Bays Harbors and Coasts, alongst the sea within the limits and Bounds aforesaid with the woods and Islands next adjoyneing to the said Lands, not being already granted by the said Councell unto any other person or persons together alsoe with all the Lands River mines Minerals of what kinde or nature soever, woods Quarries, Marshes, Waters, Lakes, ffishings, Huntings, Hawkings ffowlings, Comodities Emolumts and hereditaments whatsoever withall and singular their or to the said Lands lying within the same Limits or Bounds belonging or in any wise appertaining . . . unto the said Edward Hilton his heires, Associates and Assignes forever to the onely proper use and behoof of the said Edward Hilton his heires Associates & Assignes for ever, yielding and paying unto our Soveraigne Lord the King one fifth part of Gold and Silver Oares, and another fifth part to the Councell aforesaid and their successors to be holden of the said Councell and their successors by the rent hereafter in these p'sents Reserved, yielding and paying therefor yearly for ever unto the said Councell their successors or Assignes for every hundred Acres of the said Land in use the sume of twelve pence of Lawfull money of England into the hands of the Rent gatherers for the time being of the said Councell yr successors or Assignes for all services whatsoever."

Nearly a year and a half elapsed before the actual delivery of the land, this ceremony being performed July 7, 1631, by Thomas Lewis, acting under power of attorney from the Council. It was delivered on the premises, the witnesses being Thomas Wiggin, William Hilton, Samuel Sharpe, and James Downe.

No record appears of any history of the Dover settlement during the time between the date of the grant and the formal delivery of the land, and indeed the records of the early history of this colony are exceptionally meagre and unsatisfactory, especially when compared with those of the Plymouth and Massachusetts Bay colonies, and the reason of this difference is plain. Men possessed of peculiar ideas and identified with a movement resulting from them, naturally take care to see that full and clear records are made of the origin and progress of that movement, that their ways may be justified and their convictions and sacrifices appreciated by their successors, and in time, by all mankind. Then again, the history of such an undertaking cannot but be of peculiar interest to the student of humanity and must of necessity contain more of romance and of unusual happenings than the history of an enterprise carried on by those seeking to better merely their worldly position, and so actuated by the commonplace motives which animate people in general. The Pilgrims of Plymouth and the Puritans of Massachusetts Bay did not leave the old country because they could not gain a satisfactory livelihood there, or because they thought the New World offered more opportunities for the accumulation of wealth, but because they sought that liberty of conscience which was denied them in England ; but while this motive was common to them both there was one essential point of difference between them which is now generally overlooked, the result being that Puritan and Pilgrim are almost synonymous terms in the popular mind, the only distinction made being that the Puritans settled at one point on the coast and the Pilgrims at another.   Yet their convictions were radically different, for the Pilgrims felt themselves obliged to separate entirely from the Church of England and to discountenance its existence, while the Puritans recognized that church but had conscientious scruples concerning some of its ceremonies.   The New Hampshire colonists belonged to neither party. They held no peculiar ideas concerning Church or State and had no theories of temporal or spiritual

CENTRAL AVENUE, LOOKING SOUTH.

government differing from those accepted in England, their only object in braving the dangers and discomforts of life in the wilderness being the acquisition of wealth.   Of course this motive was mixed with various others, such as a liking for a life of adventure and an ambition to gain a social position denied to many of them in the Old World ; but they were guided in their affairs and encouraged in their efforts by no dominating, conscientious conviction peculiar to themselves, and so the early historians gave but little heed to their enterprises and the records now extant have mostly to do with the number of beaver skins and other furs obtained from the Indians, the amount of fish cured for the English market, and other prosaic happenings.

The most prominent man among those witnessing the delivery of the lands to Edward Hilton was Captain Thomas Wiggin, who probably represented the Bristol merchants who had taken that portion now comprised within Dover's limits as their own. He returned to England the following year to get men and means to carry on the work of settlement but proceedings were delayed on account of negotiations for the sale of the property, they being brought to a successful conclusion in 1633. The Bristol men disposed of their interests for the sum of 2150 pounds, and it is said that the purchasers were the Puritan Lords, Say and Brook, George Willys and William Whiting, but there were evidently others besides these judging from the subsequent records relating to the property. This change in ownership brought about a change also in the religious auspices under which the colony was conducted, for Edward Hilton was an adherent of the Church of England, while his successor, Captain Thomas Wiggin, was of Puritan sympathies. He is spoken of in a letter written June 22, 1633, to Governor Winthrop, of Massachusetts, as follows :

First Parish Church.

"Before I end, I must not forgett to put you in minde of one that is cominge to you, whoe hath deserved exceedingly of your father & the plantation, many wayes ; he discovered (under God) our enemies plotts, & helpt to prevent them ; he hath also dispossest our enemies of their hope, Pascataqua, and intends to plant him selfe and many gracious men there this sommer. Noe doubt but this may be and wil be by diverse in this shipp reported to you ; but out of the mouth of diverse witnesses the truth is confirmed. I have, and you all have cause to blesse God that you have soe good a neighbour as Capt. Wiggin."

October 10, 1633, Wiggin landed at Salem, Mass., with "about thirty" colonists for Dover, "some of whom were of good estate and of some account for religion," and the party proceeded without delay to the settlement at Hilton's Point. They were accompanied by Rev. William Leverich, "an able and worthy Puritan Minister," and a meeting-house was built the following year, or in 1634, so that this parish has the honor of being the first to be established in New Hampshire. Captain Wiggin did not long remain in control of the colony, being succeeded in 1637 by Rev. George Burdett, who was made Governor by agreement of the people who were otherwise destitute of civil government, as the corporation under whose auspices the settlement was being developed had been organized merely for planting and trading purposes and had no governing powers.

About December, 1638, he was succeeded by Captain John Underhill, who came to Dover that year on account of his being banished from the Massachusetts Bay Colony. Underhill was a brave soldier but appears to have been unprincipled and utterly untrustworthy, both in private and public life.

Underhill was succeeded as chief magistrate by Thomas Roberts, ancestor of the very large family of that name to be found throughout New Hampshire and Maine.

The Pascataqua plantations came under the jurisdiction of Massachusetts in 1641, this change being made with the full consent of the people, as important concessions were made to individuals and

to the towns, and the colonists (those of Dover especially) were tired of the confusion arising from
the contests of those favoring and those opposing annexation. They knew that no effective resistance
could be made if Massachusetts sought to gain her end by force of arms, and, as they made excellent
terms (Massachusetts granting everything in exchange for the simple title of sovereignty,) their
their course was undoubtedly the wisest one that could have been taken. The Pascataqua towns
remained under Massachusetts jurisdiction for nearly forty years, and so fully were their rights
respected and so much did they prosper while this state of affairs continued that the majority of the
people were reluctant to accept the mandate which made New Hampshire a royal province and severed
their connection with Massachusetts.

The thirty years following the annexation of Dover to Massachusetts was comparatively

MORRILL BLOCK, FRANKLIN SQUARE.

uneventful, but this period was to be followed by one the like of which the colony had never known
for they had thus far lived at peace with the Indians, who had cordially welcomed the early settlers;
but long-continued abuse, cheating and contempt of the redskins by many of the colonists at last had
their natural effect, and in 1675 the first general war with the Indians commenced, the first blood-shed
occurring at Oyster River, in September of that year.

Interesting and romantic as the history of these Indian troubles is and important as was their
influence upon the fortunes of the colony, we cannot give them even passing notice as the exigencies of
space compel us to proceed at once to the events attending the birth of the present Dover, for old as
the town is in one sense, in another it is comparatively young, for it was truly "born again" after the
advent of the manufacturing enterprises which inspired it with such life and vigor that in a few years

it caught up with and passed by every town in New Hampshire but one, Dover being second only to Portsmouth in population for nearly a score of years.

The last year in which Dover blood was shed upon Dover soil was in 1725, during the French and Indian War, but many of the townspeople lost their lives during the Revolution, for the people were heart and soul in favor of that war and were well represented in the Continental armies. The population of the town in 1776 was less than it had been in 1700, being but 1666, and at the close of the Revolution it was still less and the town, and in fact the entire country, was poor, much in debt, and struggling against the many disadvantages of a worthless currency. The effects of the war continued long after the close of the struggle, but soon after the establishment of the Constitution the industries and commerce of the country began to revive, although years elapsed before Dover began to feel the full benefits of the new order of things. The first United States census, taken just a century ago, in 1790, found Dover with a population of 1998, an increase of 132 in fifteen years, and the result of the census of 1800 was even more discouraging, while that of 1810 was but little better,

FRANKLIN SQUARE, DOVER.

and that of 1820 indicated slow progress, but from 1820 to 1830 the old town "made up for lost time" in a most decided manner, and progress was so rapid and pronounced thereafter that in 1855 it was deemed necessary to have a city charter in order that the business of voting could be carried out in one day, instead of extending over two or three as was frequently the result of the unwieldy town organization, and in order that all public business might be more efficiently and promptly transacted.

At this time the area of Dover was practically the same as now, it having been greatly reduced from the original township which included the present City of Dover, Somersworth, Rollinsford, Durham, Wadbury, Lee, Newington and probably a part of Greenland. A small portion of the lower eastern end of Rollinsford was restored to Dover in 1879.

DOVER AS A CITY.

The act incorporating the City of Dover was signed June 29, 1855, and the charter was accepted by the townspeople at a meeting held August 15, 1855, the first mayor taking the oath of office and the city government being inaugurated March 25, 1856.

The great increase in wealth and population which caused the town government after an existence of 222 years to be superseded by a city organization, was chiefly brought about by the cotton industry which had its origin here in 1812, when the Dover Cotton Factory was incorporated with a capital of $50,000, this company building a factory two miles above the Lower Falls, as it was then thought that the power at the latter point was fully taken up by the saw and grist mills there located. This establishment was long known as the Upper Factory and was not so successful as its projectors had supposed it would be ; but they had strong faith in the future of the cotton industry and in 1821 they

CENTRAL SQUARE, DOVER.

extended their operations very considerably, obtaining control of the Lower Falls and building the first cotton mill erected in the village ; the capital of the company having been increased to $500,000. It was again increased, June 17, 1823, to $1,000,000 and the name of the corporation was changed from the "Dover Cotton Factory" to the "Dover Manufacturing Company," a third increase of capital being made June 20, 1826 when it became $1,500,000. The company failed to make the enterprise profitable, however, and was succeeded by a corporation which still exists and which has made the undertaking one of the most extensive and best-known of the kind in the world. This is the "Cocheco Manufacturing Company," incorporated June 27, 1827, with a capital of $1,500,000, and now operating five mills and manufacturing some 32,000,000 yards of cloth per annum. Connected with this enterprise are the Cocheco Print Works ; their product amounting to about 50,000,000 yards per annum ; the two establishments consuming 12,000 bales of cotton a year. Employment is given to 2,000 operatives and the monthly pay-roll amounts to $50,000. The plant of machinery in these mills includes 100,000 spindles and 2,443 looms.

Some conception of the effect which the establishment of cotton manufacturing and of other industries had upon the town may be gained by comparing the increase in population in the years following their introduction with that of previous years. In 1790 the population of Dover was 1998 ; in 1800 it was 2062, a gain of 64 in ten years. In 1810 it had become 2228, a gain of 166, and in 1820 it was 2871, a gain of 643. But during the decade following, or that in which the cotton business was founded, there was an increase in population of almost 100 per cent., the number of inhabitants in 1830 being 5449, or 2578 more than in 1820. And the increase in wealth was even more decided, for the taxable property more than doubled in amount and the legitimate consequence of the era of prosperity which had dawned upon the community was to be seen in the many new streets which had been laid out, the new bridges which had been built, the hundreds of new dwelling houses which had been constructed, and the new church edifices which had been erected. Nor were these the only results of the changed condition of affairs. This same decade witnessed the opening of the Dover Bank and of the Savings Bank of the County of Strafford, the incorporation of the Dover Aqueduct Company and

CENTRAL AVENUE, DOVER, LOOKING NORTH.

the establishment of two newspapers, the *Gazette* and the *Inquirer*, making three local publications of this kind, as the *Dover Sun* had been founded some thirty years before.

From 1830 to 1840 the growth of the town was by no means so large as during the preceding decade, but this check in progress was not confined to Dover for the whole country was injuriously affected by the conditions then prevailing. There was great uncertainty as to the action of the government on the nullification and tariff questions, disastrous speculations in Eastern land had shaken confidence and unsettled values, and this condition of affairs was aggravated by the suspension of specie payments and the subsequent financial panics which destroyed some great business enterprises, crippled many more and caused capital to be as timid as it had formerly been venturesome.

The gain in population from 1840 to 1850 was almost double that of the preceding ten years it being 1728, making the total number of inhabitants 8186. This decade witnessed the advent of the railway, which worked great changes in the business of the town. As a whole these changes were beneficial but individual enterprises suffered and in some cases were utterly destroyed, notably that conducted by the Dover Packet Company, which had been in successful operation for many years as it furnished the sole means of intercourse between Dover and the business world and so transported all the freight to and from the town. Many vessels were utilized and at one time Dover's commerce with Boston was greater than that of any other place east of New York, Portsmouth excepted. Naturally "the Landing" had long been the centre of business but later the opening of the Boston & Maine Railroad, in 1841, and the building, a few years later, of the Cocheco Railroad to Alton, business deserted the Landing gradually and established itself convenient to the railroad. Within the past ten or twelve years the shipping interests of Dover have revived and a large, well-equipped fleet of coasting vessels now sail from this port.

RESIDENCE OF JONATHAN SAWYER, ESQ.

Dover's importance as a distributing point for trade in the interior declined very materially, of course, after the building of the railroads, but this was more than compensated for by the development of local interests.

But little gain in population was made from 1850 to 1860, the increase being but 316, but during this period the town became a city and many valuable improvements were inaugurated, such as the use of gas in the houses and streets, better sidewalks and roadways, a police court and a more prompt and efficient enforcing of the laws.

In 1870 the population had become 9,874, showing an increase of 1,372 during the decade, and in 1880 the figures were 11,693, a gain of 1,819 in ten years. By the census of 1890 Dover has a population of 12,790, showing an increase of 1,093 and proving that she is fully maintaining her position among New Hampshire cities.

As has before been stated, the rapid development of Dover during the years immediately preceding and following the adoption of a city charter, was not due entirely to the cotton industry but to the combined effects of this and other branches of manufacture, prominent among the latter being the woolen industry which was established here by Alfred I. Sawyer, founder of the enterprise now carried on by the Sawyer Woolen Company and known throughout the country.

The boot and shoe industry has been and is another potent factor in the building up of the town and city, it having attained large proportions since its introduction in 1847. In fact, when the business is good, more hands are employed in this than in any other local industry and the very magnitude of the trade prevents our giving it the attention it deserves, for were we to make anything like detailed mention of each of the houses engaged in it, the limits of our space would be far exceeded. As far back as 1854 there were eight shoe factories in town, some of which were very large for that period, and at the present time Dover has some establishments of this kind that will compare favorably with any in the State.

Boots and shoes are not the only leather goods that are manufactured in Dover on a very large scale, for the firm of Isaac B. Williams & Sons are extensively engaged in the production of leather belting and lacings, they operating one of the largest factories of the kind in the country.

The banks of Dover have rendered such efficient aid in developing the resources of the city, that the history of each and all of them will well repay careful study.

The educational facilities of Dover are excellent and the history of their origin and development is very interesting, but the necessity of keeping this sketch within its assigned limits compels us to pass it by. Franklin Academy, incorporated in 1805, has a high reputation and numbers among its graduates many men who have won distinction in public, professional and business life. The public schools are liberally supported and efficiently conducted, so that by no means the least of Dover's many advantages as a place of residence is the opportunity afforded to give one's children a sound, practical and thorough education.

The Church societies of the city embrace nearly all the more prominent religious sects, and many commodious church edifices adorn the streets.

Fraternal and benevolent societies are also well represented, the Masons being especially numerous and influential. Orphan Council, No. 1, was organized April 23, 1832, and has the honor of being the oldest council in the State. The Odd Fellows, Knights of Pythias, Knights of Honor, and other prominent societies have large memberships and do much to promote sociability and alleviate distress.

It is just about a century since the first newspaper published in Dover appeared, and the history of the many journalistic failures and successes since that time would make a large but very interesting volume. The great political parties have for some years been very ably represented in this city by daily as well as by weekly publications, and as regards devotion to the interests of all people, literary merit, enterprise, circulation and advertising patronage, the Dover newspaper press will not suffer by comparison with that of any other New Hampshire city.

No mention has been made in this sketch of the advantages offered by Dover as a purchasing center, for these are very fully set forth in the pages devoted to description of the more prominent mercantile and manufacturing enterprises, the high standing of which in comparison with those of other communities, conclusively proves that the conditions under which operations are carried on here are, on the whole, exceptionally favorable.

New enterprises, and particularly new manufacturing enterprises, will be cordially welcomed by the people, both in their private and in their corporate capacity, and the natural and other advantages offered are such as may well attract those contemplating the establishment of new plants or the removal of those now established under unfavorable conditions. Dover is an excellent city to live in as well as to do business in, and judging from present indications her development during the next ten years will have made her more prominent than ever among New Hampshire cities when the opening of the twentieth century finds her well on her way towards her three hundredth birthday.

LEADING BUSINESS MEN OF DOVER.

Dover Clothing Co., Clothiers and Merchant Tailors; W. S. Bradley, Proprietor. 436 and 438 Central Avenue, Dover, N. H.—The Dover Clothing Company began operations in 1880, and during the past decade have built up a business which is remarkable alike for its magnitude and its scope. The great secret of this company's general popularity lies in the fact that all classes of trade are catered to with equal care and ability. They will make you as choice a custom garment as any tailor in New England, and they will furnish you with a strong, durable garment at a very low price, for working wear; and in either case will give full value for every dollar received and spare no pains to satisfy you fully in every respect. Extensive facilities, broad experience, and exceptional executive ability are essential to the successful carrying out of so liberal and comprehensive a policy, and the fact that it *is* successfully carried out proves that none of these conditions are wanting. Mr. W. S. Bradley, the proprietor of this representative enterprise, is a native of Fairfield, Vt., and is widely and favorably known in business circles throughout this section of the State. He gives close supervision to the various departments of the undertaking, and has the business so thoroughly systematized that the responsibility for any mistake can be easily placed—and as a consequence, mistakes are of very rare occurrence. From six to ten assistants are employed in the store, and from twenty to fifty in the workrooms; so that despite the magnitude of the business callers are assured prompt and careful attention and all orders can be filled at short notice. The premises utilized comprise two floors and a basement, each measuring 40 × 90 feet, and a large proportion of this extensive space is taken up by the heavy stock of clothing, gentlemen's furnishings, hats, caps, etc., which is complete in every department and comprises the latest fashionable novelties. Goods are cheerfully shown, and visitors to Dover as well as residents of that city should make it a point to call at 436 and 438 Central Avenue, and examine as clean and desirable a stock of clothing and furnishings as can be found in the State.

Thomas H. Dearborn & Co., dealers in Foreign and Domestic Dry Goods, 452 and 454 Central Avenue, Dover, N. H.—It would require much more space than we have at our command to properly describe the stock carried by Messrs. Thomas H. Dearborn & Co., at their spacious establishment, Nos. 452 and 454 Central avenue, and even if we had the necessary space such a description would be of doubtful utility, for however accurate it might be at the time of writing it would be deficient before it reached our readers, for the firm in question make a practice of giving their customers an opportunity to choose from the latest novelties, and as a necessary consequence their stock is constantly being renewed in one department or another. They deal in foreign and domestic dry goods of every description, and two floors of the dimensions of 90 × 45 feet each are required to accommodate the heavy stock carried. The handling of cloaks, shawls, etc., forms an important department of the business, and a very varied and desirable assortment of these articles is always on hand to select from. This firm was organized in 1884, the partners being Mr. Thomas H. Dearborn, a native of Northfield, N. H., and Mr. Frank N. French, a native of Exeter, N. H. Both these gent'emen are thoroughly familiar with the dry goods business, and give their enterprise careful personal supervision, maintaining the service at the very highest standard of efficiency. Employment is given to ten competent assistants, and we need hardly add that prompt and polite attention is assured to every caller. From the very beginning, the policy of the firm has been to offer thoroughly dependable goods at the very lowest market rates, and that such methods are appreciated is proved by the extensive and steadily increasing patronage.

Clark & Aldrich, New and Second-hand Furniture and Musical Instruments, Auctioneers. No. 403 Central Avenue, Dover, N. H.—The establishment conducted by Messrs. Clark & Aldrich at No. 403 Central avenue, is popular among both buyers and sellers, for the firm deal largely in new and second hand furniture, musical instruments, etc. "Picture-framing" is also done in the best possible manner at this establishment. Messrs. Clark & Aldrich do a commission business, selling articles at auction and at private sale, and keeping the best of faith with their customers at all times. This enterprise was inaugurated a good many years ago, and in 1881 came under the control of Messrs. J. W. Foss & Co., who were succeeded by the present owners in 1890. Mr. F. G. Clark is a native of this city, and Mr. B. S. Aldrich, of Whitefield, N. H., both these gentlemen giving close personal attention to the supervision of affairs, and sparing no pains to assure prompt and satisfactory attention to every caller. The premises utilized are 20 × 75 feet in dimensions, and as they comprise one floor and a basement, opportunity is given to carry a large and varied stock. There is no establishment in town where a dollar will go farther in the purchase of dependable goods, and the assortment is sufficiently varied to suit all tastes and all purses. Money will be loaned on personal property at moderate rates, and all such business can be quickly and privately transacted.

Converse & Hammond, wholesale and retail dealers in Eastern and Western Long and Short Lumber, Lime, Cement, Calcined and Ground Plaster, Roofing, Slate, Fire Brick, Kaolin, Plastering Hair, Plum Island Sand, Super-Phosphates, Guano and Ground Bone; General Agents for E. Frank Coe's Super-Phosphates; 17 Cocheco Street, Dover, N. H.—The undertaking carried on under the firm-name of Converse & Hammond was founded in 1874, by Messrs. Converse & Blaisdell, who in 1876 were succeeded by Mr. J. Converse, he giving place to Messrs. Converse & Hobbs in 1878. In 1883 Messrs. Converse & Wood assumed control and in 1884 the existing firm name was adopted, it being still retained although Mr. Converse retired in 1889, his interest being taken by Mr. A. C. Place, a native of

New Hampshire, who is associated with Mr. M. B. Hammond, a native of Albion, Maine. The firm utilize extensive premises located at the head of navigation and comprising numerous storehouses and ample yard room, for a very heavy and varied stock is carried, made up of Eastern and Western long and short lumber, lime, cement, calcined and ground plaster, roofing slate, fire brick, kaolin, plastering hair, Plum Island sand, super phosphates, ground bone and guano. They do both a wholesale and retail business and are general agents for E. Frank Coe's Super-Phosphates, which are generally conceded by practical men everywhere to have no superiors in the market. The firm are in a position to quote bottom prices on the many commodities handled, and to fill the most extensive orders at very short notice. The office is at No. 17 Cocheco street, and as it has telephone connection, orders can be sent without trouble from any point in this vicinity.

D. Lothrop & Co., Jobbers and Retailers of Pianos, Organs and Sewing Machines, Dover, N. H. Importers and Publishers, Boston, Mass.—The story of the origin and development of the many important enterprises conducted by Messrs. D. Lothrop & Co., is of exceptional interest, but to do it justice would require much more space than the necessity of keeping this book within reasonable limits places at our disposal, and we regret this the less from feeling assured that the large majority of our Dover readers are already familiar with the more salient facts in the case. Were a novelist to present as characters three brothers, each active, enterprising and self reliant, each having strong individuality, and each a man of affairs as well as of business, and represent them as agreeing to combine fortunes and share equal profits while carrying on widely distinct enterprises, and finally represent them as implicitly keeping this agreement for more than forty years, his characters would be criticized as utterly impracticable, and yet this is the state of affairs in the firm of D. Lothrop & Co. The partners are Daniel, James E. and John C. Lothrop, all of whom are natives of Rochester, N. H. As importers and publishers the firm have an international reputation, and the members of it are also largely interested in the drug business, and the clothing business, but the present article is confined to a consideration of an enterprise which, although of quite recent origin as compared with their other undertakings, has developed so rapidly and continuously as to have become the largest of its kind in the State if not in New England. We refer to the jobbing and retailing of pianos, organs, music and musical merchandise, and sewing machines. The firm began to handle these goods in 1873 and a very fortunate venture it has proved to be—fortunate not only for the proprietors but also for the purchasing public, who find at this establishment a full selection of thoroughly reliable articles offered at the lowest market rates. The premises made use of comprise two floors, of the respective dimensions of 20 × 80 and 24 × 75 feet, and contain a very large and complete stock at all times. Employment is given to twelve assistants, and despite the magnitude of the business orders are filled with the greatest promptitude, so well considered a system being in operation that all confusion is avoided. The resident partner, James E. Lothrop, exercises a general supervision over the enterprise, and we need hardly add that the service is maintained at the highest standard of efficiency. Mr. Lothrop has been connected with the Cocheco National Bank since 1858 and has officiated as president since 1876. He has served as State Representative and as mayor of Dover, his service in the latter capacity proving of special value to this community, one of the most noteworthy features of it being the establishment of a free public library. Mr. Lothrop is the financial head of all the enterprises with which he and his brothers are identified, and although nominally supervising the Dover business only, his counsel is frequently called for in the direction of the firm's undertakings in Boston and elsewhere.

Walter H. Rines, Merchant Tailor ; Ladies' and Gents' Clothing Dyed and Repaired ; 484 Central Avenue, over Boston Branch, Dover, N. H.—To many people, a suit of clothes is a suit of clothes, and that is all there is to it. They apparently believe, that given a certain quantity of material it makes no difference how it is put together so long as it takes the shape of a suit and hence they are easily imposed upon by such dealers as are disposed to work off their goods more by their appearance when new than by their real merits. It may be taken as an axiom that the $5.00 spent for superior workmanship and trimmings are invested to better advantage than any other portion of the purchase money, and those who will accept and act on this hint, will find their reward in the improved appearance and superior durability of their wearing apparel. To assure the best of material put together in the most skillful manner, an establishment of repute must be patronized, and none better can be chosen than that conducted by Mr. Walter H. Rines, at No. 484 Central avenue. This undertaking had its inception in 1886, and has been steadily conducted since that date with constantly increasing success. Mr. Rines is a native of Dover. He has that thorough understanding of his business so essential to the highest success. A choice stock of foreign and domestic cloths is carried, and first-class clothing is made to order, a perfect fit and good workmanship being guaranteed. Ladies' and gents' clothing dyed and repaired in a most satisfactory and thorough manner, at very reasonable prices. Six experienced assistants are employed, and equitable rates prevail, while every order is given the promptest attention.

J. T. Peaslee, manufacturers of Fine Harnesses, and dealer in Whips, Blankets, Robes, Fly Nets, Horse Boots, Trunks, Bags, etc., Repairing a Specialty, 495 Central Avenue, Dover, N. H.—It is both safer and cheaper to use a good harness than a poor one, and there need be no difficulty about getting a good harness if you go to the right kind of a place. We have no hesitation in recommending that now carried on by Mr. J. T. Peaslee at No. 495 Central avenue, for this establishment was founded by Mr. Geo. W. Hayes in 1839, the present proprietor assuming full control of the business in 1888. Mr. Peaslee is both able and willing to produce fine harnesses at prices as low as the lowest for similar work. His establishment is 25×40 feet in dimensions, and is completely fitted up for the manufacture of harness of every description, and the doing of repairing in general. A well-selected stock, is constantly carried, comprising whips, blankets, robes, fly nets, horse boots ; also trunks, bags, etc., these articles being offered at moderate prices, as well as guaranteed to prove as represented. Mr. Peaslee was born in Dover, and has a large circle of friends throughout the vicinity and numbers among his customers some who have traded with the house for many years. His reputation for turning out uniformly reliable work is as high as it is deserved, and applies to repairing as well as to the making of harnesses to order. Selected material is used in the filling of every order, and as skilled help is employed, work can be done at very short notice.

J. B. Folsom & Co., dealers in Paints, Oils, Varnishes, Brushes, Artists' Materials, Window Glass, Sperm, Cylinder, Lard and Spindle Oils, Cocheco Block, Dover, N. H. —Much of the protective value of paints and varnishes depends upon the character of the ingredients used in their composition, and as these articles are used quite as much for their preservative as for their decorative qualities, it follows that care should be taken to purchase them from a concern which may be depended upon to furnish honest and reliable goods. No paint and varnish house in Dover has a better record in this respect than that conducted by J. B. Folsom & Co., and customers of this firm

enjoy an additional advantage in the fact that the stock carried is so large and varied that it is easy to find goods therein which are particularly suited to the present business in hand. This undertaking was founded in 1840 and after several changes in its management came into the possession of the present firm in 1880. The premises occupied are located in Cocheco Block, and comprise one floor and basement each 20 × 50 feet in dimensions. Two efficient assistants are employed, and an extensive retail business is done. Paints, oils and varnishes of every description will be supplied in quantities to suit at the very lowest market rates, and special attention is given to handling brushes, artists' materials and window glass ; also sperm, cylinder, lard and spindle oils of warranted quality, all orders being accurately filled without delay. Mr. Andrew P. Folsom is a native of Dover.

G. W. Parker, Hack, Livery, Boarding and Sale Stable, corner Central Avenue and Kirkland Street, Dover, N. H.—In about every community there is a more or less brisk demand for single and double teams for business or pleasure purposes, and it is to be regretted that this demand is indifferently catered to by a certain proportion of stable keepers, for on account of the poor accommodations offered at some establishments of this kind the general public have formed such an opinion of public stables that a "livery stable team" is considered as synonymous with a broken down horse and a more or less worthless carriage. There is no justice in judging every establishment by the policy followed in the management of comparatively few, and certainly no competent judge can make use of the facilities provided by Mr. G. W. Parker, at his stable, corner of Central avenue and Kirkland street, without conceding that "livery stable teams" are by no means necessarily poor. This livery stable was originally established by Wm Roberts, who gave place to Mr. Sam'l Mitchell, about fifteen years ago, he being succeeded in 1884 by the firm of Parker & Kennedy. In 1886 Mr. Parker assumed the entire control of the business, and has constantly striven to improve the service rendered. There are twenty-five stalls on the premises and an extensive hack, livery, boarding and sale business is done, employment being given to three assistants, and every order being assured prompt and careful attention. The proprietor is uniformly moderate in his charges, and as he makes every effort to please his patrons, it is not at all surprising that his establishment should stand high in public favor.

A. E. Parker, dealer in Dry and Fancy Goods, Hosiery, Gloves, Corsets, Ladies' Underwear, Infants' Wardrobe, Dress and Cloak Trimmings, 376 Central Avenue, Dover, N. H.—Every business establishment has a character of its own as surely as every individual has, and as the distinguishing characteristic of the enterprise carried on by Mr. A. E. Parker is reliability, it is natural that it should be very popular with the purchasing public, for all of us like to feel assured of getting what we pay for, and it is Mr. Parker's invariable policy to represent his goods just as they are and return full value for money received. He is a native of Wolfboro, N. H., and has been identified with his present enterprise since 1877, having at that time succeeded Messrs. Andrew Brothers. The premises occupied are located at No. 376 Central avenue, and have an area of 1200 square feet. The stock comprises dry and fancy goods, hosiery, gloves, corsets, underwear, infants' wardrobe, dress and cloak trimmings, etc., and is so complete in every department that not only all tastes but all purses can easily be suited. Mr. Parker quotes prices as low as can be named on first class goods, and with the help of four efficient assistants is enabled to give every caller immediate and courteous attention.

C. H. Trickey & Co., dealers in Coal and Wood, of every description; sole agent for Breed's "Fire King:" office, First Street, Dover, N. H.—We have no doubt but that many of the oldest and best-informed residents of Dover would be surprised to learn the total amount of coal and wood consumed in this city and vicinity, for the consumption is steadily and rapidly increasing and it is difficult for those not directly engaged in the business to keep track of it. Messrs. C. H. Trickey & Co. supply a large proportion of the local demand, for this firm have carried on operations for about eighteen years, and have built up a large trade by furnishing goods of standard quality at the lowest market rates, and by sparing no pains to ensure promptness and accuracy of delivery. The business was founded many years ago and was at one time in the hands of Mr. Moses B. Page, he being succeeded by the present firm in 1872. The partners are Messrs. C. H. Trickey and G. W. Avery, both of whom are New Hampshire men by birth. Mr. Avery has served on the board of aldermen. Mr. Trickey is thoroughly identified with the commercial growth and prosperity of this community. He is largely engaged in the purchase of timber, or standing growth, purchasing either the land and timber, or the timber alone, which is put on the market at figures very advantageous to buyers. Mr. Trickey and his ancestors have for upward of fifty years attended to all the hauling of the Cocheco Manufacturing Company and Print Works, and also attends to all heavy transportation of goods of every description for manufacturers or merchants. From fifteen to twenty-five men and some sixteen horses are employed, so that large or small orders will be filled accurately, promptly and at bottom figures. The firm deal in coal and wood of every description, special attention being given to handling the choicest brands of anthracite and bituminous coal. The office is located on First street, and yard on Cocheco street, head of tide-water, and sufficient storage capacity is available to accommodate 4000 tons.

Dr. A. J. Young, Dentist, No. 392 Central Avenue, Dover, N. H.—It would be absurd to say that any dentist, no matter how skillful and careful, or how perfectly supplied with the latest improved appliances, can practice his profession without inflicting the least pain upon his patients, but that some are more successful in this respect than others, is a fact so obvious as to be known to all. For instance, it is well understood in Dover and vicinity that Dr. Young is one of the most gentle and successful operators to be found in this section, and it is also understood that this gentleness by no means interferes with the thoroughness with which his work is done, for, on the contrary, by thus gaining the confidence of his patients, he is enabled to accomplish results which would otherwise be impossible. Dr. Young is at the head of his profession, a graduate of the Pennsylvania Dental College. Owing to failing health from a long and continued practice of his profession—of thirty-seven years in Dover—the doctor spends his winters in the beautiful city of St. Augustine, Fla., in his orange groves, returning to Dover to practice his profession at 392 Central avenue, from May to December. His rooms are large and conveniently fitted up, the comfort of patrons having been given great consideration. The facilities at hand are such that dentistry in all its branches can be successfully carried on in accordance with the most approved methods, and these facilities by lessening the labor involved in doing a given piece of work, enables Dr. Young to make his charges very reasonable—a fact which is duly appreciated by the public.

Thomas Spurlin, dealer in Glassware and Crockery, Wooden, Tin, Agate, Iron, and Fancy Ware. Agent for the Boston Dinner Set Company, always a full line in stock, 394 Central Avenue, Dover, N. H.—A tasteful dinner set or tea set adds so much to the enjoyment of a meal and to the appearance of a table, that it may justly be classed high among the things which make a home attractive, and beautiful sets can now be bought for so small an amount of money, that there is no reason why all should not possess them. Should any of our readers doubt this statement, we will not waste their time and our own in argument, but will simply advise them to visit the establishment conducted by Mr. Thomas Spurlin, for here may be found the latest novelties in glassware and crockery, besides a full stock of wooden, tin, agate, iron and fancy ware. The lowest market rates are quoted on all the goods handled, which comprise not only the styles of ware already mentioned, but full lines of the Boston Dinner Set Company's goods, for which Mr. Spurlin is the agent. The store is located at No. 394 Central avenue and is about 500 square feet in dimensions. The stock is fresh, varied and attractive, the articles composing it are guaranteed to prove as represented, and prompt and polite attention is assured to every caller. Mr. Spurlin is a native of Tuftonboro, N. H., and has carried on his present establishment since 1887. He has built up a large business by enterprising methods and fair dealing, and those who have dealt with him will agree that his success is the legitimate outcome of earnest and intelligent efforts to serve the public to the best advantage.

D. C. M. Pierce, dealer in Beef, Pork, Hams, Mutton, Fish, Oysters and Vegetables, 502 Central Avenue, Dover, N. H.—The secret of success is much the same, no matter what business may be engaged in. If you can furnish customers with reliable goods at bottom prices, and give prompt attention to all orders, you need have no fear but that a satisfactory trade will soon be built up. Such has been the experience of Mr. D. C. M. Pierce, who is engaged in the meat and vegetable trade at No. 502 Central avenue, for since he succeeded Messrs. Howard & Thompson in 1865, his efforts to extend operations have met with unquestionable success. Since 1887, Mr. Pierce has been located at his present address, having at that time bought out Mr. Horace Dearborn He is thoroughly acquainted with the wants of family trade, and has shown both intelligence and liberality in catering to the same. The premises are 20 × 40 feet in dimensions and are sufficiently spacious to accommodate a large and varied stock of choice meats, fish, oysters and vegetables. All tastes and all purses may be accommodated at this store, for the prices are in every instance in accordance with the lowest market rates, and the choicest goods are handled, as well as those of less variety and cost. Competent assistants are employed, and orders will be attended to immediately and carefully, being accurately delivered to any address.

H. L. Brewster, Electrician, Morrill's Block, 472 Central Avenue, Dover, N. H.—Many and useful have been the applications made of electricity since that subtle "fluid" or "force," or whatever you may choose to call it was first pressed into the service of mankind, and during the past decade more progress has been made than in all the previous years. The cost of electric bells, lighting apparatus, etc., has been materially reduced and these great conveniences thus placed within the means of the general public. There is now no reason why every dwelling house, store and factory should not be equipped with electrical appliances, and as the efficiency of such apparatus is chiefly dependent upon the manner in which they are put up, we take pleasure in calling the attention of our readers to the facilities offered by Mr. H. L. Brewster, of No. 472 Central avenue, for he is an expert and thoroughly practical electrician and is prepared to furnish and put up electric bells, burglar alarms, lighting apparatus, and in short to do electric work of every description. Mr. Brewster is in a position to supply electrical apparatus at manufacturer's prices, and can figure very closely on contracts to supply such appliances and put them in practical operation. Estimates will be cheerfully and promptly furnished, and work will be done under a guarantee that the results will be strictly in accordance with representations.

T. P. Cressey & Son, Fancy Goods, Fine Millinery, Laces, Kid Gloves, etc., 390 Central Avenue, Dover, N. H.—It is safe to say that no business man in Dover is more generally and favorably known than Mr. T. P. Cressey, for he has carried on operations here for more than forty years and has long been prominent in mercantile and financial circles as well as in public life. Mr. Cressey is a native of Gorham, Maine, and founded his present business in 1849. In 1872 the existing firm was formed by the admission of Mr. E. P. Cressey, a native of this city. The senior partner was formerly a director of the Dover National Bank, and has served as councilman and chairman of the school committee, holding the latter position three years. The firm are extensively engaged in the handling of fine millinery, fancy goods, laces, kid gloves, trimmings, etc., doing both a wholesale and retail business and carrying a large and varied stock, which always includes the latest fashionable novelties, and for that and other reasons is highly esteemed by the ladies of Dover and vicinity. The store is located at No. 390 Central avenue, and callers may safely depend upon receiving prompt and courteous attention. Fine millinery work to order is a very important department of the business, and during the season twelve assistants are required to properly attend to the many orders received, as the prices are moderate and the work is uniformly first-class.

H. L. White, dealer in Sewing Machines, Needles, Oil, Belts, and Attachments of all kinds. Agent for Best Makes Pianos and Organs. Repairing a Specialty. No. 350 Central Avenue, Dover, N. H.—It is all very well for sewing machine manufacturers to claim that their individual machine is the "best in the market," and in fact is "the only machine worth buying," but the public have their own ideas on such points and generally know pretty well what they want and why they want it. Therefore such an establishment as that conducted by Mr. H. L. White, at No. 350 Central avenue, is bound to be popular, for the simple reason that Mr. White deals in many of the leading sewing machines and consequently you can "pay your money and take your choice" at his store without being importuned to buy any particular make. Of course, the advantage of each style will be pointed out if desired, and any required information given, but the main point is the great latitude of choice made possible by the scope of the business. Mr. White is agent for the best makes of pianos and organs, and we may add is in a position to quote bottom prices on all the goods he handles. A large stock of sewing machine supplies is carried including needles, oil, belts, and attachments of all kinds. Mr. White is a native of Dover, and inaugurated his present enterprise in 1885. His reputation for fair dealing is of the best, and customers may depend upon all representations made and also upon getting full value for every dollar expended.

Dover Navigation Company. President, Thomas B. Garland, Dover, N. H.—That the prosperity and development of a community are directly dependent upon the transportation facilities available is a self-evident proposition, for, other things being equal, it is obvious that those manufacturers and merchants who enjoy the best facilities for the reception and shipping of goods, are best prepared to meet the sharp competition now existing in practically every line of business. The present importance of Dover as a manufacturing and trade centre is of course largely due to advantages of location, but these of themselves would have availed nothing and in less enterprising hands would not have been nearly so well utilized as is now the case. The undertaking carried on by the Dover Navigation Company is of almost inestimable benefit to this city, and indirectly to all the adjacent country, for this company offers exceptionally desirable transportation facilities, and from the origin of its business, in 1879, has shown most commendable enterprise in catering to the demands of its constantly increasing trade. Some of the most prominent business men in this section of the State are identified with it, and naturally the company is in a position to render much more intelligent service under these circumstances than would be possible were its affairs controlled by residents of other sections, no matter how able and well-meaning they might be. The president is Mr. Thomas B. Garland, and the secretary and treasurer is Mr. B. Frank Neally, while the managing committee is constituted of Messrs. Charles H. Trickey, B. Frank Neally, John J. Hanson, J. Frank Seavey, John Holland and Thomas B. Garland. The company has a capital of $186,000, and owns eight schooners now in commission, their names and capacities being as follows: *John Bracewell,* 225 tons; *Thomas B. Garland,* 319 tons; *Zinri S. Wallingford,* 205 tons; *J. Chester Wood,* 55 tons; *John J. Hanson,* 656 tons; *Jonathan Sawyer,* 400 tons; *J. Frank Seavey,* 400 tons; *John Holland,* 1000 tons. The vessels are kept in first-class condition, are in charge of experienced and reliable men, and enable the company to offer a service unsurpassed for economy and practical efficiency.

John McIntire, Meat and Vegetables, 345 Central Avenue, Dover, N. H.—It is true that the business done at the establishment conducted by Mr. John McIntire is a rapidly growing one, but those who think Mr. McIntire, the energetic proprietor of the establishment in question, is dependent upon "luck" for the popularity of the enterprise under his charge, make a great and inexcusable mistake. We say "inexcusable," for it seems to us as if no intelligent person could visit this store, examine the variety and character of the goods offered for sale, observe the uniform promptness and courtesy with which all callers are attended to and note the care shown in the delivery of orders, without acknowledging that such methods were sure to build up a large trade, quite independent of "luck," or anything like it. Mr. McIntire has been engaged in this line of business for the past ten years, and has therefore had sufficient experience to know what the public want and to know how to supply them in the most satisfactory manner. Since 1887 he has occupied his present premises, which are located at No. 345 Central avenue, and are about 400 square feet in dimensions. The stock dealt in consists of meals and vegetables of all kinds. Five assistants are employed, thus ensuring prompt and painstaking attention to every customer, and the facilities for the delivery of goods at short notice are in every way desirable. Mr. McIntire also runs four carts, and warrants his goods to prove as represented, and invariably gives all purchasers the full worth of their money.

J. Herbert Seavey, Hardware, 300 Central Avenue, Dover, N. H.—The manufacture of hardware has become one of the leading industries of the country, and as the goods produced vary as greatly in quality as they do in kind, a retail dealer who proposes to furnish articles that can be depended upon must have ability and experience as well as good will. Mr. J. Herbert Seavey has been engaged in the handling of hardware, farmer's tools, etc., in this city for a long time, and succeeded Messrs. G. F. Rollins & Co., in the ownership of the establishment with which he is now identified more than ten years ago. The natural presumption is therefore that he is thoroughly familiar with the merits of the articles in which he deals, and this presumption becomes certainty on examining his stock and noting his prices. The store is located at No. 300 Central avenue, and comprises one floor and a basement, their dimensions being 20 × 75 feet. A very complete and extensive stock is carried, a specialty being made of agricultural tools and the productions of the most successful manufacturers being represented. A full line of cutlery, general hardware, etc., is also offered, and as employment is given to two assistants callers are assured prompt and courteous attention. Mr. Seavey is a native of Rochester, N. H., and has a large circle of friends in Dover and vicinity.

J. H. Randlett, Carriage and Sleigh manufacturer, 223 Central Avenue, Dover, New Hampshire.—The establishment conducted by Mr. J. H. Randlett at No. 223 Central avenue, is regarded by many as the headquarters for carriages, sleighs, harnesses and horse goods in general, for the proprietor has carried on business in Dover for very nearly a quarter of a century, during which time he has built up a most enviable reputation for furnishing standard articles at the very lowest market rates. He is a native of Lee, N. H., and has been identified with his present enterprise since 1866. Mr. Randlett has served on the City Council, and is one of the most widely known of our local manufacturers. He utilizes very commodious premises, comprising three floors measuring 100×60 feet. Employment is given to from fifteen to twenty assistants, and order work can be turned out at very short notice; repairing of all kinds being assured immediate and skillful attention. A varied assortment of carriages and sleighs is always on hand to choose from, and the stock of single and double harness, robes, whips, blankets, brushes, and other horse furnishings is one of the most desirable and complete to be found in the State. The productions of reputable manufacturers only are handled, and every article bought at this representative establishment is fully warranted to prove as represented.

C. McClellan, Merchant Tailor, No. 30 Third Street, Dover, N. H.—We hear sometimes of the competition between custom tailors and dealers in ready-made clothing, but as a matter of fact there is no such competition, or if there is, it is confined to those tailors, who turn out garments but little if any superior to ready-made work. Really first-class custom clothing is so far superior to that bought ready-made, that there can be no comparison, and the much greater durability of custom garments goes far to compensate for any difference in the first cost. Among the merchant tailors, located in this section of the State, prominent and favorable mention should be made of Mr. C. McClellan, for this gentleman turns out work equal to the best, and his prices will compare very favorably with those quoted by others producing equally desirable garments. This merchant tailoring establishment was founded in 1881 by T. McGuire, the present proprietor assuming entire control in 1887. The premises occupied are located at No. 30 Third street, and are equipped with all necessary facilities to enable operations to be carried on to the best advantage. Ten competent assistants are employed, and a beautiful and varied assortment of imported and domestic fabrics is constantly on hand to select from. A specialty is made of ladies' garments, and suits or single garments for either gentlemen or ladies, will be made up in a uniformly superior manner, orders being filled promptly and entire satisfaction as regards fit, prices, etc., being confidently guaranteed.

H. E. Dearborn, dealer in Beef, Pork, Mutton, Veal, Lamb, Lard, Vegetables, Butter, Eggs and Canned Goods, No. 3, Fourth St., Dover, N. H. —It is not uncommon to hear people say they don't know where to get good meats; they are willing to pay a fair price for first-class goods but find it very difficult to get such articles at any figure. Now, such a statement would not excite much of any remark if made by the residents of some out-of-the-way place or other, but coming from the lips of one residing in Dover, it certainly calls for more than passing mention, for Dover is a prominent trade-center and it would be strange if first-class meats were not obtainable here. Of course they are to be had, however, and in any desired quantities, too, and as sure a way of getting them as we know of is to place the order with Mr. H. E. Dearborn, doing business at No. 3, Fourth street, for this gentleman makes a specialty of handling first quality fresh beef, pork, mutton, veal, lamb, lard, vegetables, butter, eggs, and canned goods. A store and basement, each measuring 22×50 feet, are occupied and a large stock is carried at all seasons, there being ample storage facilities to accommodate a heavy assortment. Employment is given to competent assistants, and despite the magnitude of the business customers are served with a promptness and care to be looked for in vain in many much smaller stores. The proprietor, Mr. H. E. Dearborn, is a native of Milton, N. H. He established his business in Dover in 1880, and has been located at his present address since 1889. All orders are promptly filled and the lowest market prices quoted.

Wiggin & Stevens, manufacturers of Flint, Sand, Emery and Match Papers, Emery Cloth and Glue, New England Ruby Paper, Dover, N. H.—Such of our readers as are mechanics by trade, or are engaged in any other occupation, which familiarizes them with the standing of the various flint, sand and emery papers on the market do not need to be told that the productions of Messrs. Wiggin & Stevens are equal to the best, for these goods have an unsurpassed reputation and are largely used throughout the country. New England flint paper and New England ruby paper are famous and popular brands, and their popularity is due not less to their uniformity than to their comparative excellence, for while paper of about any manufacture is occasionally good, it is but rarely a brand can be found which practically never varies from its established standard. The firm have works at Malden (Edgeworth), Mass., besides those in this city, and some idea of the magnitude of their business may be gained from the fact that while their Dover plant is devoted to the manufacture of glue exclusively, and produces from fifty to sixty-five tons per year, the concern do not sell glue, but use all they make in the manufacture of flint, sand, emery and match papers, and emery cloth, at their Malden factory. The Dover factory affords employment to from six to eight assistants, and is under the superintendence of Mr. E. Wentworth. This business was founded in 1858 and has reached its present extensive proportions by a steady process of legitimate development. The present proprietors are the estate of the late Russel B. Wiggin, and Messrs. William S. and Everett J. Stevens; both these gentlemen being natives of New Hampshire. Mr. William S. Stevens has held the position of mayor, and neither partner needs introduction to our Dover readers. We need hardly add that a concern with facilities such as we have pointed out is in a position to fill the largest orders without delay.

PHOTO ELECTROTYPE CO BOSTON

H. A. Worthen, Manufacturer of Light and Heavy Carriages, and Sleighs; Repairing Neatly and Promptly Done. Nos. 13, 16 and 17 Locust Street, rear City Hall, Dover, N. H.—The Dover Carriage Factory is the oldest established factory of the kind in town, and is probably at least as well known as any in this section of the State, for its productions have always held a high rank in the market and have gone extensively into general use. The enterprise was inaugurated forty years before the present proprietor became identified with it, and this occurred a quarter of a century ago, he beginning operations in 1865 as a member of the firm of H. A. Worthen & Co., and assuming sole control about a score of years ago. Mr. Worthen manufactures light and heavy carriages and sleighs, and the commodious premises utilized by him are fitted up with all necessary machinery, etc., to enable operations to be carried on to the best advantage. They are located at Nos. 13, 16 and 17 Locust street, rear of City Hall, and comprise two good sized buildings, one two and the other three stories in height. Employment is given to from eight to twelve assistants, and all orders are assured immediate and painstaking attention, repairing being strongly, durably and neatly done at the shortest possible notice. Mr. Worthen is in a position to quote the lowest market prices at all times, and customers may safely depend upon getting full value for every dollar they pay out, whether for repairing or new work.

G. Howard Churbuck, Retail Grocer, 112 Washington Street, Dover, N. H.—It would be very difficult to find a more popular grocery store than that carried on by Mr. G. Howard Churbuck at No. 112 Washington street, and those who argue that popularity is the result of "good luck" would do well to investigate the causes of the favor in which this establishment is held, for "luck" has had little or nothing to do with it, it having been brought about by hard, intelligent and persistent work, and a consistent policy of giving full value for all money received. The firm of Faxon & Churbuck began operations in 1880, and in 1883 the present proprietor assumed sole control. He is a native of Centerville, Mass., and has had long and varied experience in the grocery business, so that the close personal supervision he gives to the details of his present enterprise is a powerful factor in assuring its continued success. Employment is given to five assistants, and if every caller does not receive prompt and courteous attention it is no fault of the management, for the rule is equal service to all—large or small, young or old, rich or poor, —business being conducted so far as is possible on the "first come, first served" principle. An immense stock of staple and fancy groceries is constantly carried, and positively the lowest market rates are quoted on goods of standard merit.

Dr. C. W. Tasker, Dentist. No. 36 Central Avenue, Dover, N. H.—A liberal endowment of common sense is one of the most valuable legacies which any person can receive, for common sense is really one of the most uncommon attributes of character, and the fortunate possessor of a large fund of it is sure of "reasonable success in the world," and to avoid serious evils simply on account of his capacity to reason from cause to effect and thus steer clear of the errors on which so many are wrecked. For instance, one who has a fair share of common sense is not apt to abuse his teeth or to allow them to remain uncared for, until they are injured beyond repair, for he knows that good teeth are essential to the maintenance of good health, insomuch as the province of the teeth is to prepare the food for the stomach, and it is as absurd to expect badly decayed teeth to do proper work as it would be to expect broken mill-stones to turn out perfect flour. The average person is restrained from having his teeth given proper attention by one or more of three things—carelessness, fear and a desire to avoid the necessary expense. The first is no excuse at all, for everyone should appreciate the importance of having the teeth looked after; the second had some weight in former days, when instruments were crude and methods were imperfect, but does not apply to-day when science has done so much to obviate the least necessity for the infliction of pain, and the third is more than foolish, for the health is the greatest of all wealth, and imperfect teeth necessarily entail imperfect health. For dental operations we would refer our readers to Dr. C. W. Tasker, located at No. 360 Central avenue, who is conceded to be as skillful and thorough a practitioner as the State can show. Dr. Tasker is a native of Rochester, N. H., and began the practice of his profession here in 1869. His rooms are conveniently located and equipped with the most improved instruments and other facilities for operating to the best advantage. The doctor is gentle as well as thorough in his methods. He uses gas, ether and cocaine for the extraction of teeth, and the most nervous or timid may avail themselves of his services in the full assurance that all unnecessary discomfort will be carefully avoided.

Excelsior Dining Rooms, A. E. Ashby, Proprietor, No. 4 Third Street, near B. & M. Depot, Dover, N. H.— Probably each of our readers has his own ideas as to how a dining-room should be carried on for "different people have different tastes," especially where eating is concerned. The most that the proprietor of a public restaurant can do is to suit the majority, and the popularity of the "Excelsior Dining Rooms," No. 4 Third street, close by B. & M. depot, shows how well the proprietor, Mr. A. E. Ashby, has succeeded in attaining this result. He is a native of England, and has carried on his present establishment since 1889, having at that date succeeded Mr. O. B. Ireland. His rooms have sufficient seating capacity to accommodate fifty patrons at one time, and as he employs a sufficient force of experienced and efficient assistants, he is able to meet all the demands made upon him. The bill of fare is varied, the food first class, the cooking all that could be wished, and the service prompt, intelligent and courteous, so that it naturally follows that no similar establishment in the city stands higher in the estimation of the public. Meals will be served at all hours, thus accommodating all classes of patrons. The prices are very reasonable, for Mr. Ashby feeds a great many people, and, of course, not only buys his provisions, etc., in large quantities, and therefore at low rates, but can get along with a small profit on each patron. A well conducted dining-room is a great public convenience, and we take pleasure in unreservedly commending the Excelsior Dining Rooms,

Wm. W. Hayes & Elbridge A. Shorey, Dentists, No. 3 Bracewell Building, Dover, N H.—The elegant rooms of Drs. Wm. W. Hayes and Elbridge A. Shorey, No. 3 Bracewell Building, are fully equipped with the latest and most approved appliances for operations of all descriptions upon the teeth, and an extended and growing practice fully attests to the skillful treatment and thorough manner in which all operations are performed at their office. Dr. Hayes is a native of Dover, and has practiced his profession since 1871. Dr. Shorey is a native of Rochester, N. H., studied with Dr. Hayes, and took the full course at the dental department of Harvard University, receiving the degree of D.M.D. in the class of 1890.

W. A. Morrill, dealer in Carpetings, Crockery, China and Glass Ware, Feathers, Window Shades and Fixtures, No. 74 Washington Street, Cocheco Block, Dover, N. H. —It is simply impossible to properly describe the stock carried by Mr. W. A. Morrill, within the necessarily narrow limits of the present article, for that gentleman occupies two floors and a basement each 33 × 46 feet in dimensions in addition to a spacious storehouse, and deals in an immense variety of goods, including carpeting, crockery, china, and glass ware. The premises occupied are located at No. 74 Washington street, Cocheco block, and are easy and convenient to reach, but even if they were not we would still advise such of our readers as want anything in Mr. Morrill's line to give him a call, for he quotes positively bottom prices and makes it an invariable rule to represent things precisely as they are. He is a native of Salisbury, Mass., and is very widely known throughout Dover, having been connected with his present business since 1859, the business being founded at that date under the style of Morrill Brothers, Mr. W. A. Morrill assuming full control of affairs in 1872. Mr. Morrill sells his goods at extremely low prices, and certainly it would be difficult if not impossible to parallel elsewhere the inducements he offers,—a fact which is generally understood and appreciated by the residents of this city. A prominent department of the business is that devoted to the handling of feathers, window shades, and fixtures, etc. Those looking for genuine bargains in these lines may profitably give Mr. Morrill a call. Competent assistants are employed, and the assortment of goods offered is always large, varied and in short generally desirable.

Nute & Wolcott, dealers in Groceries and Grain, 555 Central Avenue, Dover, N. H.—Sixteen years is either a long or a short time, according to the point of view from which it is regarded, but it is certainly a very short time in which to build up such a business as that now carried on by Messrs Nute & Wolcott, and this firm may well congratulate themselves on the exceptional degree of success which they have attained. Still this gratifying success was not the result of luck or chance but was brought about by hard work, persistent enterprise, and by an intelligent determination to so serve the public that a heavy patronage would result as a matter of course. Business was begun in 1874 by the firm of D. A. Nute & Co., and so continued until 1882, when the firm name was changed to Nute & Foss the present firm of Nute & Wolcott being formed in 1883 These gentlemen are both well known throughout Dover and vicinity. Mr. Nute has held the office of councilman, and is a native of Wolfboro, N. H., while Mr. C. L. Wolcott is a Massachusetts man by birth. The premises occupied are located at No. 555 Central avenue, and comprise one floor 30 × 75 feet in dimensions, where is carried an extensive stock of groceries, grain, etc.; also a basement, which is used as a meat market. Considering their extensive facilities it becomes almost unnecessary to add that Messrs Nute & Wolcott are prepared to supply these commodities in quantities to suit at the very lowest market rates. These gentlemen give personal attention to the filling of orders, and as they employ only competent assistants it will be seen that customers are assured prompt and polite attention and that the heaviest orders can be filled without delay.

John Baty, dealer in Stoves and Furnaces ; Plumbing, Locust Street, Dover, N. H —Many a hot air furnace and many a steam-heating apparatus have been condemned, when the fault lay in the way in which the plant was set up and not in the furnace or apparatus itself, and therefore, when placing orders for stoves or furnaces of any kind, be sure that the setting-up receives skillful and painstaking attention. No little experience and skill are required in order to put in heating apparatus so that it will yield the best possible results for the conditions vary so greatly that what is advisable in one house would be height of folly in another, and consequently the only sure way of having the work done to the best possible advantage is to entrust it to such a man as Mr. John Baty, for this gentleman gives special attention to furnace work, plumbing, iron piping and general jobbing. He deals extensively in stoves, furnaces, etc., and is prepared to guarantee satisfaction to every customer. Operations were begun in Dover by Mr. Baty in 1878. He has had thirty years experience at his business, as a plumber, etc., and it is safe to say that no one in Dover, is better prepared to meet the wants of the public in the above lines of business. The premises occupied are about 1000 square feet in dimensions and are located on Locust street. A heavy and valuable stock is carried, plumbing work of all kinds is done in the most satisfactory manner, while the lowest market rates are quoted in every department of the business. Employment is given to six experienced and careful workmen, and general jobbing will be done in first-class style, at short notice.

Edward W. Taff, Clothing, Hats, Caps and Furnishing Goods, 479 Central Avenue, under American House, Dover, N. H.—The undertaking carried on by Mr Edward W. Taff, was founded in 1887, by Mr. Dan'l M. Hill, who was succeeded by Mr. Frank Roberts in 1888, and one year later the present proprietor assumed entire management of the businesss. The premises have an area of 1250 square feet and are located at No. 479 Central avenue. A very carefully selected stock is carried, comprising fine ready-made clothing, fashionable hats, caps, gentlemen's furnishing goods, etc. The clothing sold at the store has a well-deserved reputation for uniform superiority, and this reputation is due not only to the excellence of the materials used, the shapeliness of the garments and the perfection, with which they fit, but also to the honest workmanship, shown in every detail of their making, for this causes them to be as durable as they are handsome. A common objection to ready-made garments is their liability to become misshapen after a little wear, but this does not apply to those furnished by Mr. Taff, for they are so skillfully and carefully made that they will hold their shape equal to first-class custom work. Low prices are quoted, not only on clothing but also on all the goods handled, and, should any of our readers wish a complete "outfit" at a very reasonable expense, we can give them no better counsel than to visit the popular establishment referred to. Efficient assistants are employed, and immediate and polite attention is assured to all.

W. P. Page, dealer in fine Boots, Shoes and Rubbers ; Sole Agent for the J. F. Bliss' Ladies Fine Goods, No. 487 Central Avenue, Dover, N. H.—To obtain a shoe that combines comfort, style and durability with cheapness—such is the aim of about every buyer, and any information that will serve to make the attainment of this object easier and surer cannot fail to be of general interest. It is evident that to suit a variety of customers a variety of goods must be carried, and one of the prime reasons for the high esteem in which the establishment carried on by Mr. W. P. Page, at No. 487 Central avenue, is held, is the fact that the assortment shown contains articles suited to all tastes. The inception of this enterprise occurred many years ago, and after two or three changes in its management came into the possession of the present proprietor in 1887. Mr. Page is a native of Dover, and is, very well known throughout the vicinity. He is indefatigable in his efforts to not only maintain but to add to the high reputation so long enjoyed by his establishment. He is sole agent for J. F. Bliss' ladies' fine goods, and also makes a specialty of the Day sewed flexible shoe, which is as easy as hand sewed, being entirely free from wax thread and tacks. He keeps a close watch on the market, ready at all times to take advantage of any opportunity to offer his patrons exceptional advantages. A store measuring 20×40 feet is occupied, and two competent and polite assistants are employed. So complete an assortment of sizes and widths is kept in stock that the most difficult feet can almost invariably be fitted perfectly, and not an article leaves the store that is not fully warranted to prove just as represented in every respect.

John T. Hill, Furnaces, Ranges and Heating Stoves, Glass and Wooden Ware, Steam Washers, Clothes Wringers, Sheet Lead and Lead Pipe, Soil Pipe, Gas and Water Pipe, 19 Third Street, Dover, N. H.—The premises occupied by Mr. John T. Hill, comprise one floor and basement each 20×50 feet in dimensions, and it is safe to say that were they double that size the proprietor could profitably use them, for Mr. Hill carries a very heavy and varied stock and does a business which although already large is constantly increasing. Mr. Hill is a native of Northwood, N. H., and is widely known in Dover and vicinity, in social as well as business circles. Employment is given to six competent assistants, and in addition to dealing in glass and wooden ware, steam washers, clothes wringers, sheet lead and lead pipe, soil pipe, gas and water pipe, furnaces, ranges, heating, oil and gasoline stoves, etc., do an extensive business in plumbing, tin roofing, tin, lead, copper, zinc and sheet iron work, also all kinds of stove repairs, and wood and copper pumps made to order, all work being promptly executed, while moderate charges are made in every instance. The stock carried is exceptionally varied and complete, the prices quoted comparing favorably with those named at any establishment dealing in the same line of goods. Cooking and heating stoves are offered at very low prices, and those in need of an article of this kind, would do well to procure it of a man who guarantees his goods to prove as represented and has an enviable reputation for faithfully carrying out every agreement.

Fred H. Hayes, D.D.S., 372 Central Avenue, Dover, N. H.—Americans have been so frequently informed that they have the worst teeth in the world, that the fact should be pretty generally understood, and that American dentists are the best in the world is also a matter of common knowledge. There is nothing contradictory in this state of affairs, for demand and supply follow the same laws in professional as in mercantile life, and it is as natural to find many dentists in a country where their services are in great request, as it is to find the most lawyers in lands where labor affecting persons and property are most perfectly executed. Our American temperature has much to do with the poorness of our teeth as a nation, but there has certainly been a marked improvement since more attention has been paid to the care of these useful members. Decay of the teeth is invariably progressive, and no one, once noticing symptoms of such decay should hesitate a moment to place himself under the care of a thoroughly competent dentist. There are many in this vicinity, and one of the most popular of these is Dr. Fred H. Hayes, for this gentleman is not only an experienced and skilled operator, but is noted for the gentleness and consideration with which he discharges his responsible duties. This faculty cannot be acquired, in our opinion, its exercise can be made much more easy by education and practice. To combine thoroughness with gentleness should be the aim of every dental practitioner. We take pleasure in noting the success Dr. Hayes has gained in this respect. He is a native of Dover, and a graduate of the Boston Dental College. He is well known in this locality, having been established here since 1883. Those needing the services of a good dentist can do no better than to consult with him at his office, No. 372 Central avenue.

M. & T. Chicoine & Co., dealers in Flour, Sugars, Pork, Lard, Hams, Beans, Molasses, Teas, Coffees and Spices ; also Fresh Meat and Provisions a Specialty, corner Main and Portland Streets, Dover, N. H.—This establishment has proved very successful and popular and but a comparatively small amount of investigation is required to ascertain the cause of this popularity. Everybody likes to be sure of getting the worth of their money when they make purchases, and to know that the groceries and provisions they are consuming are as pure and fresh as the market affords. We all like to receive prompt attention and civil treatment when we have occasion to visit a store and give an order. Now when we say that all these desirable things are to be secured by dealing with M. & T. Chicoine & Co., we think no further explanation is needed, for the popularity of this store. The business was started in 1868 by M. & T. Chicoine at No. 69 Main street. They moved their store to their present location, corner of Main and Portland streets in 1889. The present firm of M. & T. Chicoine & Co. was formed in 1890. These gentlemen are dealers in flour, sugar, pork, lard, hams, beans, molasses, teas, coffees and spices. They also make a specialty of fresh meat and provisions. The assortment of the goods is excellent and the prices named for them is as low as the market will permit. Messrs. M. and T. Chicoine are natives of Canada. Mr. Frank Blair is a native of Dover.

B. Frank Nealley, Dry Goods, Bracewell Building, Central Avenue, Dover, N. H.—There is but little use of our saying that the enterprise conducted by Mr. B. Frank Nealley is a most popular one of its kind in this section of Dover, for the facts are very generally known, and there are few if any people who are at all acquainted in this section, but what have remarked the popularity gained by its proprietor. The enterprise in question was established in 1865, therefore its popularity has long been established. Mr. B. Frank Nealley is a native of South Berwick, Me., and is personally too well known in this city to render it necessary to make extended personal mention, suffice it to say that at present he is mayor of Dover, and has been representative and senator. The premises occupied comprise one floor and a basement each 20 × 65 feet in dimensions, an extensive retail business is carried on, employment being given to efficient and polite assistants. A comprehensive and skillfully selected assortment of dry goods is displayed at this store. Careful and courteous attention is extended to every caller, and as the store is conveniently located in Bracewell Building, Central avenue, the public will find it advantageous to inspect the stock before purchasing elsewhere. The prices are very low, the proprietor enjoying the most favorable relations with wholesalers and producers, and fixing his rates accordingly.

O. T. Henderson, retail dealer in Corn, Flour, Meal, Salt, Seeds, and Choice Family Groceries, Henderson's Block, corner Main and Chapel Streets, Dover, N. H.— Among the oldest established enterprises of the kind in this section of the State, is that conducted by Mr. C. T. Henderson, for its inception occured nearly half a century ago, operations having been begun about 1848 by S. H. Henderson & Son, this firm giving place to H. M. Henderson in 1858, the business finally coming into the possession of the present proprietor, Mr. C. T. Henderson, in 1870. Mr. Henderson has recently remodeled and refitted his store so it is one of the finest in the city. He is a native of Dover, and is widely and favorably known throughout the city. He occupies premises at the corner of Main and Chapel streets, Henderson's Block, comprising a store 22 × 75 feet in dimensions and a basement 40 × 22 feet. The stock handled includes corn, flour, meal, salt, seeds, and choice family groceries of all kinds. Every facility is at hand for the proper accommodation of the various commodities dealt in, and the arrangements for the prompt delivery of orders and economical handling of the stock are complete and well devised. A large retail business is done, and customers may depend upon having their commissions promptly and faithfully executed, while the lowest market rates are quoted in every department.

V. H. McDaniel, Notary Public, Auctioneer and Appraiser, dealer in Real Estate, 327 Central Avenue, Dover, N. H.—Surprise is frequently expressed because certain men are able to transact such a great amount of business and successfully carry on many enterprises varied and distinct in character, but in the large majority of such instances the explanation is to be found in the answer given by a man of this type to one who inquired how he could accomplish so much. "Simply by making use of the best obtainable facilities," was the reply. Many of us take strangely roundabout methods of doing a thing, and a prominent example is to be found in the practice of inquiring of friends and making a personal tour when searching for desirable real estate to buy or rent. This of course is all very well so far as it goes, but as long as there are well-equipped real estate agencies it is foolish to dispense with their aid, for time and money may be saved by patronizing them. There for instance is the office of Mr. V. H. McDaniel at No. 327 Central avenue. Mr. McDaniel is a native of Strafford, N. H., and has carried on business in this city for about sixteen years. He is a notary public, auctioneer, appraiser, and dealer in real estate and enjoys a very high reputation for intelligence and integrity. Commissions will be executed at very short notice in the most skillful and painstaking manner, and moderate charges are the rule in every instance. Mr. McDaniel always has some very desirable city and suburban property on his books, and is in a position to render valuable assistance to those wishing to buy, sell, exchange, or rent real estate. In addition to the above business Mr. McDaniel manages the sale of the American Rubber Paint for metal, shingle and marine uses. It is warranted not to crack, cleave or peel. It is a sure protection against fire, water and lightning. It has become generally known and meets with a rapidly increasing sale throughout the New England and Middle States.

Charles A. Tufts, Apothecary, Central Square, Dover, N. H.—If every apothecary were also a physician, the convenience of the public would undoubtedly be much better served, but as such is not the case, the best thing to do is to take advantage of the opportunities offered by those who do combine these important points. Among these we take pleasure in calling particular attention to Dr. Chas. A. Tufts, whose store is located at 85 Washington street, Central square, Dover, N. H. Dr. Tufts is a graduate of the Massachusetts College of Pharmacy, as well as the medical department of Dartmouth College, and has been proprietor of this establishment since 1847, at which time he succeeded Mr. Asa A. Tufts, who started this business in 1815. This being one of the oldest apothecary stores in the county, the premises occupied comprise a store 18 × 60 feet in dimensions and a storehouse. Two reliable and well-informed clerks are employed, and the large stock of drugs, medicines, chemicals, toilet and fancy articles, etc., is carefully selected from the most reliable sources, and always kept complete in every department. Prescriptions are compounded at short notice, and the charges made are always as low as is consistent with the use of ingredients of the best quality. Customers are assured courteous treatment and prompt attention. Dr. Chas. A. Tufts, who is a native of this city is very widely known in this country, and has been councilman, alderman, town clerk, associate judge of police court and senator.

M. P. Bennett, Junk Dealer, No. 19 New York Street, Dover, N. H.—It seems a somewhat curious thing that in civilized countries, where there are facilities at hand for the manufacturing of everything required in modern life, in any quantity that may be called for, there is actually much less waste than there is in lands where ordinary commodities are much harder to obtain, what is known in this country as a "junk store," does not exist in barbarous regions, for the simple reason that there are no means at hand to work the "junk" over again and thus greatly increase its commercial value. It is very convenient for the average householder to have a man come and carry off the accumulation of old rags, iron, etc., that gather so quickly in the ordinary home, and indeed, such a visit proves both convenient and profitable, for the junk dealer stands ready to pay a fair price for the articles that are of use to him, and thus not only carries away your rubbish, but pays you for the privilege. Mr. M. P. Bennett, doing business at No. 19 New York street, Dover, has become well known as one who pays the highest cash prices and manages his business with liberality as well as skill. He deals in old iron, rags, and all kinds of old junk, and also runs a tin cart. He is enterprising and liberal in all his business transactions, and is very generally known and esteemed throughout Dover and vicinity.

G. F. Butterfield, Agent for National Life Insurance Co.: Office 9, National Block, 450 Central Avenue, Dover, N. H.—The National Life Insurance Company of Montpelier, Vt., was incorporated in 1848 and is as successful an example of a purely mutual company as the country can show. The word "mutual" is used very loosely in its relations to insurance organizations and has come to mean almost anything, or rather almost nothing; but as an illustration of what "mutual" insurance actually should be, we would refer our readers to the insurance afforded by the instalment bonds of the National Life Insurance Company—characterized by Elizur Wright as "The grandest step in fair dealing within the history of life insurance." The claim of the company that these bonds are in many respects better than a savings bank or a government bond, is fully justified by the facts, for not only do they make the saving of money easy and sure, but from the time the first payment is made they ensure that your dependents will be provided for in case of your death, the full face value of the bond being then payable at once. The instalments are far below the premium charged for ordinary endowment policies, having twenty years to run, and the actual cost of insurance is definitely known and is reduced to a minimum. We have not the available space to make the principle and the practical workings of these bonds entirely clear, but we trust we have sufficiently interested our readers to induce them to call on Mr. George F. Butterfield, at office 9, National Block, No. 450 Central avenue, for he is agent of the company for this section of the State and is ready, able and willing to give clear and exhaustive information concerning the methods and resources of this representative corporation. Mr. Butterfield is a native of Great Falls, and has a large circle of friends throughout this vicinity. He has represented the company here since 1889 and is greatly developing its business in this section.

E. S. Tash & Co., Choice Family Groceries, Shoe Tools and Findings, 499 Central Avenue, Dover, N. H.—The establishment now conducted by E. S. Tash & Co., may truthfully be said to be one of the old business houses of Dover, having been founded in 1850. The firm of A. S. Tash & Co., assuming control in 1854. In 1865 the style was changed to G. W. Tash & Co., the present firm being formed in 1887, the individual members of which are Mr. Edwin S. Tash, and Mr. George W. Gray, both of them are natives of New Durham, N. H., and are very widely and favorably known throughout Dover and vicinity. Mr. Tash served in the army during the late Southern war, was messenger to the governor's council during the legislature of 1887, and has held the office of both councilman and alderman, while Mr. Gray has been overseer of the poor for five years. The premises occupied are located at No. 499 Central avenue, and comprise one floor and basement, each 20 × 75 feet in dimensions. An immense stock is carried, made up of teas, coffees, spices, extracts, choice family groceries, canned goods, flour, grain, produce, etc., together with shoe tools and findings. The firm do an extensive retail business and employ thoroughly competent assistants. As for their methods these should certainly be well understood in this vicinity by this time and hardly call for description in these columns. Suffice it to say that the governing principles of the enterprise is the returning of full value for money received, and so ably is this carried out that an honestly dissatisfied customer is a great rarity at this popular store.

Savings Bank for the County of Strafford, Washington Street, Dover, N. H.—"Show me a country without savings banks or their equivalent, and I will show you a people without ambition or resources," says a noted writer on economic subjects, and certainly all must allow that where savings banks most abound, prosperity, good citizenship, comfortable homes and educational privileges abound also. We hear a great deal of talk nowadays about the "capitalist" and the "wage-earner," and, many speak as though their interests were directly opposed and they could have nothing in common with each other, but it must be borne in mind that the majority of intelligent wage-earners are capitalists themselves—in a small way, it is true, but still enough so to bring it home to them that capitalists as well as wage earners have rights, and that injustice to one class works injury to all. Therefore the educational influences of savings banks cannot properly be left out of the reckoning in summing up their usefulness, and no person will deny that during the nearly seventy years that the savings bank for the county of Strafford has been in successful operation it has made its depositors wiser as well as richer. This worthy institution was incorporated in 1823, and for many years has ranked high among the representative savings banks of New England. A late statement showed deposits of $3,800,000 with surplus and premiums of over half a million dollars ; but what still more fully justifies the implicit confidence reposed in the enterprise is the standing of the men identified with it, for figures are not always conclusive, but the characters of a number of prominent men in a community are fully and generally understood, and assure the stability of any undertaking upon whose successful continuance they are dependent. The president is Mr. Charles H. Sawyer, the vice-presidents are Messrs. Elisha R. Brown and Samuel C. Fisher, and the board of trustees is constituted as follows : Charles H. Sawyer, Elisha R. Brown, Samuel C. Fisher, William S. Stevens, John H. Hurd, John Holland, B. F. Nealley, Daniel Hall, Robert G. Pike. The secretary and treasurer is Mr. Albert O. Mathur, and the executive officer is Mr. E. R. Brown. The banking rooms are located in the Strafford Bank Building, Washington street, and are so commodious and so conveniently arranged as to allow business to be speedily and accurately transacted, all unnecessary delay being absolutely avoided, and the convenience of depositors thereby greatly served.

Rooney & Burnham, Contractors and Builders, Cabinet Work, Washington Street, Dover, N. H.—It is unquestionably a fact that many people are deterred from building houses for themselves, by the stories current regarding the difficulty of knowing beforehand just what a given structure is going to cost, for there is hardly one of us but what has had stories related to him that are enough to discourage any man of humble means from building at all. But the question comes up, is there any need of this uncertainty ? In our opinion there is not. Builders are governed by the same rules that control those carrying on other branches of industry, and there is no reason why they should not as a class, adhere as closely to their agreements, as other business men do. Of course, if when your house is half finished you want one part of it made to look like the one across the way, or another part changed to correspond with some ideas you have got since accepting the original plans, you must expect to have to pay for such alterations, and it is really right here that most of the trouble comes. Place your orders with reputable builders, as for instance Rooney & Burnham of Washington street, and you need have no fear but what they will do their part if you will do yours. They employ a sufficient force of workmen to enable them to fill orders either for building or repairing at short notice. Mr. H. P. Rooney has been engaged in this business since 1884. The present firm of Rooney & Burnham was formed in 1890. Their terms are very reasonable, and their reputation for durable work is unsurpassed. They have fulfilled many commissions to the satisfaction of all concerned. They attend to orders for cabinet work, as well as for contracting and building.

Strafford National Bank, Dover, N. H.—The Strafford National Bank may be said to have had its inception some eighty-seven years ago, for it was organized as a State bank in 1803, having reorganized under the national banking laws in 1865, with a capital of $120,000 which has since been increased to $200,000. The record it has made is a most honorable and creditable one, for "brilliant" financiering has been carefully avoided, while on the other hand, undue conservatism has also been left unpracticed. It is often a delicate matter to properly discriminate between "old fogyism" and recklessness, for the principles of one age may not apply to another, and it is notorious that since the close of the war values have been revolutionized and business methods totally changed ; but the Strafford National Bank has always been managed by men who were actively engaged in business life and hence were in a position to know at the earliest possible moment of impending changes of conditions. We need not say that this bank has greatly aided in the development of Dover's interests, for were the contrary the fact it could never have attained its present popularity or have possessed the influence it now unquestionably wields. But it by no means rests its claims to patronage on past services —on the contrary, no bank in this section receives the accounts of firms, corporations, institutions and individuals on more favorable terms, or offers a more efficient service in connection with the collection of drafts, the purchase and sale of standard securities, the reception of deposits and the discounting of approved commercial paper. Finely appointed rooms are utilized, located in the Strafford Bank Building, Washington street, and the facilities available enable business to be promptly transacted. Among those identified with this bank are some of Dover's leading manufacturers and merchants, the president being Mr. William S. Stevens, the cashier Mr. E. R. Brown, and the assistant cashier Mr. C. S. Cartland. The board of directors is constituted of Messrs. Wm. S. Stevens, John McDuffee, Jeremiah Smith, E. R. Brown, C. H. Sawyer, S. C. Fisher, Geo. S. Frost.

Foot & Snell, dealers in Foreign and Domestic Hardware, Mowing Machines, and all kinds of Agricultural Implements, etc., 510 Central Av., Dover.—It is difficult to get an idea of the magnitude and the character of the business carried on by Messrs. Foot & Snell, without a personal visit to the premises occupied by them, for the simple statement that they deal in hardware and carry a very heavy and varied stock—although true enough as far as it goes—still utterly fails to convey an adequate conception of the importance of the enterprise in question. Its inception occurred about forty-five years ago, Mr. H. A. Foot, being the original founder. In 1866 he was succeeded by Mr. G. E. Foot, who conducted it alone for three years, and in 1869, associated himself with Mr. T. H. Snell, under the present firm name of Foot & Snell. Under their fostering care the ancient reputation, of the enterprise has been more than maintained, for it is now conceded that no establishment in Dover offers greater inducements to purchasers of hardware in general. The premises occupied are located at No. 510 Central avenue, and comprise two floors, each 20×60 feet in dimensions, in addition to a storehouse 90 feet long. Such ample accommodations argue a very extensive stock, and such is indeed carried, it being exceptionally complete in every department, including as it does, foreign and domestic hardware, mowing machines, and all kinds of agricultural implements. Very low prices are quoted, and sufficient assistance is employed to ensure prompt and accurate attention to every order. Messrs. G. E. Foot and T. H. Snell are both natives of Dover, and very well known throughout the social, as well as business circles of this city. Mr. Foot was in the army four years, during our late Southern war, and has also been connected with the city government as alderman and councilman. Mr. Snell has also held the the office of alderman. These gentlemen have had a long and varied experience in their present line of business, and are thoroughly familiar with it in every detail.

Charles E. Bacon, dealer in Diamonds, Watches, Clocks, Jewelry and Silverware, Spectacles a Specialty. Watches, Jewelry and Clocks Repaired. Engraving neatly executed. No. 388 Central Avenue, Dover, N. H. —This establishment occupies a prominent position among the oldest, most complete, and most attractive establishments of the kind in Dover, and contains a reliable stock of goods, embracing a fine variety of diamonds, watches, clocks, jewelry and silverware. Mr. Bacon also carries a large line of artistic brass goods that are elegant in style and finish. (Piano lamps are very attractive and useful, and make a very suitable wedding present) and hundreds of things which our limited space will not admit of mention. The store is located at No. 388 Central avenue, and is of the dimensions of 20 × 40 feet. Altogether this store is one of the most attractive in town, and has been under the able management of Mr. Charles E. Bacon since 1857, he conducts his business on a high plane of honor with fair representation of all goods, and one price, that the very lowest. Mr. Bacon is a native of Biddeford, Maine, and has conducted his business in Dover from the start in a highly satisfactory manner, both to himself and his patrons. Two competent and reliable assistants are employed and an extensive retail business is done. Mr. Bacon is sole agent for the Diamond spectacles, and gives special attention to watch, clock and jewelry repairing; also engraving is neatly executed, and the most intricate jobs will be satisfactorily performed in a thoroughly workmanlike manner at exceedingly moderate prices. No misrepresentations are permitted at this store, and callers may feel assured that all articles bought here will prove just as represented.

A. & J. Killoren. Groceries, Cigars and Confectionery. 314 Central Ave., Dover, N. H.—The store occupied by the Killoren Bro's is one of the most popular in the town, the stock is complete in every department, and is made up of carefully selected goods, which may be confidently relied upon to be precisely as represented. Messrs. Andrew and John Killoren have carried on their present enterprise for over ten years, both gentlemen are well known in political as well as business circles. The premises utilized at 314 Central ave., cover an area of over 800 feet and are very conveniently fitted up, enabling the firm to display their goods to excellent advantage, and with the aid of three assistants to handle their business without confusion or delay. Fine groceries, teas, coffees, flour, etc., cigars of all the best brands, and pure confectionery are offered at the very lowest market rates, and all goods are guaranteed to give satisfaction to the most fastidious. Callers are assured prompt and courteous attention and all orders are filled accurately and when promised, and no one who calls at this highly popular establishment will have reason to regret having done so.

Valentine Mathes, wholesale and retail dealer in Coal, Wood, Grain, Hay, Lathes, Shingles and Superphosphate, Folsom Street, Dover, N. H.—The enterprise conducted by Mr. Valentine Mathes is of the very first importance to the residents of Dover and vicinity, for Mr. Mathes deals in a variety of standard commodities, and quotes such low prices that a good deal of money can be saved by placing orders with him. He solicits a trial order from those wishing anything in his line, and feels confident that in many cases he can enable customers to save ten per cent., from the amount they formerly expended for coal, grain, etc. Mr. Mathes was born in Durham, N. H., and has carried on his present business since 1879. The premises utilized are located on Folsom street, and comprise a grain elevator, coal and wood sheds, etc., a very heavy stock of coal, wood, grain, hay, lathes, shingles, superphosphate, etc., being constantly carried, enabling the most extensive wholesale or retail orders to be filled without delay. Employment is given to fifteen assistants, and all goods are delivered in the compact part of the city free. Orders by mail or telephone are assured immediate and careful attention, and a team will call regularly to take orders if desired. Mr. Mathes makes it a rule to deliver goods promptly at the time promised, and no small share of the popularity of his establishment can be traced to this practice.

Walton R. Shaw, dealer in Boots, Shoes and Rubbers of all kinds, 101 Washington Street, Dover, N. H.—Considering the important influence that is exerted by what is worn on the feet—not only on one's personal appearance, but also on one's health as well.—it is not surprising that many people should find it harder to select a durable pair of shoes than any other article of dress, in order to obtain reliable and satisfactory foot covering dependence must be placed in the dealer, and when we say Mr. Walton R. Shaw guards the interests of his customers as though they were his own, we only voice the opinion of many of those familiar with his business methods. This establishment was originally founded by Mr. O. C. Ingraham, who conducted the business for over fifteen years. Since 1889 it has been under the sole control of Mr. Walton Shaw who is a native of Holbrook, Mass. The premises occupied at No. 101 Washington street are 20 × 60 feet in dimensions, and boots and shoes of all kinds are handled, and the stock carried is sufficiently comprehensive to include all sizes, shapes, kinds and conditions of foot-wear. The proprietor of this store warrants every article leaving this establishment to prove as represented.

G. W. Horne & Co., Brick Manufacturers, Dover, N. H.—Among the representative manufacturing enterprises which have made Dover what it now is, it would never do to omit mention of that carried on under the firm-name of G. W. Horne & Co., for this was inaugurated many years ago and has attained a reputation which is by no means confined to this section. Mr. Horne is dead, and the business is now owned by his daughter, it being carried on under the direct management of Mr. Wingate Bunker, who is well and favorably known in manufacturing and general business circles, and who is very successful in maintaining the high reputation so long associated with this undertaking. Messrs. G. W. Horne & Co., utilize spacious premises and are very extensively engaged in the manufacture of brick. The sheds used for storage purposes cover a very wide expanse of ground, and as a general thing a heavy stock of finished brick is carried. The average annual production is about 2,000,000, and the largest orders can be filled at short notice and the lowest market rates. The bricks are remarkably uniform in quality, and are highly spoken of by all who have made use of them.

George & Langmaid, Granite Cutters, and dealers in Monuments, Tablets and Cemetery Enclosures, River St., Dover, N. H.—It is undoubtedly a fact that first-class stone work is not to be had at second or third class rates, but it should be remembered that all first-class rates are by no means identical, and that there is really no need of paying fancy figures in order to get work equal to the best. A practical illustration of the truth of these assertions may be obtained by visiting the establishment conducted by Messrs. George & Langmaid, at No. 31 River street, for this firm do stone cutting in general; making a specialty of granite monuments and cemetery work, and quoting uniformly moderate prices on work that will bear the most critical inspection. This business was at one time carried on by Mr. Ira A. Butterfield, who was succeeded in 1882 by Mr. Stephen W. George and Levi Elder, and in 1886 Mr. George assumed entire control of the business and continued until 1889, when Mr. Linville F. Langmaid was admitted to partnership. Mr. George is a native of Vermont and Mr. Langmaid of New Hampshire, both partners being skillful stonecutters who have had long and varied experience. A great variety of designs is offered to choose from, and estimates will cheerfully be made on application, all orders, large or small, being assured prompt and painstaking attention. Messrs. George & Langmaid have recently opened a granite quarry in Nottingham, which is located ten miles from Dover. This granite is the best this side of Concord. It is light in color, and very nice for cemetery and building work.

———

City Employment Bureau, W. C. Williams, 327 Central Avenue, McCarty Block, Dover, N. H.—In theory, an employment bureau cannot fail to be of great public convenience and so deserves liberal support, but in practice many establishments of this kind are of no use whatever and are carefully avoided by well informed persons in search of desirable help. The fault of course is with the management, for the principle involved is sound, and when intelligently and honorably carried out the results are sure to be eminently satisfactory to all parties concerned. Therefore we take pleasure in calling attention to the City Employment Bureau, located at No. 327 Central avenue, in McCarty Block, for since this office was opened, in 1889, it has made an enviable record for efficiency and reliability. The proprietor, Mr. W. C. Williams, is a native of New York State, and served in the army during the Rebellion. He is associated with the leading employment offices in Boston, and is in a position to supply private families, hotels, restaurants, boarding, mountain and seashore houses with help at short notice. He constantly has the names of male and female help of all nationalities on his books, and can furnish new arrivals to those preferring such. The office is open from 8 A. M. to 8 P. M., and is in charge of Mrs. Williams, prompt and courteous attention being assured to every caller. All first-class help will be furnished with situations at short notice.

P. Gorman, dealer in Groceries, Fruits and Vegetables, Choice Butter, Cheese and Eggs, 11 Locust St., Dover, N. H.—It is becoming generally understood that the food we eat has more to do with our bodily health than any other one thing. Disorders and even diseases that were once treated with powerful drugs and medicines, are now corrected and almost entirely cured by careful attention to diet. It is also conceded that the man who most perfectly suits his food to his temperament and his occupation, will, other things being equal, enjoy the best health. Therefore it is of the highest importance to know where reliable food products may be best obtained. We are happy to be able to call the attention of our readers to so deserving and well-managed an establishment as that carried on by Mr. P. Gorman, at No. 11 Locust street. He commenced operations here in 1881, and has already built up a large retail trade. An extensive stock is constantly on hand consisting of groceries, fruits and vegetables, choice butter, cheese and eggs. Mr. Gorman obtains his goods from the most reliable sources, and is therefore in a position to guarantee that they will prove as represented. Two competent assistants are employed, and no trouble is spared to satisfy all customers. Mr. Gorman caters to family trade and quotes the lowest market rates on goods of standard quality.

———

Jenness & Harvey, Livery, Boarding and Baiting Stable, Hacks furnished for Funerals, Private Parties, etc. Rear of American House, Dover, N. H.—The firm of Jenness & Harvey, have shown great enterprise in catering to the public. A visit to their stable will disclose the fact, that first-class teams may be obtained there at very reasonable rates and at short notice. Horses will be taken to board at a moderate price and are assured proper care, good food and suitable stabling. The stable which is located at the rear of the American House, contains thirty stalls. Hacks will be furnished when desired for funerals, private parties, etc. These gentlemen do a large business in horse clipping. Those who have patronized them in this line, can testify to the careful and skillful manner in which the operation was performed. Four competent assistants are employed, and the interests of their customers are faithfully consulted. This enterprise has been conducted by the present proprietors since 1888. Mr. C. E. Jenness who is a native of Dover, N. H., was formerly proprietor of the Hawthorn Stable. Mr. F. C. Harvey is a native of South Berwick, Maine. All having business dealings with these gentlemen will find them thoroughly reliable and honorable. It is their aim to keep a first class stable, where first-class teams may be obtained at all times, and thus far they have succeeded to the satisfaction of all interested.

———

The City Laundry, the original Dan Guilfoyle, Proprietor, corner of Third Street and Central Avenue, Dover, N. H.—There are many people who object to having washing done at home and yet do not feel disposed to entrust their linen to public laundries. But there is no more necessity of having your clothes injured at a laundry than there is of having them done up at home, for The City Laundry now run by Mr. Dan Guilfoyle at the corner of Third street and Central avenue, does careful work and avoids injury to the most delicate fabric. Mr. Guilfoyle has conducted his present enterprise since 1884, and has built up a thriving business, employment being given to only thoroughly experienced assistants. The uniform superiority of the work turned out at this establishment is evident to the most fastidious. A very important feature of the business is the fact that all clothes are dried out in the open air, no chemicals used whatever, while the prices are so low that all can afford to take advantage of the opportunities offered. Laundry work of all kinds is done at short notice, and work is called for and delivered promptly as promised. Mr. Guilfoyle is a native of Dover, and well known throughout the city and vicinity.

James W. Hartford, Harness Maker, 9 Locust Street, Dover, N. H.,- While no man is to be blamed for trying to purchase the goods he requires as cheaply as possible, still, it should always be remembered that articles of standard merit have a much more uniform or standard price than those which are simply made to sell, as the saying is, and that the lowest priced article is therefore not necessarily the cheapest. This principle applies to every line of business and particularly to that devoted to the manufacture and sale of harnesses, whips, collars, etc., for these goods vary greatly in quality, as good material and skillful workmanship have to be paid for. Mr. James W. Hartford has built up an enviable reputation in the production of the above named goods, having been engaged in the business for over thirty years. His shop is located at No. 9 Locust street, Dover, N. H. The premises have an area of about 300 feet, while the employment of an experienced assistant enables him to serve his customers in a prompt and satisfactory manner. These articles are offered at the very lowest market rates. Mr. Hartford is a native of Dover, N. H., and is almost universally known in this vicinity as he has been deputy sheriff. Orders for custom work or repairing will be filled at very short notice.

J. Frank Roberts, dealer in Groceries, Flour and Produce, Teas, Coffees and Spices, Extracts and Canned Goods, at the lowest cash prices, 498 Central Avenue, Dover, N. H.—The great magnitude of the grocery business in this city, is significantly indicated by the number and importance of the houses engaged in this line of trade, and of these, none occupies a more prominent position than that of Mr. J. Frank Roberts, doing business at No. 498 Central avenue. This enterprise was inaugurated in 1879 by the present proprietor. In 1887 he associated himself with Mr. Foss, under the firm style of Roberts & Foss, which was continued until 1890, when Mr. Roberts again assumed entire management of the business. Mr. Roberts is a native of Maine, and is well known throughout Dover and vicinity as an enterprising and sagacious business man. No retail grocery house in this city enjoys more favorable relations with producers, wholesalers, etc., and the consequence of this state of affairs is to be seen in the exceptional advantages the proprietor is enabled to offer his customers in the purchase of many standard commodities. The premises occupied comprise a store and store-room, each 20 × 40 feet in dimensions, and are well fitted up for the accommodation of the large and varied stock dealt in, which includes groceries, flour and produce; also teas, coffees, spices, extracts and canned goods. Three competent assistants are employed and all orders are assured immediate and careful attention, while the prices quoted are invariably in accordance with the very lowest market rates.

"Boston Five and Ten Cent Store," Tin Ware, Glass Ware, Toys, Crockery, 108 Washington Street, Dover, N. H.—A very attractive establishment for the housekeeper to visit is that known as the "Boston 5 and 10 Cent Store," which is located at No. 108 Washington street, for here may be seen a fine assortment of crockery, glassware, and tinware; also a well selected line of toys, and many other goods too numerous to mention. Business was begun here in 1880, and has already attained extensive proportions. The premises utilized are of the dimensions of 20 × 50 feet, and the stock on hand is displayed to excellent advantage. Children are well provided for at this establishment, for a complete assortment of toys and games is offered to choose from, and the prices are as attractive as the goods themselves. The latest and most successful novelties may be bought here at the prices quoted, when they far exceed in value goods offered at other houses for twice the amounts. Two competent assistants are given employment and all customers are assured prompt and polite attention, while every article offered for sale will be found to be exactly as represented.

D. H. Wendell's Fire and Life Insurance Agency; corner of Main and School Streets, Dover, N. H.—A well known insurance agency is a great convenience to any business community and we therefore need make no apology for calling the attention of our readers to that of D. H. Wendell's on the corner of Main and School streets, Dover, N. H., established in 1852, and has furnished insurance of the most reliable character at the lowest market rates, and those wishing any information in relation to fire or life insurance would do well to give him a call. He is a native of Dover and widely known in the community as one of Dover's heavy tax payers, a justice of the peace and quorum for the State, was representative of the town prior to the city charter, and was appointed insurance commissioner for the State in the year 1866, but resigned on account of his other business. And at the time of the passage of the act known as the Valued Policy Law in the year of 1885, was agent for the following old well-known fire insurance companies, viz: Home Insurance Company of New York, Insurance Company of North America, Pennsylvania; Hartford of Hartford, and Phœnix and National of Hartford, representing some $25,000,000 of assets, and is now agent and broker for the Old New Hampshire Fire Insurance company of Manchester, N. H., that has more than a million and a half of assets, and is also agent for the Old Manhattan Life Insurance Company of New York that has some eleven million and a half dollars of assets.

E. H. Frost, manufacturer of Building Finish, Brackets, Window and Door Frames, Planing, Sawing, Turning, etc., to order, Folsom Street, Dover, N. H.—The use of machinery has greatly modified the building business, and there are now but very few parts of a house but what can be more cheaply and accurately made by machinery than by hand. Of course the result has been to materially diminish the cost of building and thus to enable many a man to own the house he lives in who otherwise would have to occupy less desirable rented quarters. This is a distinct gain, and it follows that such enterprises as that carried on by Mr. E. H. Frost deserve liberal patronage, for Mr. Frost is a leading manufacturer of building finish, brackets, window and door frames, etc.; being prepared to furnish anything in that line at short notice and at the lowest market rates. He is a native of Elliot, Maine, and is very well known personally in Dover and vicinity, at present being a member of the city council. He succeeded Mr. F. O. Marshall in the ownership of his present business in 1887, and gives it close personal attention, sparing no pains to fully satisfy every customer. The mill is located on Folsom street, and is two stories in height and 40 × 70 feet in dimensions. It is fitted up with improved machinery, driven by steam-power, and special attention is given to doing planing, sawing, turning, etc., to order. Mr. Frost manufactures desks and does other cabinet work to a considerable extent, quoting the lowest market rates in every department of his business and employing an adequate force of experienced assistants.

Sawyer Woolen Mills, manufacturers of Fancy Cassimeres and Suitings, Dover, N. H.—The manufacture of textile fabrics is one of New England's leading industries and represents the investment of an enormous amount of capital, but among all the many establishments devoted to this branch of production those utilized by the Sawyer Woolen Mills must be given a leading position as regards magnitude, perfection of equipment and uniform excellence of the results attained. "Sawyer woolens" are almost universally known in this country, and their high reputation is the natural sequence of the enterprising and painstaking methods which have characterized their manufacture from the first, for the aim of the producers has ever been to turn out goods that would have no superior in their special line, and to attain this end neither trouble nor expense has been spared, and a manufacturing plant has been established which combines all the most valuable improvements in machinery and methods, and is consequently a marvel of completeness and efficiency. This representative enterprise was inaugurated in 1823 by Mr. Alfred I. Sawyer and in 1849 passed under the control of Messrs. Z. & J. Sawyer, who were succeeded by Messrs F. A. and J. Sawyer in 1852 ; the present company being incorporated in 1873. Mr. Charles H. Sawyer is president, Mr. Jonathan Sawyer, treasurer, and Mr. T. M. Clark, superintendent, and the capital of the company is $600,000. The Sawyer Woolen Mills are located on Bellamy Bank River, and the company controls the power afforded by the three lower falls. In 1863-4 a reservoir was built in Barrington and in 1881 it was enlarged, its area now being 450 acres. The lower mill is located on tide-water, the stream being navigable for coal barges, light-draft sloops, etc., and further transportation facilities are afforded by the Portsmouth and Dover branch of the Eastern railroad, which has a station at these mills. The lower mill is a brick structure, three stories and a basement in height and 225 × 38 feet in dimensions, having an addition comprising two stories and a basement, measuring 90 × 25 feet. Both water and steam power are available, the latter being furnished by a seventy-five-horse Corliss engine. The upper mill is also brick, and is four stories in height and 272 × 40 feet in dimensions. Connected with or adjacent to it are various commodious structures, among which is one two stories and a basement in height, and 70 × 30 feet in size, another of similar dimensions, having three stories and a basement ; another 58 × 30 feet, with two stories and a basement ; another comprising three stories and measuring 58 × 40 feet ; another, also three stories high, 143 × 40 feet in dimensions, and also another three stories high measuring 185 × 65 feet. There are also two brick storehouses, four stories high and 126 × 40 feet in dimensions ; one brick storehouse 100 × 30 feet in size and two stories in height ; an office building, two stories high and 57 × 40 feet in dimensions, together with a dry house, repair shop, stable, etc., and fifty tenements of good size, with slated or gravel roofs. Power is afforded by two forty-inch Hercules turbine wheels and a 250-horse Corliss engine. The mills are lighted by gas and have a complete and admirably arranged fire-extinguishing plant, including automatic sprinklers of the most improved type. Employment is given to 450 operatives, and the value of the annual product is between one and two million dollars. Messrs. F. A. and J. Sawyer act as selling agents and the goods are shipped to all parts of the Union, the demand for them being steadily increasing. From the selection of the raw material to the completion of the last process incidental to production, every detail is given close and skillful supervision, and the care exercised in the designing and manufacture of the fancy cassimeres and suitings made by the Sawyer Woolen Mills, together with the enterprise and ability shown in reducing the expense of production to the lowest figure consistent with the use of dependable material, is the secret of the success the company has met with in producing goods that give the best of satisfaction to consumers and the trade and are accepted as the standard wherever introduced.

S. H. Foye, dealer in Marble and Slate Headstones, Monuments, Tablets, Grave Enclosures, Counter and Table Tops ; also Soap-Stone Work of all kinds : shop Central Street, opposite New City Building, Dover, N. H.—Mr. S. H. Foye is a native of Lee, N. H., but has resided in Dover for many years, having long ranked with the most prominent business men of this city. Although giving close attention to mercantile affairs he has found time to discharge the duties of some very important public offices. He has served on the board of aldermen two years, and was on the board of engineers from 1851 to 1872, two years of which was chief engineer. Mr. Foye has served as mayor of Dover, and was also representative during the years 1856 and 1857. He became identified with the granite business as early as 1846, and in 1855 began to handle marble also, giving up the granite business altogether in 1873. He is now extensively engaged in the manufacture and sale of marble and slate headstones, monuments, tablets, grave enclosures, etc., together with counter and table tops and soap-stone work of every description. Mr. Foye's shop is located on Central street, opposite the new City Building, the premises having an area of about 1500 square feet. Employment is given to a sufficient number of assistants to ensure the prompt filling of every order, and the finish and general character of the work turned out are unsurpassed, while the prices quoted are uniformly moderate.

Dover Steam Laundry and Dye House, T. G. Hill, Proprietor, No. 6 Orchard Street, Dover, N. H.—No more perfect sign of advanced civilization could be given than that offered by a modern steam laundry, for its presence in a community shows, first, that cleanliness prevails, and second, that the people have learned to avoid one fruitful cause of domestic trouble. There is really no more reason why washing should be done at home, than there is why our shoes should be made at home, or any other operation performed that can be more easily and cheaply attended to outside. Some of our readers may take exceptions to the "cheap" clause in that sentence, and say, that it is not justified by the facts, but if they will go to the trouble of estimating all the drawbacks consequent upon domestic washing—the extra fuel burned, the time occupied, the space taken up, the risk run, the constant and exasperating trials to strength and patience experienced—we think that they will find on comparison that we are not so far wrong after all, and then the results attained. Look at the work turned out in the ordinary course of business by the Dover Steam Laundry, and see how it compares with the best that can be done at home. Is it not superior ? every facility is at hand—skilled labor is employed, constant supervision exercised—is it any wonder that the results are more satisfactory ? The enterprise in question was originated by Mr. Webster and has been under the control of its present proprietor, Mr. T G. Hill since 1883 ; it is located at No. 6 Orchard street, and comprises spacious premises covering an area of over 1200 feet. The proprietor is a native of Biddeford, Me. In connection with the laundry a large trade is done in dyeing, scouring and cleaning, which is done in the most satisfactory manner. A specialty is made of dyeing and cleaning garments without ripping and no pains are spared to serve the public in the best manner. A large business has been established which shows every sign of a continuous and pronounced increase. Eight experienced and reliable assistants are given employment.

Walter T. Perkins, Steam and Gas Fitter ; dealer in Steam Heating and Gas Lighting Apparatus, Wrought Iron and Brass Pipe, Valves, Fittings, etc.; Gas Fixtures, Glass Globes and Shades, No. 44 Locust Street, Dover, N. H.—There are some kinds of work which may be done in a " good enough " fashion without any bad results, but when it comes to steam and gas-fitting, it is simply foolish to be satisfied with anything but the best, for inferior work in this line is dangerous, troublesome and expensive, to say nothing of its not answering the purpose for which it was designed. It is easy enough to have first-class piping if you apply to the proper party, and certainly no wiser course can be taken than to leave your order with Mr. Walter T. Perkins at No. 44 Locust street, for he is a thoroughly competent steam and gas-fitter. He has the facilities and the men to enable him to execute all commissions at short notice, and in the most approved and satisfactory manner, the best of materials being used. He is uniformly moderate in his charges, and as he gives close personal attention to his business he is in a position to keep the service to a very high standard of efficiency and to guarantee complete satisfaction to his patrons. The premises occupied comprise one floor and basement 22 × 60 feet in dimensions. Mr. Perkins is a dealer in steam-heating and gas-lighting apparatus, wrought iron and brass pipe, valves, fittings, etc., gas fixtures, glass globes, and shades, steam and water gauges, engineers' supplies, etc. Mr. Perkins, who is a native of Dover, N. H., has been the proprietor of this establishment since 1874. He has gained an honorable position among the business circles of this neighborhood. Mr. Perkins is also agent for the Gurney Hot Water Heater which is conceded to be the best hot water heater in the market. He has put in several in this vicinity which give the best of satisfaction.

Hayes & Hodgdon, dealers in Choice Groceries, Teas, Coffees, Spices, Confectionery, and Fruit, 103 Washington Street, Dover, N. H.—The ability to suit a business enterprise to the particular class of trade it is designed to reach principally, is an indispensable factor in attainment of success, and it is owing in a great degree to the skill displayed in this direction, that the firm of Hayes & Hodgdon has attained the high reputation and popularity it now enjoys. This concern is made up of Messrs. E. J. Hayes and F. P. Hodgdon. The establishment now conducted by them was founded in 1870 by Mr. W. M. Courser, Messrs. Hayes & Hodgdon assuming full control in 1889. The premises utilized are located at No. 103 Washington street, and are of the dimensions of 20 × 80 feet. A stock of fine groceries is carried, which includes all the almost endless variety of goods now handled by a first-class establishment of this kind ; also flour of all grades, selected teas and pure coffees, spices, etc.; also pure confectionery and fruits of all kinds in their season. Mr. Hayes is a native of Medbury and Mr. Hodgdon of Dover, N. H. Both gentlemen are well known and esteemed by all who know them. Employment is given to a reliable assistant and courteous and prompt attention is assured to all callers. All orders will be accurately delivered at short notice, and prices will be found to compare favorably with the lowest market rates.

Dover Trunk Factory, Whittier & Emerson, Proprietors, successors to W. O. Whittier, manufacturers of all kinds of Trunks, wholesale and retail, 62 and 64 St. Thomas St., Dover, N. H.—If anyone doubts that it is good policy to buy a thoroughly well-made trunk, let him visit the nearest railway station, especially when "business is rushing," and watch the train hands and expressmen wrestle with the baggage. Time is worth a good deal to them and the baggage belongs to other persons,—consequently they save ten cents worth of time at the expense of ten dollars worth of baggage, and think nothing of it. It is not for us to say where the fault lies, but the moral at least is plain—see that *your* trunk is of a kind that will stand the racket. Such a trunk cannot be bought for nothing, but it may be purchased at a reasonable figure if you patronize the right dealer and if that dealer gets his trunks of Messrs. Whittier &

Emerson, proprietors of the Dover trunk factory, so much the better, for in that case you may feel confident that his goods will prove as represented and give the best satisfaction. This factory was opened by Mr. W. O. Whittier, in 1887, and passed into the possession of the present firm in 1889. The premises comprise two floors measuring 25×50 feet, and are located at Nos. 62 and 64 St. Thomas street. All kinds of trunks are manufactured and both a wholesale and retail business is done, the facilities being such that the largest orders can be filled at short notice, while the smallest commissions will be promptly and carefully executed. A full assortment of sizes and kinds is carried in stock and all tastes, all circumstances and all purses can easily be suited.

J. H. Winslow, dealer in Boots, Shoes, Rubbers and Shoe Findings, French Calf Skins and Sole Leather, No. 410 Central Avenue, on the Bridge, Dover, N. H.—Mr. J. H. Winslow has been engaged in the boot and shoe business in Dover since 1861, and has conducted his present enterprise since 1885. The establishment in question was originally established in 1843 by Mr. Oliver Libey, and after several changes in its management came into the possession of the present proprietor, at the above named date. The premises occupied cover an area of about 900 square feet, and a very heavy stock is carried, for Mr. Winslow deals in boots, shoes, rubbers, shoe findings, French calf skins, and sole leather, and caters to all classes of trade. His assortment includes goods suited to all kinds of wear, and whether a dress boot, or a working shoe, is wanted, he can fill the want in the most satisfactory manner. Dealing with only reputable manufacturers' wholesalers, he is in a position to guarantee the quality of the goods he handles, and although he does not pretend to sell " below the cost of manufacture," still there is no more likely place at which to look for bargains, for Mr. Winslow is a careful and discriminating buyer, and by watching the market is often able to secure standard articles below the regular rates, but a full assortment of sizes in all standard styles is kept in stock, the result being that a perfect fit is easily obtainable. The latest novelties are offered as soon as they appear in the market, and at prices that will bear the severest comparison with those quoted elsewhere. Mr. Winslow is a native of Nottingham, N. H., and is very well known throughout the business circles of Dover. Those in want of anything included in the line of foot-wear will find it at his establishment of warranted quality.

A. N. Ward, Undertaker and Practical Embalmer. Caskets, Robes, Plates and Flowers, Hearses and Carriages Furnished ; Residence over Store, Nos. 12 and 14 Third Street, Dover, N. H.—Considerable expense as well as no small degree of executive ability is required in order to discharge the responsible duties of an undertaker satisfactorily, for it is of course highly important to so manage as to avoid all confusion or delays on the occasions when the services of an undertaker are required. Mr. A. N. Ward has often been called upon to officiate in this capacity during the past six years. He is a native of Brockton, Mass., and began operations in Dover in 1884. He is an undertaker and practical embalmer. His establishment and residence, are both conveniently located at Nos. 12 and 14 Third street. A carefully selected stock is carried, comprising caskets, coffins, burial robes, and funeral goods in general. Flowers, hearses and carriages, will also be furnished when desired. Moderate prices are quoted in every department, and the variety of goods offered is sufficiently large to admit of all tastes being suited. Orders for embalming will receive immediate and careful attention, and the entire direction of funerals will be assumed if desired, thus enabling much anxiety and trouble to be avoided.

H. A. Pattee, dealer in Carpets and Furniture, Bedding, Sideboards, Desks, Lounges, Curtains, etc., 337 Central Avenue, Dover, N. H.—The first step towards going to house keeping is to get a wife, no doubt, but after that little matter is attended to the question of furniture comes up to be settled. Some marked changes have occurred in the furniture trade of late years, and it is now possible to furnish a house at a very moderate expense. Of course you can spend money if you want to—$500 can be spent for a single chamber set, if you wish, but a small house can be very comfortably fitted up for that amount. But when it comes to exercising wise economy, the first thing to do is to find a dealer who is satisfied with a small margin of profit, and who carries a stock sufficiently large and varied to allow of all tastes being suited, and hundreds of people have solved this problem to their entire satisfaction by placing their orders with Mr. H. A. Pattee located at No. 337 Central avenue, Dover. This gentleman is a native of New Hampshire, and established his present business in Dover in 1887. He handles carpets, and furniture of all kinds, including bedding, sideboards, desks, lounges, curtains, etc. The premises occupied comprise five floors, each 20×60 feet in dimensions, thus affording ample space for the carrying of an exceptionally heavy stock. The proprietor offers some very decided bargains in every department. In regard to these bargains, we do not ask you to take our word for them, and in fact do not *want* you to do so, but what we *do* want is to have you call and see for yourself, for you will be sure to find something that you need at a price that will compel you to purchase. No detailed description of the goods dealt in is possible here, but suffice it to say that the assortment is most complete, the prices low, and that all callers are assured prompt and polite attention.

W. C. Leavitt, dealer in Meat, Fish, Poultry, Fruit, Vegetables and Country Produce, No. 5 Silver Street, Dover, N. H.—To those who are familiar with the advantages enjoyed by those dealing with Mr. W. C. Leavitt at No. 5 Silver street, the large retail business done by this gentleman needs no explanation, for self interest is a very powerful motive, and those placing a trial order with the gentleman in question, generally learn by the result that it is plainly for their interest to deal with him altogether. The enterprise was established by Mr. Geo. W. Parker, who was succeeded by Messrs. Berry & Leavitt in 1884. Mr. W. C. Leavitt, the present proprietor, assuming full control in 1889. He is a native of Massachusetts, and is well known throughout Dover. Employment is given to competent and polite assistants. The premises occupied are about 600 square feet in dimensions, and a heavy stock is carried including meats, fish, poultry, fruit and vegetables of every description together with country produce in general. The favorable relations Mr. Leavitt enjoys with producers and wholesalers are by no means without benefit

to his customers, for the prices quoted are surprisingly low, considering the character of the goods handled, and both economy and convenience are served by trading here.

N. E. Hanson, wholesale and retail dealer in Family Groceries and Provisions, Flour, Grain, Fish, etc., special attention paid in selection of choice Teas and Coffees, No. 1 Silver Street, Dover, N. H.—Among the many grocery and provision stores located in this city, few are better known than that now carried on by Mr. N. E. Hanson, for this establishment was founded in 1864 by J. T. Hanson & Co., and has long been highly popular with the most careful buyers. The present proprietor, Mr. N. E. Hanson, assumed full control of the business in 1872. Premises of the dimensions of 25 × 75 feet are occupied, and courteous and reliable assistants are required to attend to the heavy patronage enjoyed. The stock carried at this establishment will compare favorably in all essential features with that of any similar house in the city, for it is both large and varied, and comprises family groceries, provisions, flour, grain, fish, etc., special attention being paid to the selection of choice teas and coffees. Mr. Hanson does not place his prices so high that none but the favored few can afford to trade with him, but offers such decided inducements that experienced buyers feel they can hardly afford to trade elsewhere. Everything sold here is guaranteed to prove just as represented, and the prices average as low as the lowest when the quality is considered.

Rackley's Variety Store, Corner Washington Street and Central Ave., Dover, N. H.—The secret of success is much the same no matter what business may be engaged in, if you can furnish customers with reliable goods at bottom prices, and give prompt attention to all orders, you need have no fear but what a satisfactory trade will soon be built up. Such has been the experience of Samuel Rackley, who carries on a business devoted to the sale of crockery and glass and tin-ware, for since he succeeded Mr. Meldon in 1888, who was the original founder of the business, his efforts to extend operations have met with unquestionable success. Mr. Rackley is a native of Maine, and is well known in Dover; he is thoroughly acquainted with his business and has shown both intelligence and liberality in conducting the same; the premises occupied are of the dimensions of 20×30 ft. and are well stocked with a select stock of crockery, glass ware, granite-iron ware, wooden ware and 5 and 10 cent goods, also a full line of tinware, all purses can be accommodated at this store, for the prices are in every instance in accordance with the lowest market rates and the best goods are handled, as well as those at low cost.

J. W. Merrow, dealer in Groceries and Provisions, Flour, Butter, Cheese and Eggs, 5 Chestnut Street, Dover, N. H.—One of the recently established and at the same time one of the most reliable enterprises carried on in this section of Dover, is that conducted by Mr. J. W. Merrow, at No. 5 Chestnut street, for the proprietor is well and favorably known throughout this vicinity and has had sufficient experience in his present line of business to be thoroughly familiar with it in every detail. Mr. Merrow is a native of Ossipee, N. H. and as before stated is well known throughout Dover. The store is about 700 square feet in dimensions, and is very conveniently fitted up, the space available being sufficiently extensive to admit of the carrying of a large and varied stock, comprising selected family groceries and provisions of all kinds, also flour, butter, cheese and eggs. This stock is new, fresh, and "clean" in every department, and therefore, Mr. Merrow has no undesirable goods to ' work off " but is in a position to supply articles that will satisfy the most fastidious. Orders are filled at short notice and every caller may safely depend upon receiving courteous and painstaking attention. This establishment was founded about 1885, by Mr. Thos. Steel, and has been under the able management of Mr. J. W. Merrow since 1887 Those giving his establishment a trial, will find him prepared to fill either large or small orders without delay and at the lowest market rates.

H. E. Canney, Livery Stable, Boarding. Hacking and Baiting. Hacks Furnished for Weddings and Funerals, 17-23 St. Thomas Street, Dover, N. H.—The question of whether it is cheaper for one living in the city to own or hire a horse, is one that is influenced so much by circumstances in each individual case that it is impossible to answer it until those circumstances are duly considered, but at all events it will be agreed that such an establishment as that carried on by Mr. H. E. Canney at Nos. 17-23 St. Thomas street, deserves hearty support, for here a desirable, safe and stylish team may be hired at a moderate cost, or a horse may be boarded by its owner at a reasonable expense, so that all who use horses for business or pleasure can be accommodated. This enterprise was inaugurated in 1884, and now ranks among the leading undertakings of the kind in Dover. The premises in use are spacious and well-arranged, lighted with electricity, and contain every convenience, there being twenty-eight stalls and ample carriage accommodations. Single and double teams can be furnished at short notice, and the most fastidious customer will have no reason to complain of any detail of the turnout, for horse, carriage, harness, robe, etc., are all first-class, the best trade being entered to and no pains spared to assure satisfaction. Hacks for public occasions, such as balls, weddings, funerals, etc., can be supplied in any number desired, experienced and careful drivers being furnished, who will be found not only competent but courteous also. Animals boarded here will be given the best of care, and in short the high reputation of the establishment will be fully sustained in every instance.

Dover Five Cents Savings Bank, Dover, N. H.—Every well-managed savings institution is a benefit to the public, insomuch as its tendency is to encourage thrift, industry, and other qualities which go to make up good citizenship; but the Dover Five Cents Savings Bank is especially worthy of encouragement and support from the fact that, as its name indicates, it will receive on deposit so small a sum as five cents—and it is the saving of small sums that must be inculcated if prudent habits are to be established. The wage-earner who can and will save cents, can and will save dollars, and were this fact more generally understood and taken advantage of it would be of almost inestimable advantage to the community. Numberless instances might be quoted of where men have obtained their start in business life from savings accumulated when their earnings were by no means large, and it may be stated as a rule almost without exception that he who saves nothing when receiving small pay will save nothing if his wages be doubled. Once form the habit of putting aside a portion, however small, of your weekly or monthly earnings and the rest is easy. Should your pay increase, your savings will increase correspondingly, and in any event you will have 'the satisfaction of knowing that you are doing your best to improve your condition, and how gratifying that feeling is, only those who have experienced it know. The facilities offered by the Dover Five Cents Savings Bank are not surpassed by those of any similar institution, and money entrusted to its care is as absolutely secure as any funds well can be. The management is able and conservative and the financial condition of the bank is exceptionally favorable, a late statement showing that there is about $222,000 due depositors, while the guarantee fund is $11,150 and the surplus $2,700. But after all, the best evidence concerning the standing of such an enterprise is that afforded by the character of those identified with it, and we therefore take pleasure in presenting the following list, comment upon which is quite unnecessary: President,

John J. Hanson; vice-president, Eli V. Brewster; secretary and treasurer, Isaac F. Abbott; trustees, Eli V. Brewster, William A. Morrill, Ephraim H. Whitehouse, William H. Vickery, John J. Hanson, Isaac F. Abbott, Edmund M. Swan, Henry A. Worthen, James F. Seavey, Dennis Cash, Solomon H. Foye.

Dover National Bank, Dover, N. H.—The Dover National Bank is a thoroughly representative institution in every sense of the word, and since its incorporation in 1865 has exerted a most powerful influence in developing the interests of this section. It has a capital of $100,000, which has been further augmented by a surplus of $20,000. The following gentlemen, widely and favorably known in financial and general business circles for their prudence and just methods, are the officers and directors: President, Oliver Wyatt; vice-president, Eli V. Brewster; cashier, Isaac F. Abbott; directors, Oliver Wyatt, Eli V. Brewster, Joshua G. Hall, Moses D. Page, Henry A. Worthen, Richard N. Ross, John J. Hanson. The banking rooms are spacious and well-appointed, affording ample accommodations to patrons, and possessing every convenience for facilitating the despatch of business. A general banking business is transacted, including the reception of deposits, the discounting of approved commercial paper, the collection of drafts, and the dealing in government and other first-class securities. This is one of the best-managed and most popular banks in New Hampshire, and from its foundation has deserved and enjoyed the confidence of the public to an exceptional degree. The investments of the Dover National Bank have always been carefully and judiciously made, and its ventures of capital are at all times well secured; while the officers are obliging and efficient in their dealings with the public and spare no pains to extend the usefulness of the institution they represent. The following statement shows how thoroughly the public confidence is justified:

Report of the Condition of the Dover National Bank at Dover, in the State of New Hampshire, at the close of business, February 28, 1890.

RESOURCES.

Loans and discounts	$91,403.33
United States Bonds to secure circulation	100,000.00
Stocks, securities, judgments, claims, etc	31,775.11
Due from approved reserve agents	14,887.03
Banking house furniture and fixtures	8,200.00
Other real estate and mortgages owned	2,853.72
Current expenses and taxes paid	259.83
Premiums on United States Bonds	20,389.58
Checks and other cash items	1,527.50
Bills of other banks	4,713.00
Fractional paper currency, nickels, and cents	86.33
Specie	7,762.50
Legal-tender notes	3,195.00
Redemption fund with United States Treasurer (5 per cent. of circulation)	4,500.00
Total	$291,553.02

LIABILITIES.

Capital stock paid in	$100,000.00
Surplus in fund	20,000.00
Undivided profits	8,206.34
National Bank notes outstanding	88,100.00
Dividends unpaid	1,577.50
Individual deposits subject to check	69,388.25
Cashier's checks outstanding	4,280.93
Total	$291,553.02

State of New Hampshire, County of Strafford, ss:

I, Isaac F. Abbott, Cashier of the above named bank, do solemnly swear that the above statement is true to the best of my knowledge and belief. ISAAC F. ABBOTT, *Cashier.*

Subscribed and sworn to before me this 10th day of March, 1890. GEORGE W. BENN, *Notary Public.*

Correct—Attest:

OLIVER WYATT,
ELI V. BREWSTER, } *Directors.*
HENRY A. WORTHEN, }

JOHN A. GLIDDEN,
Furnishing and Funeral Undertaker.

SPECIAL CARE IN PREPARING FOR BURIAL.

MY PERSONAL ATTENTION TO ALL ITS DETAILS.

Residence and Office, 20 and 24 Locust Street.   Dover, New Hampshire.

George B. Wentworth & Co., manufacturers of Brogans and Plow Shoes, Central Avenue, Dover, N. H.—The enterprise carried on under the firm-name of George B. Wentworth & Co., was inaugurated about thirty-five years ago and has long held a leading position among other New Hampshire undertakings of a similar character. Mr. George B. Wentworth, the founder of the business, died in 1888, and it has since been conducted by his sons, Messrs. Charles B. and Fred N. Wentworth, no change being made in the firm name. The concern are extensively engaged in the manufacture of brogans and plow shoes for the Southern and Western trade, and their productions are highly thought of by dealers and consumers as they are unsurpassed for ease, strength and durability—the three fundamental characteristics of desirable working shoes. Some of our readers may be surprised to learn that there are degrees of merit in such coarse goods as brogans and plow shoes, but such is the fact and no little experience and skill are required in order to attain the best results in their manufacture. The premises utilized by this firm comprise four floors of the dimensions 45 × 65 feet, and are very thoroughly fitted up, power being furnished by a twenty-five horse engine and employment being given to 100 operatives. The output averages 1000 pairs per day and the firm are prepared to fill the largest orders at comparatively short notice, and to quote the lowest market rates. The business is conducted under the immediate supervision of Mr. Chas. B Wentworth who spares no pains to maintain the high reputation of the product.

Mary Byrne, Millinery and Fancy Goods, 63 Washington Street, Dover, N. H.—An old established and very popular enterprise of its kind is that of which Miss Mary Byrne is the proprietress, and which is carried on at No. 63 Washington street, founded in 1847 by Miss Byrne and which is the oldest millinery establishment in town. This business has since been continued without change of any kind in its ownership, and the experience gained by its manager through all these years, now enables her to offer inducements to her customers which it would be very hard to equal elsewhere. One floor is occupied of the dimensions of 25 × 40 feet, and the stock carried is not only large but varied, containing as it does, ribbons, laces, feathers, embroideries, collars, handkerchiefs, hosiery, white goods, underwear and fancy goods of all kinds, and in fact a complete assortment of such goods as are only handled by a first class establishment of this kind. Miss Byrne is very well known in Dover and vicinity, in both business and social circles. She employs an efficient assistant and assures all customers prompt and polite attention, and handles only goods that she can recommend, and guarantees that they will prove strictly as represented, and no trouble is spared to fully maintain the enviable reputation for enterprise and fair dealing this establishment has held so long.

A. P. Drew, Photographer ; Picture Frames and Mouldings of the latest patterns ; Life Size Crayons a Specialty ; 420 Central Avenue, Rooms 16, 17 and 18, Dover, N. H.—Those who deny the title of " artist " to any photographer no matter how skillful he may be, or how beautiful the work he may produce, occupies a precisely similar position to that held by those asserting the same thing in connection with the process of engraving on wood. There may be room for an honest difference of opinion on this subject, but it is difficult for us to see how any competent judge can declare art to be entirely absent from some of the wonderful photographic work to be seen nowadays, notably that produced by Mr. A. P. Drew, at his studio, No. 420 Central avenue, for this gentleman ranks with the leading photographers, and does the largest business of the kind in Dover. Mr. Drew is an artist of high merit, he gives special attention to all branches of photography, and has produced portraits that are worthy of the name, and that have called forth much favorable comment throughout this community, life size crayons being a specialty. Mr. Drew is a native of Dover. He established his profession in 1859, and now occupies three large rooms, 16, 17 and 18, at No. 420 Central avenue, where every provision is made for the comfort and convenience of patrons. Mr. Drew does not confine his business to photography alone, but deals in picture frames, and mouldings of the latest patterns. The extensive business transacted by Mr. Drew requires the services of seven competent assistants. Art lovers can visit this studio with pleasure and profit, for a fine selection of finished work is to be seen. The views of Dover illustrated in this book were taken by him.

C. H. Horton, Book Binder, 97 Washington Street, Dover, N. H.—Mr. C. H. Horton was born in New York City, but has been engaged in active business life in Dover for nearly forty years, during which time he has become thoroughly identified with the advancement of the best interests of that city, and has done much to bring about that advancement by the zeal, intelligence and fidelity with which he discharged the responsible duties devolving upon him in the various official positions to which he has been elected. Mr. Horton has served as councilman, as alderman, as mayor and as representative. He is now councilor of district No. 1 to Governor Goodell, and we need hardly add that few if any of our local business men are more universally known. He carries on a book binding establishment at No. 97 Washington street, and is prepared to fill either wholesale or retail orders at short notice and at moderate rates. As his facilities for binding pamphlets, books, etc., are well known to neighboring printers, publishers, etc., we will not dwell upon them, but will call attention to the service he is prepared to render in connection with the binding of magazines, music, etc., for retail customers. The work is done in a neat and durable manner and the charges are uniformly moderate.

Woodbury Brothers, wholesale manufacturers of Buskins and Slippers, and Women's and Misses' Boots and Shoes. Boston office: 31 Lincoln Street. Factories: Beverly, Mass., and Cor. Park and Dover Streets, Dover, N. H.—Shoe manufacturing is steadily increasing in New Hampshire, and present indications are that it will increase still more rapidly in the future, for manufacturers find that operations can be carried on in this State to excellent advantage, and it is becoming common for the leading Massachusetts concerns to establish branch factories here. The establishment conducted by Messrs. Woodbury Brothers can hardly be called a "branch," however, for the firm manufacture all their women's and misses' boots and shoes at this factory, the one in Beverly, Mass., being utilized for the production of buskins and slippers. Messrs. Woodbury Brothers rank with the leading boot and shoe houses of New England, their goods being very widely known among consumers and the trade. They have carried on operations in Beverly for about a score of years, and opened their Dover factory in 1886. This is located in a five-story building, 236 x 40 feet in dimensions, situated on the corner of Park and Dover streets. The plant of machinery in use is of the most improved type, and power is furnished by a seventy five horse engine; the capacity of the establishment being 2,400 pair per day. Employment is given to 250 persons, and operations are carried on under the direct supervision of Mr. J. T. Woodbury. No trouble is spared to maintain the high reputation of the product, and as the firm are in a position to quote the lowest market rates they find no difficulty in disposing of the output. The Boston office is located at No. 31 Lincoln street, where a full line of samples may be seen.

C. W. Smith, Books, Stationery, Picture Framing and Wall Papers, Bracewell Block, Dover, N. H.—This popular bookseller and stationer, during the six years he has been established here, has attained a prominent position among Dover's business men. He occupies a store 20×80 feet in dimensions, located in Bracewell Block, Central avenue, which contains a fine selected stock of books, stationery, picture frames, wall papers, etc. This business was originally established by Mr. C. H. Hovey who was succeeded in 1884 by the present proprietor. Under the able management of Mr. C. W. Smith, the establishment has been greatly extended and has become the local headquarters for books, stationery, picture frames, wall papers, artists' materials, etc. The goods displayed in the above named lines, show marked taste and judgment in their selection. Capable and reliable assistants are constantly employed. The store is neat and attractive in all its appointments, and every customer is treated in a polite and attentive manner, and the wants of the public are studied in every respect. Mr. Smith is a native of Maine, and a gentleman combining business talent with fairness in all his dealings. He is well qualified to push his business to still greater usefulness and importance. He is well known throughout this vicinity and is regarded as a reliable and representative business man.

DOVER FOUNDRY AND MACHINE WORKS,

Iron and Brass Castings, Machine Work,

C. E. MARSTON, Prop.,

Dover, - - New Hampshire.

The Dover Foundry and Machine Works may be said to have been established more than half a century ago, for the enterprise had its inception as far back as 1838, and after various changes in ownership, passed under the control of C. E. Marston, the present proprietor, about fifteen years ago. Mr. Marston is a native of Great Falls, N. H., and is very widely known in manufacturing circles, he having filled many important contracts and being accepted and often quoted as a competent authority on matters relating to piping, steam heating and constructional iron work. The Dover Foundry and Machine Works are spacious and well equipped, the foundry alone having an area of about 6,000 square feet. There is a large two-story machine shop, besides various out buildings, etc. Every facility is at hand for the production of iron and brass castings and the doing of general machine work ; and among the more important articles manufactured may be mentioned plumbers' pipe and fittings ; steam and hot water heating and ventilating apparatus, radiators ; lamp posts, hitching posts, iron columns; pulleys, shafting, and hangers; feed-water heaters, pumps, Babbitt metal, etc. Mr. Marston also deals extensively in wrought iron pipe, radiators, engines, gas fittings, steam fittings, gas fixtures, brass valves and boilers, and is in a position to figure very closely on piping, steam or hot water heating, and on iron work of all kinds. Estimates will cheerfully be made on application, and we need not dwell upon the advantages gained by placing orders in such experienced and responsible hands. Employment is given to from twenty to forty assistants, and the most extensive commissions can be executed at short notice, while the smallest orders are assured immediate and careful attention.

I. B. Williams & Sons, Tanners and manufacturers of Oak-Tanned Leather Belting, Rawhide, and Tanned Lace Leather, Dover, N. H.—Never before was there so extensive a demand for strictly first-class leather belting as is now the case, and it is easy to account for this condition of affairs, for the tendency is to constantly increase the speed of machinery and, other things being equal, the higher the speed the better the belt required. It is well-known that electric dynamos call for especially high grade belts if the best results are to be attained, and the rapidly increasing number of dynamos in use is of itself enough to account for a large share of the demand noted. Under these circumstances it is not surprising that the productions of Messrs. I. B. Williams & Sons should meet with a ready sale, for the purchaser of belting has to depend chiefly upon the reputation of the maker to ensure being supplied with a satisfactory article. The belting and lace leather made by this firm have an unsurpassed reputation throughout the country. The business was founded nearly half a century ago by Mr. I. B. Williams. The existing firm name was adopted in 1878, and remains unchanged, although the senior member Mr. I. B. Williams died in July, 1885. His sons, Messrs. F. B. and G. H. Williams, still continue the business and are now sole proprietors. They are both natives of Dover, and prominent citizens. The firm are tanners and manufacturers of oak-tanned leather belting, raw hides and tanned lace leather, producing a full line of these goods, and quote the lowest market rates on goods of standard excellence. The Cocheco raw hide lace leather (one of their specialties) being as famous and popular a brand as can be found in the market. A very large and complete plant is operated; the main building being four stories in height and 150 × 50 feet in dimensions. The most improved machinery is used throughout the works and power is afforded by a sixty-horse engine. Employment is given to sixty men, and some idea of the extent of the business may be gained from the fact that 500 butts, equaling 1000 sides of leather, are consumed weekly into belting, and 300 green hides per week are made into lace. The productions are shipped throughout the United States and hold a leading position wherever they have been introduced.

Crawford, Tolles & Co., Insurance, Rooms 13 and 14 National Block, Dover, N. H.—Messrs. Crawford, Tolles & Co., began operations in this city in 1889, and the magnitude and character of the business built up since that comparatively recent date, show better than anything else could what is thought of the facilities they offer by the property owners of Dover and vicinity. The firm is constituted of Messrs E. A. Crawford, A. D. Tolles and E. A. Leighton, Messrs. Crawford and Leighton being natives of New Hampshire, while Mr. Tolles was born in Vermont. Offices are maintained at Great Falls and Farmington in addition to the one in this city, and Mr. Crawford represents the firm here and also has charge of the Farmington agency. No concern in New Hampshire is better prepared to place large lines of insurance on desirable risks at short notice, and the smallest commissions will be promptly and faithfully executed, and no pains spared to make the service reliable and satisfactory in every respect. Insurance is placed on the most favorable terms and some idea of the facilities offered may be gained from the following list of companies represented: *New Hampshire Department.*—Ætna Insurance Company, of Hartford, Conn., in Great Falls and Farmington; Anglo Nevada Insurance Company, of California; Insurance Company of North America, of Philadelphia, Pa.; Liverpool and London and Globe Insurance Company, of England; London & Lancashire Insurance Company, of England; National Insurance Company, of Hartford, Conn.; Sun Fire Insurance Company, of England; Springfield Fire and Marine Insurance Company of Springfield, Mass.; Fitchburg Mutual Fire Insurance Company of Fitchburg, Mass.; Peoples' Fire Insurance Company of Manchester, N. H.; Granite State Fire Insurance Company of Portsmouth, N. H.; Portsmouth Fire Association of Portsmouth, N. H.; Capital Fire Insurance Company of Concord, N. H.; Underwriter's Fire Association of Concord, N. H.; also eight New Hampshire mutuals. *Maine Department.*—Royal Fire Insurance Company of England; Queen Fire Insurance Company of England; Pennsylvania Fire Insurance Company of Philadelphia, Pa.; Union Fire Insurance Company of California; Traveller's Accident Insurance Company of Hartford, Conn.; State Agents for New Hampshire of the Mutual Benefit Life Insurance Company of Newark, New Jersey.

C. E. HODSDON JEWELER
WATCHES, SILVERWARE, BRONZES, ETC.
DOVER, N. H.

Charles E. Hodsdon, Diamonds, Jewelry, and Rich Fancy Goods. Repairing and Engraving skillfully done, 444 Central Avenue, Dover, N. H.—The stock carried by Charles E. Hodsdon is worthy the careful inspection of all who contemplate the purchase of anything in the line of diamonds, jewelry, and rich fancy goods, for the assortment shown is unusually complete in every department, and what is more, the prices quoted are remarkably low, considering the quality of the goods. Mr. Hodsdon was born in Dover, and is well known throughout the city. The premises occupied are located at No. 444 Central Avenue, and is shared with Mr. Cash, dealer in boots and shoes. Some very beautiful designs in jewelry and fancy goods, are offered to select from, and the most fastidious cannot fail to find articles to please them at this establishment, for not only a full line of staple goods is carried, but also many of the latest and most fashionable novelties in jewelry, watches, clocks, etc. While especial attention is paid to the quality of the optical goods dealt in, eye glasses and spectacles suited to all defects of vision being always on hand. The proprietor has with him Mr. Geo. R. Hodsdon, a practical optician and graduate from Dr. Bucklin's School of Optics, N. Y. Five competent assistants are employed, and particular care is taken to make no representations that are not fully justified by the facts, and hence the most inexperienced buyer may trade here with the assurance of obtaining just what he pays for. Special attention is given to repairing and engraving, and those who have valuable articles that need cleaning or repairing, will find Mr. Hodsdon prepared to do the work in a skillful as well as perfectly satisfactory manner.

E. Morrill Furniture Co., dealers in Furniture, Carpets, Bedding, Draperies, Curtains, and Upholstery Goods, American Hall Building and 95 Washington Street, Dover, N. H.—The enterprise now conducted by the E. Morrill Furniture Co., was established about forty years ago by Mr. Edward Morrill, the present company being organized in 1889. It is composed of Messrs Henry J. Grimes and Mr. Charles E. Cate, these gentlemen are natives of Dover, and both are too well known in the vicinity to render extended personal mention necessary. This company occupy premises consisting of a furniture store including three floors at No. 95 Washington street, also a factory about 7,000 square feet in dimensions, located in the American Hall Building. Accuracy and economy are combined in the various processes of production, and explains in a great measure the ability of the company to supply thoroughly first-class goods at bottom prices. Employment is given to thoroughly competent assistants in both establishments, the company doing one of the largest business in furniture transacted in New Hampshire. The heaviest orders can generally be filled at very short notice, and it is worthy of note that durability as well as appearance is provided for in the construction of all work done at the factory, the stock being carefully selected and every detail of the work is executed under intelligent supervision. The legitimate result of such methods, is to be seen in the large and increasing demand for the company's goods. The stock dealt in comprises furniture, carpets, bedding, draperies, curtains, and upholstery goods, and the public will find that no more popular and desirable goods can be obtained than those offered by this enterprising company.

A. T. Ramsdell, Architect, 450 Central Avenue, National Block, Dover, N. H.—There are many advantages gained by obtaining the services of a competent architect, and in the large majority of instances it is much cheaper to employ such aid than to try to get along without it. This is true, whether a dwelling house, a factory or a warehouse is to be built, and in a somewhat extended experience we have yet to see the man who regretted employing a skilful architect, while we can recall many cases where an opposite course was bitterly regretted, we take pleasure in calling attention to the facilities offered by Mr. A. T. Ramsdell, for he is thoroughly well equipped to practice his profession and is very careful in his methods and regardful of the best interests of his clients. He is a native of York, Maine, and began operations in Dover in 1889. His office is located at No. 450 Central avenue, in National Block, and all communications to that address are assured prompt and painstaking attention. Plans and specifications will be drawn up at very short notice, and particular attention is given to putting the ideas of patrons as to construction, arrangement, etc., into practical and convenient form. The work of building will be personally supervised if desired, and the contractors kept strictly up to their agreements as regards material, workmanship, etc.

Richard A. Drew, Carriage Making and Repairing. Broadway, Dover, N. H.—People have been so often told that a thoroughly built vehicle was the cheapest as well as the best, and that it is always advisable to place orders for anything of this kind with a thoroughly reliable concern, that it would seem entirely uncalled for to repeat such advice were it not for the fact that the sale of cheap and worthless wagons and carriages is steadily increasing. If these vehicles gave satisfaction, or anything approaching

, satisfaction, we would have nothing to say against them, but the fact is they are made merely to sell, and are not only the most expensive but also the most dangerous to use in the long run. Compare them with the carriages that are made by Mr. Richard A. Drew, and the difference is plain even to one who has not had much experience in the selection of such articles, and the longer the vehicles are put to practical use the greater will be the difference in their appearance. Mr. Drew is a native of Barrington, N. H., and has carried on his present business in Dover since 1849. The premises occupied are located on Broadway and are of the dimensions of 30 × 40 feet, they are fitted up with improved tools and other facilities to enable first-class work to be done at short notice as well as at moderate rates. Mr. Drew is in a position to guarantee entire satisfaction to customers. Carriage making and repairing of all kinds will be done in a careful and durable manner at very reasonable prices.

O. L. Churbuck, Exchange Market, Meat, Fish and Vegetables, Canned Goods, etc., No. 6 Third Street, near Franklin Square, Dover, N. H.—The trade in meat, fish and vegetables has long been one of Dover's leading sources of wealth, and the establishments devoted to this line of business here located will compare favorably as regards resources and general standing with any in the State. Some of them have of course special claims upon the favor of the public, and that carried on by Mr. Orlando L. Churbuck is of particular interest from the fact that it is one of the most ably managed in the city. This establishment was originally founded by Mr. E. S. Trask, who was succeeded in 1886 by Messrs. Seavey & Randall, and they in 1888, by the present proprietor. Mr. Churbuck was born in this city and it is unnecessary to add, needs no introduction to our Dover readers. The premises occupied are located at No. 6 Third street, and known as the Exchange Market. It is about 800 square feet in dimensions. A very large stock is constantly carried, Mr. Churbuck being an extensive retail dealer in fresh and salt meats of all kinds; also fresh and shell-fish, vegetables, canned goods, etc. Employment is given to four competent assistants and the business is so thoroughly systematized that every order is assured immediate and careful attention. Mr. Churbuck keeps three teams constantly employed in delivering goods.

HISTORICAL SKETCH OF GREAT FALLS.

The village of Great Falls is located in the town of Somersworth, which was originally a part of Dover, but was set off and incorporated as a separate parish by an act passed December 10, 1729.

The first settlement in the territory comprised within the original town was made about 260 years ago, in 1630, or perhaps a year or so earlier, and about 1634 a saw mill and a "stamping mill for corne" (as it is described in the early records) were built at Salem Falls in the present town of Rollinsford, which is made up of territory set apart from Somersworth in 1849. The first settlement within the present limits of the town was made about 1670, near Hussey's Pond, so it will be seen that the section afterward incorporated as Rollinsford had a start of about forty years over the northern section; and for many years the "meeting house," the "training lot," and the centre of business of the parish and town of Somersworth were located close by what is now Rollinsford Junction.

The original township of Dover comprised so large a territory that the residents of the more remote portions found themselves greatly inconvenienced, and in 1729 the inhabitants of the northeastern section asked to be set off as a separate parish, for reasons clearly presented in the following petition:

"The petition of the subscribers inhabitants of the North East part of the town of Dover, humbly *sheweth*—That the dwelling places of yor petitioners are at a great distance from the houses of the public worship of God in the town of Dover where your petitioners live by which their attendance thereon is rendered very difficult more especially to the women and children of their families and that in the winter season and in stormy weather, So yt they cannot pay that Honour and Worship to God in publick as it is their heart's desire they could, therefore for the advancing the interest of Religion and for the Accommodation of yor Petitioners it is humbly prayed by them that your Excellency and the Honourable Assembly will please to sett them off as a Parrish for the maintaining the public worship of God amongst themselves and that they be dismiss'd from the Town of Dover as to the supporting of the Settled Minister there, And that the Bounds of that their Parish may begin , at the Gulfs a place so called at Cocheco river, and from thence to run to Varney's Hill and from thence the Town bounds on a North West point of the Compass & Your Petitioners shall ever pray as in duty bound," etc.

The petition was read in the house of representatives, April 25, 1729, but action was delayed on various accounts so that it was not until December 19, 1729, that the parish was incorporated.

The first minister was the Reverend James Pike, who had began preaching in this part of Dover in the latter part of 1727 and was regularly ordained in 1730. He lived to a ripe old age and was the "guide, consoler and friend" of the people of Somersworth for more than sixty years, his last sermon being delivered in 1790. Mr. Pike was a very powerful man, a fact which was of much service to

BIRD'S-EYE VIEW OF GREAT FALLS.
(From High School Building.)

him in the settlement of disputes. It is said that he and another minister in the course of a walk happened upon two men who were fighting. The combat was brought to an abrupt end by a summary separation of the fighters, each minister taking one bodily upon his shoulders and walking off with him. Mr. Pike made every one in his large parish his personal friend, and meagre as his salary was he refused to accept any of it during the hardest period of the Revolution. About all the legal documents of the parish and town relating to that time were written by him.

The parish became a town April 29, 1754, and by the setting apart of Rollinsford, July 3, 1849, the township was reduced to its present size.

Somersworth was a prosperous and quite largely populated town when the Revolution broke out, although the number of inhabitants had diminished somewhat during the preceding decade, the population being 1044 in 1767 and but 965 in 1775.

A meeting was held Friday, April 21, 1775, at which it was "voted that twenty men immediately march from town to meet the enemy, and those who shall go shall have wages." Liberal bounties were voted from time to time and more than fifty men were furnished before the war was over.

In 1783 the total population was but 888, eighteen of that number being negroes.

There were 285 buildings in town,—126 dwelling houses and 159 barns. The people were very poor, and the unsettled condition of affairs following the Revolution prevented much progress from being made, so nothing of special note occurred until 1820, when Isaac Wendell came from Dover, purchased the privileges at the Great Falls, together with a large area of land adjoining the privileges on both sides of the Salmon Falls River; his idea being to establish the manufacture of cotton goods. This scheme was destined to revolutionize the quiet old town and to give birth to one of the most beautiful and prosperous villages in New England.

A saw-mill and grist-mill had been built at this point in 1750, by Andrew Horn, who bought all the land in the vicinity, and the name of "the Great Falls" had been given to this part of the stream years before because the largest fall on the Salmon Falls River is here located, the water dashing from ledge to ledge down a distance of a hundred feet or more.

Mr. Wendell erected a wooden building for a cotton factory, carding houses, work shops for the

HIGH STREET, GREAT FALLS.

building of cotton machinery, and a store; this property being purchased in 1823 by the Great Falls Manufacturing Company, which had been incorporated June 11th of that year with a chartered capital of $500,000. The corporation held its first meeting at Dover, July 10, 1823, Abraham Wendell being elected president, and Jacob Wendell treasurer.

A contract was made with Isaac Wendell to furnish by the following January 1,280 cotton spindles, with all other machinery essential to the production of cotton goods, at $25 per spindle, Wendell to receive for this contract and for the property previously described the sum of $76,224.18. He was also made resident agent of the corporation. At this time there were but two dwelling houses on the site of the present village.

In 1824 a second cotton factory of 4000 spindles was built, and in 1825 a woolen mill, having a capacity for producing 200 yards of fine broadcloth daily was erected. Another building was utilized for carpet weaving and as a woolen picker and dyeing house. In 1826 the charter was so amended as to authorize a capital of $1,000,000, and in 1827 it was again amended, the authorized capital becoming $1,500,000 at which amount it still remains. The company made every effort to establish woolen manufacturing on a paying basis; expensive experiments being carried out and goods being produced that compared favorably in texture, color and finish with the finest fabrics then imported; but the business was found to be unprofitable and was gradually discontinued, the manufacture of carpets being given up in 1833, and in January of the following year the directors were empowered to stop the production of all woolen goods. All the stock and machinery were sold by July, 1835, and cotton machinery was substituted.

The work of improving the water power, adding machinery and otherwise developing the undertaking went steadily on and by 1859 the company had seven mills, 83,120 spindles, and 2120 looms. Steam power was first utilized in 1849, when a 180-horse engine was put into operation.

A reservoir for water for fire purposes and ordinary uses in the mills was built on Prospect Hill, at a cost of $100,000, in 1864; and water pipes have since been laid through all the chief streets in the village, the service being very efficient for the extinguishing of fires as the water has a " head " of some 130 feet.

GREAT FALLS AND DAM FROM BERWICK SIDE.

Between 1866 and 1869 some $700,000 were expended in adding new buildings, substituting turbine for breast-wheels, and in otherwise improving the plant, and in 1872 a new stone dam was built in place of the old wooden one on the upper level, and the Milton Three Ponds dam was raised two feet. The whole amount expended for this and other work from 1870 to 1874 exceeded $900,000. The mills have been consolidated from time to time, and a striking illustration of the extent to which this has been carried out is afforded by the fact that only three mills are now operated as compared with seven mills in 1859, but these three mills contain nearly 115,000 spindles and nearly 3000 looms, while the seven mills contained but 83,120 spindles and 2120 looms.

Employment is given to from 1800 to 2200 operatives, and between twenty and thirty million yards of shirtings and sheetings are produced annually.

The company control one of the most extensive and valuable water privileges in New Hampshire, it being estimated that there is about 4,000 horse-power on the three levels at Great Falls. A large amount of steam-power is also available, so the mills can be run to excellent advantage under all circumstances. George P. Gardner is president of the corporation, J. Howard Nichols is treasurer, and Charles H. Plummer, agent. The selling agents are Minot, Hooper & Co., of Boston.

The Somersworth Machine Company is another corporation which has done much to build up the town during the past forty years. It was incorporated in 1848 but did not begin business until 1851, when the manufacture of the once-famous " White Mountain " wood stove was begun at Salmon Falls. This stove was for a long time the best and most popular in the market, and even now a demand exists for it. The company still manufacture stoves and ranges of all kinds, together with furnaces, sinks and hollow ware at Salmon Falls; and at Great Falls and Dover they manufacture pulleys, shafting and hangers, and iron castings of all descriptions; employment being given to sixty men at the Great Falls works. O. S. Brown is president of this corporation and E. H. Gilman is treasurer.

The Great Falls Woolen Company was organized in 1862 and its mills were completed in 1863. They are located at Woodvale, about a mile-and-a-half from Great Falls village, and are very finely fitted up for the manufacture of fancy cassimeres and other woolens. Employment is given to from 75 to 100 assistants, and the total value of the annual product approximates $300,000.

VIEW OF DAM FROM GREAT FALLS SIDE.

The Great Falls Gas Company originated with the Great Falls Manufacturing Company and is said to have been the first gas company incorporated in New Hampshire, the necessary act having been passed June 29, 1850. The service is reliable and efficient and is very generally utilized.

The manufacture of boots and shoes seems destined to become a very important local industry and even now is extensively carried on here, a single firm, that of C. D. Packer & Sons, employing 400 hands and producing from 2300 to 2500 pairs daily. This enterprise was not inaugurated until 1885 and its immediate and decided success affords significant indication of the advantages of the village as a manufacturing centre.

Tanning is also largely carried on here and so are wood-working and stone-working, there being extensive and valuable granite deposits in the immediate vicinity of the village.

The banking facilities are excellent, being furnished by the Great Falls National Bank and the Somersworth Savings Bank.

The former was incorporated as a State bank in 1846 and reorganized under the national banking laws in 1865. It has a capital and surplus exceeding $200,000, and the bank building is equipped with burglar-proof vault, safe and locks, costing more than ten thousand dollars.

The Somersworth Savings Bank was incorporated in 1845 and has been and is of great benefit to the village and town. It is very ably managed and its affairs are in a most prosperous condition, the total surplus profits amounting to $102,532.23 January 1, 1890, the increase for the year being $7,272.84.

As a trade centre Great Falls has a more than local reputation, for the stores of the village are numerous, commodious, varied in kind and excellent in character. The magnitude of the trade enjoyed and the excellence of the railway facilities enabling local merchants to buy cheap and sell cheap,—a fact very generally appreciated by the residents of adjoining sections as well as of this town. The stocks carried are large, varied and very carefully and skillfully chosen, and it is but simple justice to say that the merchants of Great Falls as a whole have a thoroughly well-deserved reputation for practicing strictly legitimate methods and selling goods on their true merits, the natural result being that their trade is established on a sound and permanent basis.

Few villages offer more varied attractions as a place of residence ; the magnitude and diversity of the local industries affording exceptional opportunities for obtaining congenial and remunerative employment, and the cost of living being low both as regards rents and the prices of clothing and food products.

The climate is healthful and agreeable, and the surface of the country round about is so diversified as to make the scenery notable for its beauty even when compared with that of other New Hampshire towns.

The school system is well-considered and efficiently conducted so that ample opportunity is given for the obtaining of a good common school education, and there is an excellent library in town, known as the Manufacturers and Village Library, and containing some nine thousand volumes. It was organized in 1841 and during its nearly half-century of existence has been of very great benefit to the community.

Several of the more prominent religious bodies have large and prosperous church societies in Great Falls, and take it all in all the village lacks nothing to make it a fine example of a typical New England manufacturing community.

LEADING BUSINESS MEN OF GREAT FALLS.

Somersworth Savings Bank, Great Falls, N. H.—It is obvious that knowledge of a perfectly secure and reasonably remunerative means of investment is of great aid to one desirous of saving money, for when a safe and profitable place of deposit for small sums is known to one he is encouraged to go ahead and put by every dollar of his surplus earnings, first, because "money makes money," and a snug sum will soon accumulate with the aid of interest, and second, because every man worthy of the name wants to secure his dependents and himself against being dependent upon charity in case of sickness or other trouble. Therefore the Somersworth Savings Bank has unquestionably been the means of causing many thousands of dollars to be saved during the forty-five years of its existence, for it has always stood high in the confidence of the public and that confidence has never been abused, but, on the contrary, been more fully deserved with every succeeding year. At the present time there is more than one million dollars on deposit in this institution, and the surplus over all liabilities is such as to prove very conservative management and to indicate that no safer place of deposit can be found in New England. This impression will be confirmed by an examination of the following statement, issued April 1, 1890 :

LIABILITIES.

Due depositors	$1,041,646.64
Guarantee fund	48,000.00
Undivided earnings	47,520.76
Premium	43,371.00
	$1,180,508.40

RESOURCES.	Market value.
Loans on real estate	$125,586.19
Loans on personal security	22,811.54
Loans on collateral security	19,110.00
State bonds	12,000.00
County, city, town and district bonds	549,481.00
Bank stock	63,300.00
Railroad bonds	245,150.00
Other bonds	24,000.00
Real estate	68,478.29
Cash	20,561.38
	$1,180,508.40

That the progress of the bank is "upward and onward" is shown by the increase in surplus profits, as given below:

SURPLUS PROFITS

January 1, 1884	$65,193.15
January 1, 1885	68,203.61
January 1, 1886	74,132.28
January 1, 1887	76,945.87
January 1, 1888	86,380.18
January 1, 1889	95,350.39
January 1, 1890	102,532.23

These figures tell their own story, and if further assurance of the standing of the institution be needed it may be found in the names of those identified with its management, as this is in the hands of men prominent in financial and general business circles and widely known as prudent investors ; the officers for the current year being as follows:

The Great Falls National Bank, corner Market and Prospect Streets, Great Falls, N. H.—The banking facilities of Great Falls are at least equal to those of any community of no greater size in the State, and indeed it is probable that they exceed those available in the majority of villages of similar population. There are reasons for this gratifying condition of affairs of course, but it is not within our province to consider them here, our present purpose being to call attention to the excellence and comprehensiveness of the service offered by the Great Falls National Bank, the oldest bank of discount and deposit in town, and one which has been of inestimable service in aiding in the development of local and adjacent resources. It was incorporated nearly half a century ago, being organized as a State bank in 1845, and receiving a national charter twenty years later. The institution has ever been ably and conservatively managed, and as a natural consequence has steadily held the full confidence of the public, but conservatism has never been allowed to degenerate into stagnation, the management being progressive as well as prudent. The banking rooms are located at the corner of Market and Prospect streets, and are very completely and conveniently fitted up, the equipment including a burglar-proof vault, safe and locks costing more than $10,000. In this connection it is pertinent to note that the bank will receive any amount of money and issue certificates of deposit, payable only to the order of the depositor, and on demand. As fire proof safes afford no protection against the professional burglars who infest the country and make the keeping of any considerable sum in one's house positively dangerous, the value of this service is obvious. Deposits subject to check at sight are also received, and in short a general banking business is done ; checks, drafts and coupons being cashed and received on deposit. Drafts on Boston, good throughout this country and Canada, sold at moderate rates. Orders for the purchase or sale of all marketable stocks and bonds in Boston or New York markets executed, etc. Collections are assured prompt attention, blank forms being furnished on application. The banking hours are from 9 to 12 a. m., and 2 to 4 p. m. daily, with the exception of Saturday afternoon, when the bank is closed. The institution has a capital and surplus of $200,000, and its financial condition is excellent in every respect. The officers are as follows : President, Albert A. Perkins ; Cashier, J. A. Stickney ; Directors, Joseph A. Stickney, William S. Tibbets, John C. Lothrop, Isaac Chandler, Albert A. Perkins, John W. Bates, S. Augustus Seavey.

Wimpfheimer & Company, dealers in Dry and Fancy Goods, corner Main and Fore Streets, Great Falls, N. H.— It is now forty-five years since Mr. A Wimpfheimer started this house as a dealer in dry and fancy goods of all kinds. In 1866 he was succeeded by Wimpfheimer Bros. & Co. The present firm of Wimpfheimer & Co. assumed control in 1873. This establishment certainly merits prom-inent mention among the enterprising firms of this section as a representative business undertaking in this class of trade. Energetic men who believe in building up their trade by honesty and fair dealing, are sure to accomplish their desired project and will sooner or later obtain a large and remunerative patronage, which is not to be obtained in any other way. It did not take long for this house to gain popularity or custom and this has been retained through the several changes of firms and managements, and it stands to-day as an example of well directed energy and application to business. The premises consists of two floors, one 24×60 feet in dimensions, the other 24×40 feet. Employment is given to four competent assistants. The stock is large and varied, comprising foreign and domestic dry goods in almost endless variety. We heartily recom-mend this establishment to the attention of our readers as an excellent one for those who wish to supply themselves with really good and desirable articles. They will not be disappointed.

James & Sons, Tea and Coffee Store, High Street, Great Falls, N. H.—The admirably equipped store known by the name of James & Sons' tea and coffee store, is in all respects an excellent and noteworthy house and is one of the finest and best ordered concerns devoted to this important branch of commercial activity in Great Falls, where patrons may at all times feel assured of receiving only first class goods and the most courteous treatment. It is one of the old establishments, having been conducted by Mr. Samuel James for about ten years, when the firm name became James & Sons and has so continued for about twenty years, thus having been known to this vicin-ity for thirty years. A large stock is carried comprising every thing usually kept in a first class grocery. Three floors and basement, each 15 × 50 feet in dimensions, are required for this stock, Mr. A. H. James is well known as breeder of Light Brahmas and Pekin Ducks. He also sells eggs for hatching and is manufacturer of Orange Farm Egg Food. Mr. Samuel James with his sons A. H. and L. M. James, who constitute the firm, are natives of Lebanon, Maine. Orders are filled in the most careful and accurate manner. Mr. A. H. James also makes a specialty of raising strawberry plants in great variety for market; the demand for them has become quite extensive.

Thomas P. Duffill, The Cash Tailor, Burleigh Block, High Street, opposite Band Stand, Great Falls, N. H.— There is no question but that it "pays" to be well dressed when one's occupation is such that "good clothes" can be worn without injury, for appearances go for a good deal in business as in social affairs, and, other things being equal, the well-dressed man will make a much more favor-able impression, sell more goods, and attract a more desir-able class of customers than one who is shabby and slouchy in his apparel. This may seem singular to some of our readers, but it is a fact, nevertheless, and one that many successful business men appreciate and profit by. The residents of Great Falls and vicinity are very favorably situated to obtain first class clothing at moderate rates, and no local establishment does more valuable service in this direction than that conducted by Mr. Thomas P. Duffill, for he is an experienced and skillful merchant tailor, carries a fine assortment of imported and domestic fabrics and is prepared to make garments to order in accordance with the latest dictates of fashion, the work-manship, trimmings, fit, and style being satisfactory to the most critical. He was born in England, where he learned his trade, working on the bench with his father—

afterwards working in New York City, and in Haverhill, Weymouth, and Quincy, Mass. Was afterwards cutter for H. Veschoff, one of New Hampshire's best known tailors, whom he left in 1878 to enter business in his own name and established his present business in Great Falls in 1878. He occupies premises located in Burleigh Block, on High street, comprising a store and work room of the respective dimensions of 20 × 40 and 18 × 50 feet, and employs from fifteen to twenty competent assistants— being prepared to fill all orders at short notice. Mr. Duf-fill's prices are uniformly moderate, and as his work is strictly first class we have no hesitation in guaranteeing satisfaction to all who may take advantage of the facilities he offers.

Great Falls Hotel, Henry S. Gray, Proprietor; oppo-site Boston and Maine Depot, Great Falls, N. H.—It is important to have good hotel accommodations in any community, but particularly so in such a place as Great Falls, for there are few if any towns of no greater popu-lation in the State which are called upon to entertain so many non-residents at all seasons of the year. Great Falls is not only an important manufacturing and mercan-tile centre, but also a very popular summer resort, and when we come to sum up the number who visit here on business or pleasure trips in the course of a year the result is surprising. The Great Falls Hotel average a very large amount of arrivals per annum, and the prospects are that this average will be materially increased in the near future, for not only are more being attracted to Great Falls every year but a larger proportion are putting up at this house, which, under its present management ranks with the most popular in this vicinity. Mr. Henry S. Gray, the proprietor, is a native of New Durham, N. H., and has had charge of the Great Falls Hotel since 1882, the house having been originally established over sixty years ago. He makes no extravagant announcements and does not profess to give two dollars worth of accommodation for every dollar paid, but he does take pains to see that each patron gets full value for his money and he spares no effort to keep his hotel in first-class condition throughout, and to promote the comfort of his guests in all possible ways. The beds are comfortable, the bill of fare varied and abundant and the service prompt and efficient, so the popularity of the Great Falls Hotel is not at all difficult to account for. The hotel contains fifty guest rooms, and the dining room has a seating capacity for a very large number. The house is centrally and conveniently located opposite the Boston and Maine depot, it is heated by steam and lighted by electricity, and offers many solid advan-tages to both commercial travelers and pleasure tourists.

F. C. Ham, Druggist, No. 2 Fore Street, Great Falls, N. H.—The business conducted by Mr. F. C. Ham has held its present position for so long a time that it is safe to say no one at all familiar with Great Falls can be unacquainted with it. This business was started several years ago by Mr. F. C. Ham, and in 1883 Mr. Chas. E. Cater entered the employ of the proprietor and in 1888 became manager. There is probably no other branch of trade known to commerce in which so great a responsibility is incurred as there is in that carried on by the druggist. Dealing as he does in drugs and chemicals unfamiliar to the general public, many of which agents are deadly in their effects when used in certain quantities, or when combined improperly with other materials, he must rely absolutely and entirely on the knowledge, care and skill of himself and employees for the assurance, that by no fault of his, or those for whom he is morally, if not legally responsible, shall the life, or even the comfort, of the hundreds whom he daily serves, be endangered. This store managed by Mr. Cater is an example of what a prescription pharmacist's should be. The premises are 20 × 40 feet in dimensions, and contain a valuable stock of drugs and chemicals. He has also a good assortment of toilet articles and fancy goods such as are generally to be found in a first-class store of this kind. Customers are served promptly and carefully. Mr. F. C. Ham is a resident of South Berwick, Me., and is worthy the confidence of the public whom he so faithfully serves.

Thomas Morgan, Groceries, South Street, Great Falls, N. H.—One who has had a long and varied experience in the grocery business in Great Falls ought to be well qualified to cater to the demands of local trade, and the popularity of the establishment conducted by Mr. Thomas Morgan affords convincing evidence that the experience of its proprietor has not been thrown away, and also shows that the residents of Great Falls and vicinity are prompt to recognize efficient and reliable service. Mr. Morgan founded his present enterprise in 1889, and is so well known throughout this section as to make extended personal mention entirely unnecessary. He gives very close supervision to every detail of the business, is where business expenses are very low and customers are accorded the benefit, and as only thoroughly competent assistants are employed, orders can be promptly and accurately filled at all times in spite of the magnitude of the trade. Spacious premises are occupied on South street, and a very heavy stock of staple and fancy groceries, teas, coffees and spices, etc., is always on hand to choose from ; the goods being especially selected for family trade and being guaranteed to prove just as represented. The prices are invariably as low as the lowest, quality considered, and the service is so carefully systematized that delay or mistake in the delivery of orders is of very rare occurrence—a point experienced housekeepers will thoroughly appreciate.

A. D. Faunce & Son, Furnishing Undertakers, manufacturers and dealers in Coffins, Caskets, Robes, Habits, etc. Flowers loose or made in any shape for Funeral Decorations. Salesroom : Rollins Block, High Street, Residence, Highland St., Great Falls, N. H.—Mr. A. D. Faunce has been engaged in the undertaking business in this town for the past fourteen years, during which time he has become widely and favorably known throughout this section, and has attained a high reputation for promptness, reliability and good taste in the discharge of the difficult and responsible duties which an undertaker is called upon to perform. Mr. A. D. Faunce succeeded Mr. Benj. Hill in business in 1876, and in 1883 admitted his son, Mr. A. L. Faunce, as partner. These gentlemen are both natives of Oxford, Maine, and have actively interested themselves in public as well as in business affairs of Great Falls. Mr. A. L. Faunce served in the Army during our late southern war. Messrs. A. D. Faunce & Son's

salesroom and workshop are located in Rollin's Block, High street. A heavy and very carefully chosen stock is constantly carried, for this firm are furnishing undertakers, and manufacturers as well as dealers in coffins, caskets, robes, habits, etc. They are prepared to furnish anything in their line at short notice. Also flowers, loose or made in any shape for funeral decorations. Their residence is on Highland street, and orders left here or at their salesroom are assured prompt and careful attention.

E. W. Folsom, Jeweler and Optician, Watches, Clocks, Jewelry, Silver and Plated Ware, No. 8 Main Street, opposite B & M. Depot, Great Falls, N. H.—The stock offered for sale by Mr. E. W. Folsom at his spacious store at No. 8 Main street, is remarkably attractive and the more closely it is examined the more attractive it becomes, for it is made up of goods that have been obtained from the most reliable sources and are fully guaranteed to prove as represented. No detailed description of it is possible within the limited space at our command, for it is as varied as it is extensive and includes full lines of watches, clocks, jewelry, silver and plated ware, sporting goods, etc. Inspection is cordially invited, and our readers will find the time spent in looking over this stock both profitable and pleasant. The goods are displayed to excellent advantage and callers are sure of receiving prompt and courteous attention, while the prices quoted are strictly in accordance with the lowest market rates. This house is of very long standing, having been founded in 1850 by Mr. S. B Cole, who was succeeded in 1870 by Mr. A. F. Chandler. In 1875 Folsom & Foss assumed control of the business and so continued until 1878 when Mr. E. W. Folsom became sole proprietor. The premises occupied will measure 18 × 50 feet in dimensions. Employment is given to three competent assistants, thus assuring prompt attention to customers. Mr. Folsom gives his personal attention to his business for which he is admirably adapted.

E. A Tibbets & Son, wholesale and retail dealers in Hardware, Paints, Oils and Varnishes, Carpenters', Mechanics' and Manufacturers' Tools and Supplies. and every variety of Carriage Wood and Iron Work ; Steam Fitting a specialty ; Plumbers' Supplies a specialty; Great Falls, N. H.—There are few if any business centres having a larger proportion of old established enterprises than Great Falls, but the undertaking conducted by Messrs. E. A. Tibbets & Son is exceptional for the length of time it has been carried on, even in that community of time honored establishments. The business in question having been founded about half a century ago. The earliest proprietor being Mr. Luther C. Tibbets, who founded it in 1841, the firm name being changed in 1845 to Tibbets & Brooks, and again in 1847 to Tibbets Brothers, the present firm assuming control in 1881. It is constituted of Mr. E. A. Tibbets, a native of South Berwick, Me., and his son, Mr. W. S. Tibbets, of Great Falls. Mr. E. A. Tibbets has held the office of representative of Great Falls, and both members of the firm are so well known in this vicinity as to render extended personal mention unnecessary. The business, which is both wholesale and retail, has reached very large proportions, but has by no means attained its full growth yet. for its development is still steadily going on, and with a continuance of present methods can hardly fail to keep doing so. The premises in use comprise four floors, 24×49 feet each in dimensions, and a storehouse in Great Falls in addition to a spacious storeroom in Berwick. A very heavy stock is constantly carried, made up of hardware, paints, oils and varnishes. Also carpenters', mechanics' and manufacturers' tools and supplies, as well as agricultural tools of all kinds. A large assortment of plumbers' supplies are also dealt in, and a specialty is made of steam fitting and every variety of carriage wood and iron work. Employment is given to thoroughly competent assistants, and small as well as large buyers are assured immediate and painstaking attention.

Z. Provencher & Co., Druggists, Main Street, Great Falls, N. H.—It is very natural that particular confidence should be placed in a druggist who is thoroughly educated in his business, for although we are happy to say that the large majority of our New Hampshire pharmacists are educated, competent and reliable men, still there is a prevailing impression that he who fills such a responsible and exacting position as that held by a dispenser of drugs and medicines to the general public, cannot know too much concerning the properties and effects of the agents he handles. Consequently the popularity of the establishment conducted by Z Provencher & Co., on Main street, is not to be wondered at in the least, for Mr. Provencher is master of his profession. This business was established in 1887 by Ager & Provencher, then the present proprietors succeeded them in 1890, and have become widely and favorably known in this vicinity. The premises occupied by them are 22 × 50 feet in dimensions, and contain a large and varied stock, made up of drugs, medicines, chemicals, toilet articles, and the usual line of selected fancy goods to be found in a druggist's store. The compounding of physician's prescriptions is given the most careful personal attention, and we need hardly say that no trouble is spared to avoid the least possible error, while the charges made are very moderate. A careful assistant is employed and polite attention is given to every caller.

Dorr & Hobson (Successors to M. Bates & Co.), dealers in Dry and Fancy Goods, Central Building, Great Falls, N. H.—The establishment now conducted by Messrs. Dorr & Hobson is one of the oldest in town, and although comparisons are odious, it would not be just the proper thing to say it is the most reliable, it is certainly as trustworthy and popular an establishment as can be found in the entire State. The business was founded in 1832 by Moses Bates, the name being changed to Bates & Son, and then to Moses Bates & Co., the present firm assuming full control of affairs in 1886 The present firm is made up of Mr. C. M. Dorr, a native of Great Falls, and Mr. J. E. Hobson, of Limerick, Me., and for many years a resident of Steep Falls, Me. They are both so generally known in Great Falls and vicinity that we feel extended personal mention would be absurdly superfluous. Nor is any eulogy of their methods necessary in these columns, for those who know the men know that their business policy in a nut shell is, "full value for money received," and the magnitude of their trade shows how successfully this is carried out. The premises made use of comprise a store 1750 square feet in dimensions, and containing a heavy, varied and skillfully chosen stock of dry and fancy goods, the styles offered comprising the latest novelties as well as full lines of staple goods. The prices are always in strict accordance with the lowest market rates, all classes of trade being successfully catered to, and the employment of three competent assistants assures prompt, intelligent and courteous attention to every caller.

H. M. Hanson, dealer in Meats, Provisions, and Groceries, Green Street, Great Falls, N. H.—Although the advantages of housekeeping far outweigh its disadvantages, it must be confessed that the trials and disappointments of the average housekeeper are many, and that the larger portion of them are connected with the obtaining of food supplies, for it is at times very difficult to obtain food, and especially meats, that will prove altogether satisfactory. This is by no means entirely the fault of the dealer, but nevertheless a great saving of time, money and patience, may be made by trading with a reputable and well equipped house, and hence we feel that we are doing some of our readers a service by calling to their attention the facilities possessed by Mr. H M. Hanson, for furnishing meats, provisions, and groceries of standard quality at the lowest market rates. The store is located on Green street, and is sufficiently roomy to accommodate a complete line of the commodities mentioned, the assortment

being so varied that all tastes and purses can be suited. Employment is given to two efficient assistants, and no trouble is spared to insure prompt and polite attention to every caller, and to fill orders in a manner that will prove satisfactory to the most fastidious. Mr. Hanson was born in Maine, and needs no extended personal mention in these columns. He has been identified with his present establishment since 1889, having at that time succeeded the firm of Hanson & Herson. He has attained a high reputation as an enterprising and honorable merchant, and his methods have made his store popular among all classes in the community.

Daniel Hodsdon, manufacturer of and dealer in Stoves and Ranges of every kind ; also Plumbing, Roofing and Gas Fitting, furnished promptly and at low prices, 26 Market Street, Great Falls, N. H.—In view of the great number and enormous variety of stoves, ranges and furnaces to be found in the market it seems almost incredible that one need not be so very old to be able to remember when stoves were almost unknown outside the larger cities, but such is the fact, and it affords an impressive example of the progress made during the past quarter of a century. The great trouble nowadays is to choose satisfactorily from the many styles offered, but this may be easily overcome by telling a reputable dealer of the attending circumstances and being guided by his advice for of course he knows what is best suited to your purpose, and it is for his interest to satisfy his customers. No better plan can be followed than to place the order with Mr. Daniel Hodsdon, for he is an extensive dealer in stoves, ranges and tinware of all kinds, and not only handles the most popular styles but has a well earned reputation for uniformly fair dealing. Mr. Hodsdon is a native of Piermont, N. H., and has been identified with his present business since 1865, it having been established by Messrs. Pierce & Hodsdon, who were succeeded by Hodsdon Brothers in 1870, the present proprietor, Mr. Daniel Hodsdon assuming full control of affairs in 1883. Mr. Hodsdon invented and put in market the Tip Top range—in eight different styles—in 1880. Improved same in 1884, and again in 1890, said range now being the most convenient and durable range the market affords. Four thousand of these celebrated ranges have been sold, and hundreds of testimonials been given as to their value as a complete cooking apparatus. The premises are located at No. 26 Market street, and comprise one floor and a basement, each covering an area of 1500 square feet. Besides carrying a full line of stoves, tinware, etc., Mr. Hodsdon is prepared to do plumbing, roofing and gas fitting in a thoroughly workmanlike manner at moderate rates. Employment is given to ten competent assistants, and all work undertaken will be most thoroughly and satisfactorily executed.

J. W. Preston, M. D., Drugs and Medicines, Orange Street, Great Falls, N. H.—There are many skillful and reliable pharmacists in New Hampshire, though but few can be found who can do the good work with the actual experience of J. W. Preston, M. D., who now carries on the business on Orange street. This store was opened many years since, and after several changes it passed into the control of J. W. Preston, M. D., in 1884. The premises occupied measure 20×50 feet. He carries as carefully chosen a stock of drugs, medicines and chemicals as can be found in this section of the State, for a specialty is made of the compounding of physicians' prescriptions, and all necessary materials and apparatus are at hand to enable such orders to be satisfactorily, accurately and promptly filled at moderate rates. A fine assortment of fancy goods, toilet articles, stationery and notions is also always at hand to choose from. Mr. J. W. Preston, who is a native of Canada, formerly kept a drug store at Bristol, N. H. He practiced medicine for seventeen years in Plymouth, making a total practice of thirty-five years in that profession.

Chas. F. Blake, dealer in Groceries, Provisions, Country Produce and Ice, corner Orange and Washington Streets, Great Falls, N. H.—Among the various dealers in food supplies doing business in this vicinity, Mr. Chas. F. Blake should be given prominent mention, for he is very successful in catering to all classes of trade, and makes it an invariable rule to sell goods strictly on their merits, being convinced that such a policy is for his own interests as well as for those of his patrons. Judging from the present extent and the steadily increasing magnitude of his trade, his methods are appreciated by the residents of this section. It is certainly pleasant to note a success won by the employment of such a legitimate and liberal policy. His store has an area of 1,200 square feet and contains a heavy stock of groceries, provisions and country produce, the assortment being so varied that all purses, as well as all tastes, can easily be suited. Ice is also dealt in extensively, and as he is the only dealer in this commodity in town, the demand is great. He is prepared to supply this very desirable article in any quantity that may be ordered. Employment is given to twelve assistants, thus assuring every customer immediate and courteous attention. Mr. Blake is a native of New Hampshire and is well known, having been in the grocery business about twenty years. He has also been selectman.

Eastman & Davis, Millinery Novelties, Trimmed Goods in great variety, Savings Bank Building, High Street, Great Falls, N. H.—Were a vote to be taken to establish the comparative popularity of the various mercantile establishments located in Great Falls, it is sure that the ladies would come out very strong in favor of that conducted under the firm name of Eastman & Davis, for this is of especial interest to the fair sex, as the firm deal exclusively in millinery goods and offer inducements which are very hard to parallel elsewhere. The business was founded in 1889 by the present firm, the individual members of which are Mrs. E. Eastman, a native of York, Me., and Miss H. L. Davis, of Newfield, Me These ladies have a large circle of friends and patrons in Great Falls and vicinity. They give personal attention to the filling of orders, employing sufficient assistance to enable commissions to be executed at short notice. The stock of millinery includes the latest fashionable novelties as well as trimmed goods in great variety. The premises occupied are located in Savings Bank building, High street, and cover an area of some 800 square feet. The prices quoted here will bear the severest comparison with those named elsewhere on equally desirable and fashionable goods.

F. A. Hussey, dealer in Crackers, White Bread, Cake, and Pastry, Great Falls, N. H.—If it were possible to make first-class bread, cake and pastry out of second class materials, more public bakeries would be worthy of patronage than is now the case, although it is only fair to say that our New Hampshire bakers will as a class compare very favorably with those of other States, but still there are some establishments which deserve special commendation and among these the bakery conducted Mr. F. A. Hussey holds a leading position. This was originally opened by J. A. Locke, who after several changes was succeeded by the present proprietor in 1878 He is a native of Great Falls, and knowing his business thoroughly is enabled to turn out crackers, white bread, cake, and pastry of the finest quality, at prices which puts his productions within the means of all. A store is maintained on High street, and a rapidly growing business is done both wholesale and retail, orders being accurately filled at short notice and at the lowest market rates. This bakery covers an area of about 1300 square feet, containing a stock which is so frequently renewed as always to be fresh and attractive. Mr. Hussey uses first-class materials, also employs six competent assistants and can safely guarantee satisfaction to the most fastidious customer He has been a member of the board of selectmen, and is highly reputed throughout town as an energetic and reliable

W. H. Tasker, Wall Papers, Borders and Ceiling Decorations, also Curtains, Fixtures, Drapery Poles, Sash Rods and Trimmings. Upholstering and Furniture Repairing and old Furniture Re-covered. Burleigh Block, High Street, Great Falls, N. H.—One of the most complete and desirable stocks of imported and domestic wall papers to be found in Great Falls, is carried by Mr. W. H. Tasker, located in Burleigh Block, High street, and as he quotes bottom prices on all the goods he handles, it is well worth while to visit his establishment when anything in the line of wall papers, borders and ceiling decorations is wanted. There is a sufficiently large force of assistants employed, and callers may depend upon receiving prompt and polite attention and being given every opportunity to make deliberate and satisfactory choice, while goods are guaranteed in every instance to prove just as represented. The latest artistic designs in curtain fixtures, drapery poles, sash rods and trimmings are included in this stock, and new styles are constantly being received. Orders for upholstering and furniture repairing will be executed in a superior manner at short notice. Furniture re-covering forms a very important department of the business, a force of experienced workmen being employed and all orders executed under a guarantee that both stock and workmanship shall be strictly first-class, every detail of the work being done under careful supervision.

John A. Dumas, Dry and Fancy Goods, Small Wares, etc., Bank Building, High Street, Great Falls, N. H.—We have no fear but what the ladies of Great Falls and vicinity will agree with us when we say that no "shopping" tour in this vicinity is looked upon as complete unless it includes the establishment conducted by Mr. John A. Dumas on High street, for this store is in some respects unique and always offers many attractions impossible to find elsewhere. And then, again, these inducements are constantly varying; because you have visited the store Monday is no reason why you cannot profitably visit it again Tuesday or Wednesday, for the stock is constantly being renewed, fresh novelties being added at such frequent intervals that the only way to "keep up with the times," so far as this popular store is concerned, is to visit it early and often. The business was originally founded by Mr. S. S. Chick, the present proprietor assuming control in 1887. Mr. Dumas is a native of Canada and is too generally known hereabouts to render extended personal mention necessary. He gives close attention to the supervision of affairs, and spares no pains to maintain the enviable reputation so long associated with this enterprise. Mr. Dumas is an extensive retail dealer in dry and fancy goods, small wares, cloaks, etc., and is prepared to quote the lowest market rates on large or small orders. The stock is exceptionally varied and complete and is made up of articles that can safely be guaranteed to prove as represented. Employment is given to seven well informed assistants.

Smith & Son, dealers in all kinds of Fresh, Pickled and Smoked Fish, Oysters, Lobsters, Clams, Fresh Halibut, Mackerel and Salmon in their season, corner of Washington and Green Streets, Great Falls, N. H.—This business was formerly conducted by Mr. Bradford Jones, who was succeeded in 1875 by the present firm of Smith & Son. They carry on a large trade in fresh oysters, fish and lobsters, as well as all kinds of fresh, pickled and smoked fish, oysters, lobsters and clams. Fresh halibut, mackerel and salmon in their season. Those wishing anything in this line and desiring strictly fresh and reliable goods at moderate prices would best serve their own interests by giving this enterprising firm a call. This house is run on true business principles in which a genuine spirit of accommodation prevails, and prompt and courteous attention may be confidently expected by every patron. The store occupied contains about 300 square feet, and it is completely fitted for the first class retail trade carried on here. Mr. L. E. Smith is a native of Sandwich, N. H., and his son, Mr. J L. Smith, was born in Great Falls. Orders are promptly attended to and delivered when promised.

C. S Beacham & Son, dealers in all kinds of Flour, Grain, Feed and Shorts, Market Street, Great Falls, N. H. —Among the prominent New Hampshire houses engaged in the handling of flour, grain, feed, shorts, etc., the firm of C. S. Beacham & Son must be given a leading position, both on account of the magnitude of its business and the many years that it has been successfully conducted. The enterprise has been controlled by various firms, among the earliest being that of Wright & Co., who were succeeded by Messrs. Blood & Co., who conducted it for many years, they giving place to the present concern in 1882. It is composed of Mr. Charles S. Beacham and his son, Mr. C. Arthur Beacham. Both these gentlemen are natives of Ossipee, N. H., and are personally well known throughout Great Falls and vicinity. An exclusively retail business is done and exceptional facilities are enjoyed for filling the heaviest orders without delay. The premises occupied are located on Market street and cover an area of some 1,470 square feet, and is fitted up with every facility and convenience for handling the stock dealt in, the railroad running by the rear door. Every order given in person or sent by either mail or telegraph is assured immediate and painstaking attention, while the firm are in a position to quote bottom prices on all the commodities they handle.

John S. LeGro, dealer in Beef, Pork, Veal, Mutton and Lamb, Poultry and Vegetables, Washington Street Market, Great Falls, N. H.—There is no article of food that varies so much in quality as meat, and as a natural consequence there is no other kind of food which is so difficult to select, for even experts are deceived sometimes, and it is really impossible to always judge correctly. The only sensible way to do is to find the most experienced and reliable dealer within your reach, tell him just what you want and take what he selects, for, although he will make a mistake himself occasionally, still he will cheerfully correct it when his attention is called to the matter, for it is plainly for his interest to satisfy his customers, and he will spare no pains to do so. Mr. John S. LeGro, who is the proprietor of the "Washington Street Market," does business on this basis, and the magnitude of the trade he has built up since he commenced operations here in 1863 shows that this method has been a successful one. He is a native of Lebanon, Me., and is widely known throughout this section. His market always contains a fine stock of beef, pork, veal, mutton and lamb, poultry and vegetables of all seasonable kinds. All classes of trade are catered to, and every order is assured prompt and careful attention. The lowest market rates are quoted, and all the commodities dealt in are guaranteed to prove as represented.

Edwin A. Lewis, Cigar Manufacturer, Moore's Block, 261½ Market Street, Great Falls, N. H.—There are few persons who are not in the cigar business that have any idea of the immense number that are consumed in the United States every year, and not the least remarkable thing about the demand for cigars is its rapid and steady increase. In spite of all that is urged against smoking, the habit has become so general that the man who does not smoke is a rare exception, for the sensible man can see that it is the abuse of tobacco which is hurtful, and the enjoyment derived from its proper or moderate use can be obtained in no other way. The finer grades of tobacco are especially harmless, and therefore it is gratifying to know that Mr. Edwin A. Lewis, who makes a specialty of manufacturing fine cigars, is meeting with great success in his efforts to introduce a superior article among the trade. His brand "Great Sachem," is a delicately flavored Havana hand made cigar, and is in great demand. He started business in Great Falls in 1871, but removed to Berwick, Me., in 1873. He has been located in Moore's block, Market street, Great Falls, since 1888. The premises that he occupies contain about 300 square feet. Employment is given to six assistants, as he does a wholesale business. Goods will be delivered promptly, as all orders are attended to as soon as received.

Granite State Hotel, C. L. Bodwell, proprietor. Good Livery Stable connected. High Street, Great Falls, N. H. —The more experienced a traveler is the more readily he puts up with unavoidable discomforts and the less growling he does when no responsible person is at hand to complain to ; but all the same he means to be comfortable if any act of his can make him so, and when he comes across a well managed hotel he notes the fact and takes particular pains to put up there again should he revisit the locality. This is one reason for the steady patronage enjoyed by the Granite State Hotel, for it has been in operation for many years, and traveling men and others appreciative of good hotel accommodations, have long since learned that such may be found at this commodious hostelry. The Granite State Hotel has been under the able management of its present proprietor since 1889 and has always held a leading position among the representative hotels of this section of the State. Mr. C. L. Bodwell is a native of Sanford, Me., and is highly respected throughout Great Falls. The premises are located on High street ; they are spacious and well arranged and can accommodate forty guests. The sleeping rooms are attractive and comfortably furnished and the hotel is kept in excellent condition, employment being given to six assistants, and the service at the table and elsewhere being prompt and courteous. An abundance of the best food the market affords is supplied at all seasons, and as the terms of the house are moderate it certainly well deserves its high and extended popularity. A good livery, sale and boarding stable is also maintained.

A. Gaudette, dealer in all kinds of Wood and Kindling, and Job Teaming, Washington St., Great Falls, N. H.—In spite of the great quantity of coal used in this vicinity, there is still a large demand for hard and soft wood, and one of the most prominent of the local dealers engaged in supplying this demand is Mr. A. Gaudette, doing business on Washington street. He carries a large stock of hard and soft cut wood, slab wood and kindlings. He is prepared to give prompt and painstaking attention to every order and to fill the same at the lowest market rates. Mr. Gaudette is a native of Canada and has a well earned reputation for enterprising and reliable business methods. In addition to his wood business he does an extensive job teaming business, and is prepared to execute all orders in this department of his business promptly, carefully and satisfactorily. Employment is afforded to six efficient assistants and no pains are spared in either branch of the business to maintain the high reputation this establishment has borne so long. Mr. Gaudette began operations here in Great Falls about 1880, and has for some time ranked with the leading men in his line of business.

N. Roy, Meat Market, Union Street, Great Falls, N. H. —It is all very well to argue that meat is by no means essential to health, and that a person can work hard and thrive on a diet composed exclusively of vegetables, cereals, etc.; but the great majority of us can't consider anything a "square meal" unless it includes meat in abundance, and when we are really hungry meat is the only thing that will actually satisfy us. Even assuming that one may thrive on a strictly vegetable diet, that is no reason why we should give up the enjoyment of meat eating, for little if any money would be saved by so doing, and the enjoyment lost could not be gained so cheaply in any other way. Of course in order to really enjoy meat it must be of good quality, and one sure way to get such is to buy of Mr. N. Roy, for he makes a specialty of meats, and offers grades suited to the most critical taste. He occupies a spacious meat market, located on Union street, and carries a full assortment of beef, pork, mutton, veal and lamb, together with poultry and game in their season. The lowest market rates are quoted at all times and the stock is sufficiently varied and complete to admit of all tastes and all purses being suited. Mr. Roy is a native of Canada and is almost universally known in this vicinity, and has been connected with his present business since 1888.

J. Guttman, Dentist, established 1857, Market Square, Great Falls, N. H.—Whatever may have been the case in days gone by, those who neglect and abuse their teeth nowadays can advance no admittable excuse for doing so, for the matter has been so often and so thoroughly discussed that every person of average intelligence must appreciate, to some extent at least, the importance of keeping the teeth in proper condition. The many who fail to do this excuse their action or rather inaction by various more or less ingenious pleas, but when all of these are summed up and divested of side issues it will be found that they may be classed under not more than four heads, as follows: First, lack of time; second, lack of money; third, lack of courage, and fourth, lack of disposition. Regarding the first, it need only be said that those who have not time to care for their health have no time to live at all, for without health life is not worth living; regarding the second, competent dental service may be obtained at moderate rates, and is within the means of all who really desire it; regarding the third, improved apparatus, facilities, and methods have combined to do away with the pain formerly attending dental operations; and regarding the fourth, that of course is no excuse at all, and requires no answer. There are many excellent dentists practicing in Great Falls and vicinity, and occupying a leading position among them is Dr. J. Guttman, who has finely furnished and conveniently located premises in Market square, Great Falls. The most improved facilities for the practice of dentistry in all its branches are provided, and operations are executed at short notice and in a skillful, durable and thoroughly satisfactory manner. Special attention is given to manufacturing and administering Nitrous Oxide Gas. Dr. Guttman is a native of Prussia in Germany, and has become widely and favorably known in Great Falls since he began the practice of his profession here in 1857, having gained an enviable reputation as a competent, gentle and careful operator. His charges are moderate, and his methods are in accordance with the accepted principles of modern dentistry, insuring results that can scarcely fail to be permanently satisfactory in every instance.

J. Bickford, Groceries and Provisions, Market Square, Great Falls, N. H.—It is always a good idea to trade with an enterprising house whenever such a course is possible, for the customers of a wide-a-wake and progressive concern are sure to be treated with liberality and are also sure to receive their share of any increase in the concern's prosperity. The latter statement may be disputed by some people who pride themselves on their shrewdness, and who will say that no firm is going to give its customers anything more than it has to; but all the same we know it to be true, and we also know that the really successful business men are not those who keep every advantage to themselves, but rather those who share with customers and thus largely increase their trade and income, although they may lessen the percentage of their profits. The enterprise now conducted by Mr. J. Bickford in Market Square is a good example to mention in this connection, and we hold that Mr. Bickford is in a much better position to day than he would have been had he pursued the shortsighted policy too common in his business. A co-operative store was established in 1864, Mr. Bickford being the manager. In 1872 Mr. Bickford assumed full control of the business, since which date the name has been as at present, J. Bickford. He has built up a large retail trade, requiring the services of well informed assistants. The premises occupied comprise one floor and a basement, each covering an area of 800 square feet. A large stock is carried, including choice staple and fancy family groceries of all kinds. Mr. Bickford is a native of Rochester, N. H., and is very well known throughout Great Falls. He has every facility at hand to enable the many orders received to be filled with promptness and accuracy. The prices quoted are very low and the goods are strictly first-class in every respect.

S. C. Horne, dealer in Choice Family Groceries, Teas, Coffees, Sugars, Spices, etc., High Street, Great Falls, N. H.—There is no question but that the taste of the community has been educated up to a point where the difference between superior and inferior teas, coffees and spices can be readily detected, for there is a constantly increasing demand for really desirable goods of this kind, while the inferior grades once so popular, are rapidly becoming practically unsalable. Mr. S. C. Horne, dealer in choice family groceries, teas, coffees, sugars, spices etc., is entitled to much credit for enabling the residents of this section to become familiar with these choice goods, for he has handled them for several years. He began operations here in 1880, as a member of the firm of Plummer & Horne. In 1887, Mr. Horne became sole proprietor. He is a native of this place, and we need hardly say has a large circle of friends here. His store is large, being 25×50 feet in dimensions, and he also occupies a basement for some of his stock. Visitors may always find a large and varied stock to choose from, the goods being warranted to prove as represented, while the prices are wonderfully low, quality considered. A large business is done here, and his trade is steadily growing. Mr. Horne has been a member of the school committee.

Mrs. A. H. Webber, Pure Soft Candies at wholesale and retail, made fresh every day. Old fashioned Molasses Candy a specialty. Fore Street, Great Falls N. H.—There are very few people but what are fond of nice confectionery, that is when it is made of first-class materials and is properly flavored and invitingly displayed. It is very easy to get such articles if you only know where to go for them. Mrs. A. H. Webber, who keeps a store on Fore street, is a wholesale and retail dealer in pure soft candies that are made fresh every day, as Mrs. Webber makes her own candy. She also has a fine assortment of bread, cake and pastry, and her ice cream will bear comparison with any in this vicinity. Mrs. Webber has recently enlarged her business by opening a dining room, where she will furnish meals at all hours and also table board for regular boarders. In her store she makes a specialty of old-fashioned molasses candy, for which she has become well known. The premises occupied are 20×40 feet in dimensions. Careful assistants are employed that customers may be promptly attended to. Mrs. Webber, who is a native of Boston, Mass., commenced business here in 1889, and the large and increasing patronage which she has gained proves that she understands her business and has served her customers in a satisfactory manner. Her stock is kept fresh and her prices moderate.

Hurd & Grant, dealers in Family Groceries, Flour, Corn, Meal, Pork, Lard, Molasses. Cash paid for Country Produce. Opposite No. 2 Mill, Main Street, Great Falls, N. H.—The business conducted by Messrs. Hurd & Grant is located opposite No. 2 Mill, Main street. For many years it has held a deservedly high reputation for furnishing first class family groceries. The business was founded in 1873 by Cowell & Hurd, who were succeeded in 1875 by Hurd & Cate. In 1888 the present proprietors, Messrs. E. P. Hurd and G. F. Grant, assumed control. These gentlemen are both natives of Maine. Mr. Hurd has been representative. They have spared no pains to maintain and even to increase the high repute of the enterprise, the result being that it is constantly growing in popularity, and with increased patronage the firm are enabled to offer increased inducements to their customers. The premises occupied are 25×50 feet in dimensions. A heavy stock is carried, including flour, corn, meal, pork, lard, molasses, syrup, butter, cheese, fish, salt, sugars, teas and coffees, spices, fruit, confectionery, extracts, and a complete line of family supplies These goods are carefully chosen and are fully guaranteed to prove as represented. The lowest market rates are quoted on all these goods. Prompt attention is assured to every caller. Orders are carefully filled and delivered.

O. Marin, Meats and Vegetables, Main Street, Great Falls, N. H.—That the successful management of a retail meat market is by no means the easy task it may seem to some is not likely to be disputed by any one who has had a practical experience in the matter; for in point of fact, to so carry on an establishment of this kind as to be prepared to meet all of the reasonable, and not a few of the unreasonable, demands of customers, and at the same time avoid being loaded down with an overstock, requires both experience and brains, and cannot be accomplished by everybody. But, however, there are not a few who seem to "have the business down fine," as the saying is, and among these due mention should be made of the market conducted by Mr. O. Marin, located on Main street, Great Falls. This business was originally founded by Boucher Brothers in 1887, they being succeeded in 1890 by the present proprietor. This gentleman has already attained a liberal patronage, and may be fairly considered as one of our representative business men. Mr. Marin is a native of Canada by birth, and has not a few friends in this community. He is steadily adding to them by the liberal and enterprising business methods he makes constant use of, and we can strongly advise any one who appreciates first-class provisions and square dealings to patronize Mr. Marin, as both of these are assured to every customer. Competent assistants are employed, and the stock of meats, vegetables, etc., carried is varied enough to satisfy all tastes and conditions of purses.

Anson Chick, Picture Framing and Job Carpentering, Washington Street, Great Falls, N. H.—It may be safely set down as an invariable rule that it is always best to obtain the advice and assistance of a practical man when an enterprise of any importance is contemplated, and yet, obvious as this may seem, it is often neglected by those who propose to build or who require the services of a reliable carpenter. A reputable and experienced builder can give many valuable hints as to the details of a plan, even if it is not desired to have him draw it up altogether, and it should always be borne in mind that alterations made in a plan, after contracts are signed and the work is well under way, are apt to cost double what they would had they been suggested in the preliminary stages. Mr. Ansel Chick is a job carpenter as well as a picture frame maker, and is well able to give advice relating to the planning of a house, or the alterations that may be desired in stores or houses. Mr. Chick does quite a business making screen doors and windows to order. He is prepared to do general jobbing, also saw filing, and those desiring the services of a careful and thorough workman will do well to obtain such a man. Picture frames will be made to order in a neat and substantial manner at short notice, and at moderate prices. A large variety of styles being on hand from which a selection can be made, that cannot fail to please those who are familiar with fine work.

S. E. Pattee, Livery, Sale and Boarding Stable, Orange Street, Great Falls, N. H.—There are some livery stable keepers who seem to think that their customers are either millionaires or else are prepared to spend half their earnings on horse hire, for the charges made are away beyond the means of the most of us, and the consequence is we are obliged to do without the enjoyment and healthfulness of driving. Now, of course it costs money to keep horses, to pay help and to maintain carriages, harness, etc., in good order, and no sensible man expects to get "something for nothing," but still there is reason in everything, and many stable keepers would make more money by charging lower prices. Mr. S. E. Pattee has struck the "happy medium" in his charges, for his prices are high enough to enable him to furnish first class turnouts at a fair profit and at the same time are low enough to suit anybody who doesn't want the earth for a ten-acre lot. It is evident that Mr. Pattee means to do the square thing by his patrons, and his livery, sale and boarding ness indicate that his policy is appreciated. Mr. Pat

tee is a native of Goffstown, N. H., and has been identified with his present enterprise since 1888, succeeding at that time the firm of J. O. Lord & Son. He gives close personal attention to the supervision of affairs, and is prepared to let single or double teams for pleasure or business uses at very reasonable terms. The stable is located on Orange street, and callers may depend upon receiving prompt and polite attention at all times. Horses are also taken to board, and will receive every attention and care requisite for their comfort and health. Special attention being given to selling horses for either cart or driving purposes. Many fine horses suitable for such purposes being constantly on hand.

A. B. Jeneau & Co., one price Clothiers and Gents' Furnishers, Corner Fore and Main Streets, Great Falls, N. H.—The question of where to get fashionable, well made and durable clothing at the lowest market rates is one of great importance in every civilized community, for proper self-respect prompts us to dress well, and ordinary prudence counsels us to get the largest possible return for our money. A large proportion of the residents of Great Falls and vicinity have answered this question to their entire satisfaction by making their purchases at the establishment conducted by Messrs. A. B. Jeneau & Co., and all competent judges who will examine the goods there offered and note the prices, will agree that one might easily go a great deal farther and fare a great deal worse, for the stock is remarkably complete and attractive and the prices are as low as the lowest. Messrs. A. B. Jeneau & Co. founded their business in Great Falls in 1886, and the clothing business under their direct management is maintained at a high standard of efficiency. The store is located on Main street and covers an area of some 1200 square feet of space. It is well arranged and contains a full line of ready-made clothing, together with a complete assortment of gentlemen's furnishings, hats, caps, trunks and bags. The latest fashionable novelties are well represented and the goods are sold strictly on their merits and at bottom prices. Five competent and well informed assistants are employed, and every caller is assured courteous, as well as prompt attention.

Belleville & Daigle, dealers in Groceries and Provisions, Flour, Fruit and Confectionery, cor. Franklin and Union Streets, Great Falls, N. H.—There is often as much ingenuity shown in explaining the success as in accounting for the failure of a business enterprise, but when an undertaking has been successfully conducted for several years it is always safe to assume that its popularity is due to solid merit. Such is the case with that now carried on under the firm name of Belleville & Daigle, for this enterprise was inaugurated by Messrs. Gagnon & Demers in 1882. In 1887, Mr. O. Demers assumed the entire management of the business, and so conducted it until 1890, when he was succeeded by the present firm of Belleville & Daigle, who now hold a leading position among similar undertakings in this section of the State. The gentlemen comprising this firm are Mr. Fred. Belleville and Mr. Napoleon Daigle, both natives of Canada, and are energetic and reliable business men. The premises are located at the corner of Franklin and Union streets, and cover an area of 2400 square feet, and are fully occupied by a heavy and complete stock of groceries, provisions, flour, fruit and confectionery of the best quality. The policy which has made this enterprise so prominent among Great Falls' mercantile undertakings is followed to-day as strictly as ever, and when one has remarked the reliability of the goods, the lowness of the prices, and the promptness and accuracy of the service, he is not obliged to ask what that policy is, nor need he be told that its effect is to assure entire satisfaction to every reasonable customer. Employment is given to three competent assistants, and all orders are assured immediate and careful attention.

John Martin, Boots and Shoes, 30 Market Street. Proprietor of the "Somerworth Mineral Spring," Great Falls, N. H.—It is always provoking to be imposed upon, but especially so when you are purchasing anything in the line of foot wear, for one's comfort is so dependent upon the quality and fit of the boots or shoes worn, that unsatisfactory foot-wear is enough to make the best natured man "cranky." Hence one way to maintain that even, good temper which makes friends, prolongs life and is one of the most valuable possessions a man can have, is to buy your boots, shoes and rubbers of Mr. John Martin, who has a newly fitted up store at No. 30 Market street, where he has a complete and carefully chosen stock of boots, shoes, slippers and rubbers, suited to all needs in size, widths and quality, adapted to all ages, all occupations, both sexes and all tastes, and he sells them for what they are, giving every customer the bottom facts regarding the goods, and also bottom prices. Mr. Martin is a native of Vermont, but has long resided in Great Falls. He opened this store in 1890, but was formerly in the same line of trade in this town ; the store now occupied is 20 × 60 feet in size and is conveniently fitted up for this business. Mr. Martin is the owner of a valuable mineral spring located on his place, but a few moments' walk from the depot. The water comes boiling up out of the earth from a white, sandy bottom, is cold, of pleasant taste, but medicinal in its effect. Many in this vicinity have tested its merit and give unqualified testimony of its virtues. It is the purpose of Mr. Martin to introduce this valuable spring to the public so that its benefit may be enjoyed by thousands who now are ignorant of its benefit.

Charles H. Mellen, wholesale and retail dealer in Groceries and Provisions, Flour, Tea, Coffee and Spices, Market Street, Great Falls, N. H.—The wholesale and retail grocery business is not one to be chosen by a man who dislikes exertion, for if there is a business outside of sawing wood or shoveling dirt that demands hard work and plenty of it from those carrying it on, it is just that which we have mentioned. This may seem an extreme statement to those who have not "been there," but we have no fear that anyone who has had any personal experience in the trade will contradict us in the slightest degree. Grocers who really strive to accommodate their patrons earn every cent they make, and it is therefore with pleasure that we note the prosperity of Mr. Charles H. Mellen, who succeeded Mr. Moses Weeks in business in 1889. Mr. Mellen has conscientiously endeavored to render an adequate equivalent for every cent paid to him and fully deserves the large measure of success he has attained. His store is located on Market street and covers an area of some 1,200 square feet. A large stock is carried, including groceries and provisions of all descriptions, flour, tea, coffee and spices. With a well stocked and well equipped store, with every facility for handling goods economically and expeditiously, customers can rely on having their orders promptly filled. Mr. Mellen is a native of Great Falls and is one of our most energetic and public spirited local dealers and one who has the respect and confidence of the people in general.

B. Etter, Artistic Photographer, Market Square, Great Falls, N. H.—The eminent painter who replied " with brains, sir," when asked with what he mixed his colors in order to obtain the wonderful effects noticeable in his work, concisely stated a truth which is too often overlooked. Want of ability is not to be compensated for by the most improved facilities, and this principle applies as forcibly to the work of the photographer as to that of the artist in colors. Anybody can procure photographic apparatus, and, by the way, about everybody nowadays does do so, but to attain artistic results in photography is quite another matter. Therefore, when we say that Mr. B Etter is an artistic photographer and has the latest improved apparatus at his studio, we by no means explain the great success he meets with in making accurate and beautifully

finished portraits ; but when we add that he "mixes brains" with his chemicals the cause of his success becomes evident. Mr. B. Etter, who is a native of Nova Scotia, succeeded Mr. John R. Parker in the proprietorship of the studio in question in 1887. He carries on this work in all its branches. Portraits will be copied and enlarged and finished as desired. The scale of prices will be found to be remarkably moderate, considering the excellence of the work. Two assistants are employed that orders may be filled at short notice, satisfaction being guaranteed in every instance. All kinds and styles of picture frames are furnished to order at short notice.

Peter Guilmet, wholesale and retail dealer in Groceries, Provisions, Beef, Mutton, Pork, Lamb, Poultry, Tripe, Sausages, Butter, Cheese, Eggs, etc. Also Fresh Fruit and Vegetables of all kinds in their season, corner Franklin and Main Streets, Great Falls, N. H —The house of Peter Guilmet enjoys an enviable reputation in connection with the sale of groceries, provisions, meats, etc., and on visiting the store carried on by this gentleman at the corner of Franklin and Main streets, it soon becomes evident that his reputation is well deserved, for one meets with prompt and courteous attention, and the stock on hand to choose from is certainly large and varied enough to suit the most critical taste. It embraces the leading brands of groceries and provisions, as well as a superior quality of meats of all kinds, with fresh fruits and vegetables in their seasons, of excellent variety. The goods are all right, the prices are all right, and the service is all right, so the natural conclusion is that Mr. Guilmet must be doing a very large wholesale and retail business—a conclusion which we are happy to say is fully warranted by the facts. Mr. Guilmet began operations in 1879, and his trade has been steadily developing ever since. He is a native of Canada, and is widely known in social as well as mercantile circles. Giving close personal attention and employing five competent assistants, it is not to be wondered at that orders are promptly filled to the entire satisfaction of his customers.

J. H. Beacham & Son, Life, Fire and Accident Insurance, Central Building, Great Falls, N. H.—There are but few business men in a position to personally investigate the soundness of the claims made by the various fire, life and accident insurance companies, and, therefore, it is obvious that a competent and reputable insurance broker, who has made a special study of the subject, is, in a certain sense, indispensable to a community, as he is competent to give valuable advice and information regarding the companies that will best suit the individual requirements of his patrons, and offer valuable suggestions to those who consult him. The firm of J. H. Beacham & Son are doing this, and the very extensive business they enjoy is sufficient evidence that the public appreciate the courteous and liberal methods pursued by this firm. The firm is composed of Mr. John H. Beacham, Wolfboro, who has for many years been engaged in the business, and his son, Mr. John L. Beacham, the junior partner, who has charge of the office at No 7 Central Building, Great Falls, N. H. The firm also have a branch office in Cloutman's Block, Farmington, N. H., while the main offices are in Goodman's Block, Wolfboro. The firm do a general insurance business in life, fire and accident, and are prepared to place risks in first-class companies on the most favorable terms, and claims and losses are adjusted promptly. Messrs. J. H. Beacham & Son represent both stock and mutual companies, their list including some of the strongest companies in the world. Any information regarding life, fire or accident insurance is gratuitously given on application, by mail or in person

SULLIVAN SQUARE.

HISTORICAL SKETCH OF BERWICK, ME.

The town of Berwick was originally a part of the ancient town of Kittery and was set apart and incorporated under its present name in 1713. Since that date the size of the township has been greatly reduced ; South Berwick being taken from the south side, in 1814, and North Berwick from the northeastern side, in 1831. A small portion of York was annexed in 1854. The present town is bounded on the north by Lebanon ; on the east by North Berwick ; on the south by South Berwick, and on the west by the towns of Rochester, Somersworth and Rollinsford which are in New Hampshire, being separated from Berwick by the Salmon Falls River, on which is located the village of Berwick in which the business of the town is concentrated. The stream is crossed by a bridge of 100 feet span, and the railway station is on the New Hampshire side, on the line of the Portsmouth, Great Falls & Conway Railroad.

Berwick village began to be a manufacturing centre about 1854 and its growth, especially during the past score of years, has been both rapid and steady. Police protection has been provided since 1819 and a fire department was established in 1873 ; while the educational facilities are excellent, the schools being liberally supported and very efficiently managed.

One of the most prominent of the public buildings is Odd Fellows Hall, dedicated in 1879. This is a fine brick edifice, three stories in height and thirty-two by fifty-five feet in dimensions. It is utilized by Echo Lodge, No. 52, and Golden Gate Encampment, No. 24 ; both these having been instituted in 1876. Another flourishing society, the Independent Order of Good Templars, is represented by Wilson Lodge, No. 75, organized in 1878.

Saw mills were erected on the site of the village at a very early date and wood-working is still quite extensively carried on ; the local establishments including a sash and door factory, a bobbin factory, a modern equipped saw-mill, etc., as well as a large tannery, reed and harness factories, iron and steel shops, soap factories, carriage factories, marble works, etc.

There are also some excellent stores in the village, including a very successful co-operative store established by the Sovereigns of Industry, in 1874.

The majority of the dwelling houses have been erected since 1870 and are consequently modern in style as well as neat and attractive in appearance. In short, both as regards public and private buildings, Berwick makes a very favorable showing and has no reason to fear comparison with any village of no greater population.

Leading Business Men of Berwick, Me.

S. P. Horne & Co., manufacturers of and dealers in Ready-Made Doors, Sash, Blinds and Mouldings; also Stair Work and Brackets of all sizes, Berwick Side, Great Falls, N. H.—The importance of placing building contracts with reliable and responsible parties cannot be overestimated, for the most carefully prepared plans and specifications will not protect the interests of the builders if their carrying out be entrusted to incompetent, careless or dishonest hands. Therefore the residents of Great Falls and vicinity have reason to congratulate themselves on having so dependable a firm as that of S. P. Horne & Co. to place their orders with, especially as this house is prepared to figure very closely on all work submitted. This business was started by Mr. S. P. Horne, who is a native of Rochester, N. H., and carried on until 1886, when he took in as partner, Mr W. L. Butterfield, a native of Vermont. The shop, located on the Berwick side, consists of a building two stories and attic, 25 × 40, and storehouse, employing six men and having a ten horse-power engine to turn out all their mouldings, doors, window frames, blinds, etc., etc. Orders for jobbing work will be filled at short notice in a satisfactory manner and at moderate prices, the proprietors giving their personal supervision to all.

L. M. Nute, Shoe Manufacturer, Berwick Side, Great Falls, N. H.—This business was founded in 1870 by Messrs. L. M. and D. H. Nute, and changed in 1882 to the present proprietor who is a native of Milton, N. H., and very well and favorably known. Realizing that there is a continuous demand among the trade for durable and thoroughly-made footwear at fair prices he has endeavored to fully meet it. His shop comprises three stories, 30 × 175 feet in dimensions, with a fifteen horse-power engine and well equipped with every facility in the way of new machinery, etc., for doing the best work. He gives employment to from 100 to 150 people, turning out about 1000 pairs per day of men's, boys' and youths' calf buff and flesh split shoes. The largest orders can be filled at short notice. Mr. Nute has an office in Boston at 28 High street, where samples are shown, but he is always pleased to see visitors at the factory, where they receive courteous attention, and to which place all mail orders should be addressed.

James W. Harriman, Machinist; all kinds of Repairing done in the best mechanical style; and at very reasonable rates; Steam, Gas and Water Piping a Specialty; Berwick Side, Great Falls, N. H.—One of the best places to get machine repairing of any kind done with which we are familiar is at the shop carried on by Mr. James W. Harriman at Great Falls on the Berwick side, for this is a very well-equipped establishment and Mr. Harriman is an expert machinist, employs experienced help, and spares no pains to thoroughly satisfy every customer. He is a native of Great Falls, and in 1896 succeeded Messrs. H. W. Pierce & Son, who had carried on the business since 1887. While doing all kinds of repairing in the very best style and at moderate rates, Mr. Harriman makes a specialty of steam, gas and water piping and of the building of pipe fence for graves, lots and enclosures of any kind, being prepared to fill orders at very short notice. He is agent for stationary engines and boilers of the most approved type and also for the Spence hot water heater.—conceded to have no superior in its special line. Mr. Harriman is making a specialty of this branch. Turned and cold rolled steel shafting is also dealt in to a considerable extent, and all kinds of mill work and supplies will be furnished at prices as low as the lowest in every instance.

Grant's Hotel, E. Grant, Proprietor, H. W. Niles, Clerk. Free Conveyance to and from Depots. Berwick side, Great Falls, N. H.—Great Falls is one of the most attractive towns in New Hampshire, and as it is also quite a business centre, it is visited by many strangers at all seasons of the year. Under these circumstances the question of hotel accommodations assumes no little importance, and it is perfectly safe to assert that the enviable reputation Great Falls enjoys among non-residents is due to the nature of the accommodations provided at Grant's Hotel, for this is a well-managed establishment. The proprietor, Mr. E. Grant, is a native of Acton, Maine, and has been in business since 1873. He spares no pains to secure the comfort of guests and together with his genial head clerk, Mr. H. W. Niles, employs a staff of seven assistants, so that the hotel and its appointments are kept in first class condition and the service is uniformly prompt and dependable. The Grant Hotel is very pleasantly located on the Berwick Side, and can accommodate some thirty people. The table is supplied with an abundance of seasonable food at all times, and the terms of the house are very reasonable.

John C. Nutter, manufacturer of and dealer in Doors, Sashes, Blinds, etc., Sullivan Square, Berwick, Me.—One of the most fruitful causes of discontent and even anger in the occupancy of a new house is to be found in the liability of the doors and sashes to "bind" and "stick" so firmly in some cases as to defy all efforts to stir them. Now of course this is at times unavoidable owing to a variety of causes which it is unnecessary to mention here, but in many instances the true explanation of the difficulty is to be found in the defective construction of the doors and sashes themselves. These defects may be in the workmanship, or they may be in the stock used, but in either case they occasion much annoyance which might easily have been entirely obviated, had well made articles been purchased originally. The productions of Mr. John Nutter, doing business on Sullivan square, will be found to be always satisfactory and reliable and it is owing to the growing appreciation of this fact that his business shows a marked and steady increase. This business was founded by Nutter & Tibbets, who were succeeded in 1887 by Mr. John C. Nutter. Mr. Nutter is a dealer in and manufacturer of doors, sashes, blinds, etc., the best of work being done and strict attention paid to the quality of the stock used. Orders will be filled at short notice, and the work will be guaranteed satisfactory.

ORRIN KNOX,

Wholesale dealer in Country Produce; Retail dealer in Family Groceries..

Railroad Mileage Tickets Bought, Sold and Rented,

SULLIVAN SQUARE.　　-　-　-　-　BERWICK, MAINE..

A. B. Spencer, dealer in Choice Family Groceries, Country Produce, Flour, Grain, etc.; also Furnishing Undertaker and manufacturer of and dealer in Burial Caskets and Coffins; Sullivan Square, Berwick, Maine —Mr. A. B. Spencer is a native of Berwick, Maine, and started the undertaking business in 1868, having become so thoroughly identified with the best interests of the town, is looked upon as a representative citizen, in the full sense of the word, having served n the army and holding the position as town treasurer. Mr. Spencer has had long and varied experience as a funeral director, and is prepared to fill all orders entrusted to him in that capacity with fidelity, intelligence and despatch. He will assume entire charge of funerals and furnish everything that is required, his facilities enabling him to execute all commissions at very short notice and at uniformly moderate rates. He retails and wholesales in coffins, occupying a store three stories h, 30 × 55 feet in size, and always carrying a varied and are stock of funeral and undertaking materials and emp. ing some five assistants. In 1886 Mr. Spencer combines with his other business a large choice family grocery store, located at Sullivan square, and his stock is always complete in every department, and sufficient assistance is employed to assure prompt, careful, and polite attention to every caller, while he is in a position to quote the lowest market prices on all the commodities dealt in.

Jesse R. Horne, manufacturer, wholesale and retail dealer in Hemlock, Pine and Spruce Timber and Boards of all kinds. Sawing, Planing, Jointing, Matching and Box making, Packing Boxes, etc., Berwick Side, Great Falls, N. H.—The extensive mill and box factory carried on by Mr. Jesse R. Horne is located in Berwick but may be classed among Great Falls' establishments for Mr. Horne lives here and has for years, at one time representing Great Falls in the State legislature. He was born in Rochester, N. H., and has been identified with his present enterprise for more than fifteen years. The premises utilized by him are two-stories in height and 55 × 70 feet in dimensions, and are fitted up with an elaborate plant of improved wood-working machinery, driven by an engine of seventy five horse power. Mr. Horne is a large manufacturer of packing boxes, his facilities being such as to enable him to meet all honorable competition by furnishing boxes of standard quality at the lowest market rates. Sawing and planing, without undue delay, employment being given to from sixteen to twenty five assistants. Mr. Horne deals extensively in lumber and can furnish it in any desired quantity at the lowest market rates.

L. E. Grant, Physician and Druggist, Berwick, Me.—It would be difficult to find an establishment of more genuine value to the community than that carried on by Mr. L. E. Grant, who being a native of Candia, N. H., started this undertaking in 1888, and under his able management has largely developed into a successful trade; drugs, medicines and chemicals are supplied at both wholesale and retail at the lowest rates that can be named on first class goods, and as the filling of prescriptions is given especial attention, customers may feel assured of their favors being appreciated and of their orders being handled with that skill and accuracy so desirable in this connection. Every precaution is observed that will tend to reduce the liability of error to the smallest possible amount, and every facility is at hand that can aid in attaining this result. Mr. Grant is moderate in his charges, and certainly has solved the problem of combining reliable service with popular prices. Stationery, choice brands of cigars and tobacco and druggists' sundries, form another important department of his business. The stock carried is fresh and acceptable, two assistants are employed, customers are treated with courtesy and consideration. His store is 15 × 40 feet in size.

DAM AND STONE BRIDGE, ROCHESTER.

HISTORICAL SKETCH OF ROCHESTER.

Lines of railroad as represented on a map have been described as "index fingers, pointing out the more prosperous and important towns and villages," and by following their indications on the map of Strafford county, even one entirely unacquainted with that section cannot fail to appreciate to some degree at least the comparative importance of Rochester, for railroads enter that town from six different directions and form a junction at and near Rochester village. From the north comes the Portsmouth, Great Falls and Conway Railroad, starting at Conway where connection is made with the railway systems of Vermont, New York, Canada and the West and Northwest ; from the northwest comes the Dover and Winnipesaukee Railroad, starting at Alton Bay at the southern extremity of Lake Winnipesaukee, where connection is made with steamers to and from all the lake ports, and with the Lake Shore Railroad, a branch of Concord and Montreal system ; from the northeast comes the Portland and Rochester Railroad, giving direct communication with Portland, and extending from Rochester in a southerly and south-easterly direction under the name of the Nashua and Rochester Railroad to Nashua, N. H., and thence to Worcester, Mass. The Portsmouth, Great Falls and Conway Railroad takes a south-easterly course from Rochester and joins the Boston and Maine Railroad at Rollinsford Junction, and the Dover and Winnipesaukee Railroad proceeds south to Dover and thence under the name of the Portsmouth and Dover Railroad to Portsmouth. All these railroads are included in the great Boston and Maine system and by them Rochester is given direct communication with all parts of this country and Canada.

Being directly on the line of travel between the sea-shore and mountain resorts an immense passenger traffic passes through the town during the vacation season, and at all times of year the passenger and freight services are frequent and efficient.

It is obvious that a town so situated must offer many advantages for the carrying on of great manufacturing enterprises and for the conducting of mercantile undertakings, and the magnitude and high standing of the industrial and commercial establishments of Rochester show that these advantages are largely and successfully availed of, while the steady growth of the town in population and in wealth proves that it has hardly begun to reach its ultimate development, and gives ground for the

HIGH SCHOOL, ROCHESTER.

prediction that the early part of the coming century will see Rochester occupying a prominent position among New Hampshire's cities. There is certainly no good reason why such should not be the case for no community has better transportation facilities, none gives more cordial welcome and assistance to deserving new enterprises, and few towns are more healthfully located or are inhabited by a more law-abiding, sociable and agreeable people. Low cost of living, remunerative employment in varied industries, and healthful climatic and hygienic conditions will do much to build up any community and all these are to be found in the Rochester of to-day.

The town lies in the eastern part of of Strafford County and is separated from Maine by the Salmon Falls River, this stream forming Rochester's eastern boundary, while Farmington and Milton bound it on the north; Somersworth, Dover and Barrington on the south, and Barrington, Strafford and Farmington on the west. The township is one of the largest in the county and contains three villages: Rochester, East Rochester, and Gonic.

Its surface is rolling and the soil is generally fertile, some of the farms being highly cultivated and very productive. There are three rivers in town : The Salmon Falls River extending the whole length of the township from north to south ; the Cocheco River entering about midway on the northern boundary and flowing out at the southern corner where it is joined by the Isinglass River, which first enters Rochester from Barrington at about the point that the Nashua and Rochester Railroad leaves the latter town, the stream then making an abrupt turn in its course and re-entering Barrington which it again leaves to enter Rochester just before the Dover line is reached.

The village of Rochester is located to the east of the centre of the township ; Gonic is in the southern centre, and East Rochester is near the Salmon Falls River about midway between the Somersworth and Milton lines.

By far the greater part of the business and population of the town is centered at Rochester village which indeed appears more like a prosperous city than a village and contains many large and substantial mercantile edifices, many handsome stores with plate-glass windows and other modern appointments, and many factories, some of which are very large and are fitted up with elaborate plants of the most improved machinery. Such a community naturally requires extensive banking facilities, and these are furnished by one national bank and three savings banks, or rather, to be strictly

MARKET STREET, ROCHESTER.

accurate, by one national bank, one institution that combines the functions of a bank of discount and deposit with those of a savings bank, and two regular savings banks. The two institutions doing a general banking business have capitals aggregating $150,000 and each has a large surplus. The amount of savings held on deposit approximates $1,500,000.

Manufacturing was begun in Rochester at a very early period in the town's history, among the first establishments being saw and grist mills, fulling and finishing mills, a nail factory, a scythe factory, a cotton yarn mill, etc., but the first corporation to begin operations was the Mechanic's Company, incorporated in 1834, with a capital of $15,000. This company manufactured blankets, but failed in 1841 and was succeeded by the Gonic Company, which also failed. The business was continued by private parties for a time and in 1840 passed under the control of the Norway Plains Company, incorporated with a capital of $60,000 which has since been increased to $150,000, for the company have been very successful in carrying on and developing the enterprise, and now operate three large mills run by water and steam power ; employ 440 assistants, and manufacture a fine line of woolen blankets, flannels and suitings.

RESIDENCE OF HORACE L. WORCESTER.

The manufacture of textile fabrics is also carried on successfully at Gonic and at East Rochester, but that industry is no longer the representative one of the town, for of late years the business of manufacturing boots and shoes has attained immense proportions and now gives employment to more hands than all other branches of manufacture combined. One of the local shoe factories is said to be the largest in the State, and certainly there are very few in all New England equal to it either in size or in completeness of equipment. The plant includes two large shoe shops, a tannery, a machine shop, a box factory numerous out-buildings and a large fire-proof store-house. The tannery, box factory, and machine shop do no outside work whatever, they being utilized exclusively in connection with the shoe business, and some idea of the magnitude of the latter may be gained from the fact that the capacity of the factory is 4,000 pairs per day. The tannery can produce 1,200 sides of leather per week. A 150-horse engine furnishes the motive power, and employment is given to 750 assistants.

Another large factory which turns out over 2,000 pairs per day and gives employment to some 250 operatives is carried on by one of the largest and best known shoe manufacturers in New England. He is a resident of Lynn, Mass., and maintains shops in Athol and Marblehead, in that State.

There are some large lumber mills in town, besides sash and blind, house finish and box factories. The quarrying and working of granite are also carried on to some extent ; and a comparatively new but very promising industry is that conducted by the Kiesel Fire Brick Company, incorporated in 1888 with a capital of $200,000.   This company make a superior grade of fire brick, tile, etc., and employ about fifty assistants.

We have already spoken of Rochester's fine mercantile edifices, and need only add that their contents are worthy of the buildings, for the local merchants as a rule carry very extensive and skillfully chosen stocks and offer inducements which draw trade from all the adjacent country. Some of the more prominent business men are very liberal and persistent advertisers, and the firm carrying on the largest store in town not only make liberal use of printers' ink but have their advertising signs spread throughout the State from the White Mountains to the sea.

MAIN STREET, ROCHESTER.

The local newspapers are well edited and well supported, the latter fact being due in no small degree to the good sense shown by their managers in looking after and advancing their local interests.

The earliest record relating to schools among the archives of the town shows that it was voted to have a school in 1750, but the next year the vote was the other way and as a natural consequence it was soon necessary to hold a special meeting to choose agents to defend the town which "lies under a presentiment for want of a school being kept, and to be heard and tried at the next Court of Quarter Sessions." Thereafter schools were kept for a number of years but finally the town became reckless and voted to hire no teachers but to pay whatever fine might be recovered by presentment.   This un-American state of affairs did not last long, however, and now for many years the schools have been liberally supported and are very largely attended.

There has been a Masonic Lodge in Rochester for eighty years, "Humane Lodge," F. & A. M., having been incorporated October 24, 1810.   The Odd Fellows also have lodges here, and there are other fraternal societies of lesser note.

The first meeting-house to be built in Rochester was erected in 1731 and divine worship has been regularly engaged in since that date. The various religious societies are in a generally flourishing condition, and maintain commodious and well-appointed church edifices.

We have left ourselves but little space in which to present the early history of the town, our idea. being to give a sketch of the Rochester of to-day rather than an account of the Rochester of the past. The town was incorporated May 10, 1722, and was named in honor of the Earl of Rochester, a. brother-in-law of King James II. The proprietors held their first meeting at Cocheco, July 9, 1722, they being assembled " to consider, debate, and resolve such matters and things" as were essential to a proper observance of the conditions of the charter, the first of these being that the proprietors. should build a house and settle a family therein within three years, and plant or sow three acres of ground within four years, those failing to comply with these requirements forfeiting all their rights in the property. So the proprietors arranged to have the most commodious part of the township laid out into what they called " home lots," and a committee was chosen to select the best location and to. lay out roads and a proper " train field." So carefully was every detail looked after that the proprietors' clerk was authorized to obtain a " book consisting of three quires of paper bound up in parchment, at the charge of the commoners" in which to keep the records. But " the best laid schemes. of mice and men" sometimes went wrong in those days even as they do now, and the beginning of trouble with the Indians put an end to all attempts at frontier settlement for a time and so prevented the doing of anything that could fitly be recorded in that book provided " at the charge of the commoners."

The second meeting was held April 24, 1727, at which a board of selectmen consisting of Captain. Francis Matthews, Captain John Knight, and Paul Gerrish, was appointed, and these selectmen instructed the committee, which had been appointed at the first meeting, to reconsider a plan of division. At the end of five months a plan was submitted but was not satisfactory, and a surveyor was appointed to lay out the plantation in one hundred and twenty-five lots of sixty acres each, in ranges from Salmon Falls River to the Barrington line. Each share was to consist of one lot, and the location of that assigned to any individual proprietor was decided by a veritable " drawing of lots," it being governed by chance entirely. The drawing was begun in Cocheco, December 13, 1727, and finished the next day at Oyster River. The comparatively small size of the lots left by far the larger portion of the granted tract undisposed of and December 17, 1730, another drawing was held, each lot consisting of at least two hundred and forty acres. The land then divided included a large part of the territory now in Milton and Farmington, and also a level tract which was called Norway plains on. account of its being covered by Norway pines. A considerable portion of this tract was left common and is now the site of Rochester village, this fact putting one in mind of the biblical saying, " The stone the builders rejected has become the corner stone of the temple."

The first settler was Captain Timothy Roberts, he established himself in Rochester, December 26, 1728. The proprietors held their last meeting June 28, 1784, at which time the town clerk became proprietor's clerk, all documents were placed in his custody, and the office was vested in him and his successors forever.

June 27, 1746, is a memorable day in the annals of Rochester for it was then that the first concerted Indian attack upon the settlement was made, four men being killed and one wounded and captured. For several years thereafter the town suffered considerably from the Indians, but when the Revolution broke out she was in a position to render great service to the cause of freedom, and made a record of which she may well feel proud. The same may be said of her Civil War record, for she furnished two hundred and seventy-three men, and paid in bounties the sum of $64,914 ; responding promptly to all calls for aid.

Since theiclose of the Rebellion the town has gained wonderfully in wealth and population and her best friend can wish her no greater good than that the promise of the past and present be justified by her future.

Leading Business Men of Rochester, N. H.

The Rochester Loan and Banking Co., Rochester, N. H.—The Rochester Loan and Banking Company was incorporated in 1887 by virtue of a special charter given by the New Hampshire legislature, and is under the direct supervision of the bank commissioners, and the extensive use which has already been made of the facilities offered is not the result alone of the legal safeguards afforded to investors, but of these safeguards combined with the prestige given by the high business and social standing of those identified with the company, the officers and directors being known throughout the State as solid and representative business men, as will be readily agreed after reading the annexed list of names : Hon. Edwin Wallace, president ; Sumner Wallace, vice-president ; John L. Copp, cashier ; directors, Edwin Wallace, Rochester, N. H.; Hon. Frank Jones, Portsmouth, N. H.; G. W. Wattles, Carroll, Iowa ; Sumner Wallace, Rochester, N. H.; Charles B. Gafney, Rochester, N. H.; I Salinger, Rochester, N. H.; C. F. Caverly, Rochester, N. H. The company has a capital of $100,000, paid in, and as a recent sworn statement showed a surplus of $30,000 and a total absence of bad or doubtful accounts and protested or overdue paper, the financial condition of the enterprise must be conceded to be exceptionally sound. Briefly stated, the advantages offered by the corporation are as follows : Receives deposits subject to check ; pays five per cent. interest (free of taxes) on savings deposits ; acts as trustee for individuals and corporations, and officially, under appointment by the court of this or other States, as financial agent ; offers for sale choice and conservative investment securities paying a safe rate of interest. These securities are in the form of debenture bonds, bearing six per cent. interest, payable semi-annually at the bank. They are issued in series of $100,000, and in denominations of $100, $200, $500 and $1,000 ; each series being entirely separate from the others and secured by an equal amount of real estate first mortgages on improved property worth at least two and one-half times as much as the amount of the loan. These mortgages are duly transferred to trustees, who hold them in trust for the benefit of purchasers of the bonds, which run ten years but may be redeemed in five should occasion require. Well informed investors regard these debentures as being practically as good as government bonds, and say that the claim of the company, that its aim is absolute security to the purchaser and the prompt payment of principal and interest, is fully justified by the facts. At all events, these bonds are largely held by banks, insurance and trust companies, educational and benevolent institutions, trustees and guardians, as well as by private individuals, and the demand for them is constantly increasing. But few corporations have entered the business field under more favorable auspices or with brighter prospects, judging either by its past experience or future outlook. Its affairs will continue to have the same energetic, enterprising and conservative management which has gained for itself that high standing which is a guarantee to all the holders of its securities that their interests will be protected to the fullest extent. The officers of the company whose names have already been given are men of wealth and experience, and are large holders of its stock, which is a sufficient guarantee that the affairs of the company will be faithfully administered.

E. G. & E. Wallace, manufacturers of Leather, Boots and Shoes, Rochester, N. H.—The enterprise conducted by Messrs. E. G. & E. Wallace well deserves very prominent mention in any review of Rochester's representative industries, and its history has that peculiar interest which always attaches to the story of an undertaking built up to vast proportions from small beginnings. Operations were begun away back in 1845, by Mr. James Bodge who was succeeded by Messrs. Onion & Richards, the present firm assuming control in 1854. Both partners are natives of Berwick, Me., and both have served as representatives, Mr E. Wallace having also served as senator. They are identified with other important enterprises besides the one under consideration, and rank with the most widely known and influential business men of New Hampshire. When Messrs. E. G. & E. Wallace assumed control of the business it was confined to the tanning of leather and even that was carried on on a small scale, whereas now, although the firm tan only for themselves, they operate a tannery having a capacity of 1200 sides per week and find that not a bit too large at times. The manufacture of medium and low price boots and shoes is very extensively carried on, the total capacity of the shops being 4,000 pairs per day. The plant of machinery in use is not only very elaborate but is of the most improved type, and it comprises not only machines for the carrying out of the various processes incidental to shoe manufacturing but also for the production of boxes and for the doing of machine repairing, etc., for the firm make their own boxes and repair their own machinery as well as tan their own stock. The premises utilized include one shop containing three stories and a basement and measuring 170 × 35 feet, with an ell 65 × 35 feet, another shop of the dimensions of 120 × 50 feet, and four stories and a basement in height, a very large tannery, a commodious fire proof storehouse, and many out-buildings of various sizes. A 150 horse engine is located in the centre of the works and power is transmitted in four directions. Employment is given to about 750 assistants, and we need hardly add that the annual product is of very great amount and value. The boots and shoes made by this concern are very favorably known among consumers and the trade, they ranking with the most uniformly durable and comfortable goods in the market. No trouble is spared to keep them fully up to the standard in their several grades, and they are supplied at the lowest market rates, the most extensive orders being filled at very short notice.

F. E. Wallace & Co., Hardware, Rochester, N. H.—
Even a stranger in Rochester who had no knowledge of
the fact that it is one of the most important trade centres
in the State and distributes goods over a very wide extent
of country would be very liable to guess pretty near the
truth after inspecting the establishment conducted by
Messrs. F. E. Wallace & Co., for this concern do an
extremely large business, and its magnitude is indicated
by the size of the premises occupied and the extent and
variety of the stock carried. The premises comprise three
floors and a basement, measuring 30 × 100 feet, together
with a two story addition and a three-story storehouse 40
feet square, and the stock includes full assortments of
hardware, agricultural tools, paints, oils, varnishes, glass,
harnesses, horse furnishings, etc., the productions of the
leading manufacturers being represented and the lowest
market rates being quoted on all the articles handled.
Despite the magnitude of the business orders are assured
prompt and careful attention, for employment is given to
from three to six assistants, and the members of the firm
exercise close supervision over the many details of the
service and thus maintain it at a high standard of efficiency. The partners are Mr. F. E. Wallace, a native of
Vermont, and Messrs. E. G. and E. Wallace, both of
whom were born in Berwick, Me. The junior partner
has served as town treasurer, and both his associates have
held the position of representative, all three gentlemen
being very widely and favorably known not only in business but also in social circles, while the enterprise with
which they are identified is one of the most truly representative in this section of the State.

Dodge's Hotel, J. Thorn Dodge, Proprietor, Central
Square, Rochester, N. H.—Dodge's Hotel is so truly one
of the "institutions" of Rochester that those who know
the town must of necessity know the hotel also, and it
would be well if every city and town had a public house
at which guests would be made so thoroughly comfortable
as they are here. This hotel has been carried on by the
Dodge family for many years, and the present proprietor,
Mr. J. Thorn Dodge, has fully maintained its high reputation since assuming control, for he gives the service very
careful personal supervision and is always ready to do
anything in reason to further the comfort and happiness
of his guests. Dodge's Hotel is very conveniently located
in Central square and is a commodious and well-arranged
structure having accommodations for about seventy. The
sleeping rooms are light, airy and pleasant, the beds and
other furnishings are very comfortable and well kept, the
entire house is thoroughly heated during the colder
months, and in short the appointments, conditions and
management are such as to make Dodge's Hotel a very
desirable place to put up at at any time of year. The
bill of fare is varied, the quality of the food is excellent
and the quantity abundant, and the cooking is satisfactory
at all times. There is an excellent livery connected,
teams being furnished at all hours, at short notice and at
uniformly moderate rates.

L. B. Moulton, Contractor and Builder, Elm Street,
Rochester, N. H.—The work of the contractor and builder
may be said to precede that of nearly every other trade,
for houses and stores must be built before they can be
occupied, and no surer index of the commercial prosperity
of a community is known than that afforded by the condition of the building industry. We take, therefore, given
this branch of trade considerable prominence in this book,
and take pleasure in mentioning among the most reliable
contractors and builders to be found in this town Mr. L.
B. Moulton. This gentleman has been engaged in business
in Rochester and vicinity for twenty seven years, and is
well known throughout the trade for the thorough character of his work and the conscientious manner in which
all agreements are carried out. The premises utilized are
located on Elm street and all necessary facilities are at
hand to give prompt and skillful attention to orders for
building of all descriptions. The shop is located over a
blacksmith shop where Mr. Moulton also attends to carriage repairing and wheelwright work, and also the filing
of saws. From one to six men are employed according to
the season. Mr. Moulton is very moderate in his prices,
and by using honest material and insisting upon honest
workmanship he has gained a high and well-deserved reputation.

Harrison Soule, Iron and Brass Founder; Castings of
all kinds made at short notice; Foundry near Boston &
Maine Depot, Rochester, N. H.—The manufacturing
establishments located in Rochester and vicinity are so
many and varied that there is a wide and increasing field
for the operations of the enterprise conducted by Mr. Harrison Soule, in carrying on a very thoroughly equipped
brass and iron foundry and being prepared to make castings of all kinds at short notice. Mr. Soule was born in
Middleboro, Mass., and has been identified with his present enterprise since 1870, during which time he has won
a high reputation for turning out uniformly accurate work
and for filling all orders, large or small, without undue
delay. The premises utilized are located near the Boston
& Maine depot and are 32 × 60 feet in dimensions,
exclusive of an engine and boiler room, containing a
twelve horse-power engine. Mr. Soule employs three
competent assistants and gives personal attention to the
filling of orders no defective work being knowingly
allowed to leave the shop. The charges made are uniformly moderate, and in short there is abundant reason
for the wide popularity of this most useful enterprise.

Edward Davis, Wholesale Confectioner, Cocheco
Block, Rochester, N. H. Experienced and enterprising
grocers, apothecaries, variety store keepers and many
others that could be mentioned find that it pays to carry a
stock of first class confectionery, for aside from the profits
made on its sale it attracts custom to other departments of
their business, and very desirable custom too, for those
who appreciate high grade confectionery are almost invariably large buyers of other first class goods also. Dealers
who wish to obtain confectionery that will give the best of
satisfaction would do well to place a trial order with Mr.
Edward Davis, carrying on operations in Cocheco Block,
Market street, for he does an exclusively wholesale business and is prepared to furnish thoroughly satisfactory
goods at the lowest market rates. This business was
founded in 1878 by Messrs C. A. Davis & Co., and came
under the sole control of the present proprietor in 1883.
He is a native of Albion, Me., and is very widely and
favorably known in trade circles; his straightforward and
enterprising methods having gained him many friends.
Every order is assured prompt and painstaking attention
and the goods are exceptionally uniform in quality and
may confidently be guaranteed to prove as represented.

David Hayes, dealer in Coal, Wood, Hay, Ice; also
Cement and Fertilizers; Central Square, Rochester, N.
H.—The business now carried on by Mr David Hayes was
founded several years ago under the firm name of D.
Hayes & Son Mr. Hayes is a native of New Hampshire,
and has been in business in Rochester for over twelve
years, and is too well known here to need extended personal mention. Mr. Hayes has an office on Central square,
and handles coal, wood, hay, ice, cement and fertilizers at
wholesale and retail, carrying a large stock and having
storage capacity. It is hardly necessary to say that he is
in a position to quote the very lowest market rates on both
large and small orders, and to guarantee that the quality
of product should be up to representations in every
respect. Employment is given to five assistants, and
despite the large business done all orders can, and will, be
given immediate and careful attention. The business is
given the personal attention of the proprietor who has the
interests of his patrons in view at all times. The system
of delivery is unusually good, thus avoiding all unnecessary delays, and the goods furnished are strictly first class.

N. C. Phillips, dealer in Fresh and Salt Fish, Oysters and Clams, Central Square, Rochester, N. H.—There is hardly a physician of any note but what will agree that it would be well for the health of the community as a whole if more fish and less meat were consumed, for although meat is a valuable and healthful article of food, still it is hurtful when eaten to excess, and three families out of five do unquestionably consume too much of it. The residents of Rochester are very fortunate as far as the fish supply is concerned, for our local markets are supplied at all seasons with an abundance of fresh and salt water fish of all descriptions. Among Rochester's dealers in these products we take especial pleasure in calling attention to Mr. N. C. Phillips, doing business on Central square, for he not only carries an attractive stock of thoroughly reliable fish, oysters and clams, but he quotes prices as low as the lowest and caters to all classes of trade, making it a point to show uniform courtesy to every caller. Mr. Phillips is a native of Swampscott, Mass., and founded his present business in 1884, quite an extensive wholesale and retail trade is now carried on. Mr Phillips employs only competent assistants, and all orders are given prompt and painstaking attention, and every care is taken to handle only such articles as will prove just as represented.

I. A. Collins, Photographer, Hanson Street, Rochester, N. H.—Probably in no branch of the arts have more improvements been made during the recent years than in the art of photography, and the avidity with which inventions of latter days have been availed of by the profession, is a convincing proof of the spirit of enterprise, which has been a distinguishing feature of those interested in this most available of all arts. Business in this line was begun at the place mentioned at the head of this article in 1881 by Mr. J. C. Whittimore, who was succeeded in 1884 by the firm of Lampson & Smith, who managed matters until the present proprietor, Mr. I. A. Collins, became possessor of the premises. He is a native of Vermont. The appliance and apparatus used are of the best, and comprise as perfect an establishment of the kind as can be found in this section. Nothing but the very best work is here executed, while the prices are very moderate. Great care and attention is paid to each individual in regard to proper light, position and other surroundings, which are very essential in the making of a pleasing as well as a correct picture. Mr. Collins has also half of the store on the street floor where he manufactures and sells picture frames, and also sells mouldings and pictures. He employs only thoroughly experienced assistants, who give polite attention to all callers.

O. A. Hoyt, dealer in Foreign and Domestic Dry Goods, Fancy Goods, Hosiery, Ribbons, Laces, Underwear, etc., Hayes' Block, Central Square, Rochester, N. H.—An establishment which stands very high in the estimation of the residents of Rochester, is that conducted by Mr. O. A. Hoyt, and located in Hayes' Block, Central square. This establishment was opened by the present proprietor in 1882. The premises occupied comprise a spacious store, 30 × 80 feet in dimensions, which contains a stock of both foreign and domestic dry goods, and fancy goods, hosiery, ribbons, laces, underwear, etc., which would not suffer by comparison with a similar stock offered by any first-class dry goods house. Those who wish to examine all the latest novelties in dress goods, etc., will save time and trouble by going direct to this popular store. The stock is given close and painstaking attention, and will be found to be complete in every detail. Low prices rule, for the maxim, "quick sales and small profits," is fully carried out, the result being that the assortment is constantly in process of renewal, and is composed exclusively of fresh and seasonable goods. Employment is given to from four to six competent assistants, and every caller may depend on receiving immediate and courteous attention, goods being cheerfully shown on application. Mr. Hoyt is a native of New Hampshire, and very well and favorably known in Rochester.

S. Stringer, manufacturer of Soda and Mineral Waters, Belfast Ginger Ale, Lager, Tonic, Ginger, Pineapple, Birch and Root Beers, Rochester, N. H.—The development of the business conducted by Mr. S. Stringer since its foundation in 1884, is due to the honorable business methods of the proprietor. He is a native of Portsmouth, N. H., and well and favorably known in Rochester. The premises utilized by him in his business are located on Hanson street, and are of the dimensions of 50 × 70 feet, and are well equipped with all the necessary facilities for carrying on the business. Mr. Stringer is a manufacturer and wholesale dealer in soda and mineral waters, Belfast ginger ale, lager, tonic, ginger, pineapple, birch and root beers, and customers may be sure of getting first-class articles when dealing with this house. Refined cider bottled for family use, and soda in syphon bottles may be obtained here, and soda fountains are charged to order. Mr. Stringer employs three competent and reliable assistants, and as he gives the business his own personal supervision, all orders are sure to receive prompt and painstaking attention. He is prepared to furnish his goods in quantities to suit, and is also prepared to give prices on same which cannot fail to prove satisfactory.

C. A. Davis, Manufacturing Confectioner, Cocheco Block, Rochester, N. H.—While it is a demonstrated fact that pure confectionery is not only harmless but beneficial, it is also a fact that impure or carelessly made confectionery is an excellent thing to leave alone, and hence when buying candies of any kind it is good policy to take some little pains to patronize a reputable dealer. One sure way to get first class confectionery at the lowest market rates is to place the order with Mr. C. A. Davis, doing business in Cocheco Block, for he is a manufacturer as well as a wholesale and retail dealer, and has won an enviable reputation for integrity and enterprise since beginning operations here in 1877. Mr. Davis is a native of Belfast, Me., and has had long experience in the confectionery business, being thoroughly conversant with it in every detail. The premises utilized by him have an area of 1700 square feet, exclusive of a basement and a spacious store-house, and his manufacturing facilities are such as to enable him to fill the largest orders at short notice. A complete and attractive stock is constantly carried, and as the confectios are skillfully made from carefully selected material they give uniform satisfaction even to the most fastidious.

Charles M. Bailey, manufacturer of and dealer in Stoves and Kitchen Goods, Furnaces and Hot Water Heating, Tin Roofing and Tin Shingles a Specialty, Job Work done at short notice, Market Street, Rochester, N. H.—The establishment conducted by Mr. Chas. M. Bailey on Market street was founded about ten years ago by Mr. Chas. E. Ricker, who was succeeded by the present proprietor in 1896. This gentleman is a native of Littleton, N. H., and is thoroughly experienced in his present business. The premises occupied consist of three floors and basement 30 × 100 feet in dimensions and two spacious store-houses, where an extensive manufacturing and retail business is done. The stock handled includes stoves and kitchen goods, pumps, lead pipes, sheet lead and zinc, all of which are offered at market rates, and the tin, wooden, glass and plated ware and table cutlery sold at this establishment has an enviable reputation for general excellence. Furnaces and hot water heating apparatus are made a specialty of, as is also tin roofing and tin shingles, and all kinds of tin ware is made to order at short notice. Mr. Bailey has another store in Pittsfield, N. H., where he carries on an extensive trade in coal, flour and grain, in addition to the class of goods handled here. He is prepared to do all kinds of job work at short notice, having every facility at hand for the proper execution of such work. Employment is given to five competent and reliable assistants, and low rates are quoted on both labor and goods.

A. S. Parshley, General Insurance, Rochester, N. H.—The general insurance agency carried on by Mr. A. S. Parshley at Rochester was established by him in 1870. A very large amount of insurance has been placed through this agency during the past twenty years, and its record for efficient service and prompt and satisfactory settlements of fire losses is one of which those responsible for its management have every reason to be proud. The proprietor, Mr. Parshley, is a native of Stafford, N. H., and has long since become thoroughly identified with the interests of Rochester, and is now chairman of selectmen. He is a pushing, energetic business man, and has been very successful in placing insurance in a manner which has given entire satisfaction to all parties concerned. He represents a goodly list of strong stock and mutual companies, and is prepared to write policies at the most favorable rates. Two thoroughly experienced assistants are employed, and all communications by mail are given immediate and careful attention. The following list shows the nature of the services Mr. Parshley is prepared to render : Stock companies, assets —.Ætna, Hartford, Conn , $10,071,510 ; Insurance Company of North America, Philadelphia, $8,731,160 ; Anglo-Nevada, Cal., $2,569,553 ; National, Hartford, $2,443,937 ; London, Lancashire, Liverpool, Eng., $2,104,080 ; Phoenix Assurance Corporation, London, $1,966,132 ; Sun Fire Office, London, $1,956,331 ; Providence Washington, Providence, R. I., $1,164,983 ; New Hampshire, Manchester, N. H., $1,588,817 ; Peoples' Manchester, $623,593 ; Granite State, Portsmouth, N. H , $456,673. Mutual companies: Portsmouth Fire, Fire Underwriters, Fitchburg, Cheshire Co., Concord & H. M. & T. Mutuals. Also National Life Insurance of Vermont. Mr. Parshley also deals in real estate, will negotiate the purchase or sale of same, negotiate loans or take charge of the renting of property.

E. W. Emerson & Co., Druggists, Main Street, Hayes' Block, Rochester, N. H.—The position of the pharmacist unites the requirements and responsibilities of both the professional and business man, and as is always the case it thus involves peculiar fitness and the combination of rare and opposite characteristics of mind, which we seldom find in one individual, in order that the duties and cares may be properly met. To the fact that these conditions of scientific knowledge and business enterprise have been exceptionally well filled, is chiefly owing to the marked and increasing success which the establishment now conducted by E. W. Emerson & Co. in Hayes' Block on Main street. This establishment was founded by Mr. S. F. Sanderson, who was succeeded by G. N. Shaw & Co., and so continued until the present firm assumed control in 1889. The premises are of the dimensions of 18x85 feet, and are fitted up with all necessary facilities and stocked with a complete assortment of pure drugs and first-class druggists' sundries. Also books, stationery, toilet and fancy goods. Two reliable assistants are employed, and special attention is paid to the prescription department, which is managed with unusual accuracy. Mr. Emerson is a native of New Hampshire, and is one of our most successful and popular pharmacists He has had thirteen years' experience, having been in the business eleven years in Farmington, N. H., and has justly earned the esteem and appreciation of his fellow citizens.

Harry M. Hoyt & Co., Crescent Bargain Store, Imported and Domestic Dry and Fancy Goods, Ribbons, Gloves, Hoisery, Trimmings and Ladies' Furnishings, No. 4 McDuffee Block, Rochester, N. H.—"All is not gold that glitters," according to the proverb, and no doubt there is not one of our readers but what has learned from sad experience that all is not "cheap" that is claimed to be so. Indeed, the word "cheap" has a very elastic meaning, and it may be so used as to convey precisely opposite ideas at different times, but take it in the sense of "below the regular rates," or synonymous with the word "bargains," and it applies very forcibly to the establishment conducted by Harry M. Hoyt & Co , at No. 4 McDuffee Block, for the "Crescent Bargain Store." is indeed a " bargain " store and no mistake, the proprietors being very close buyers and giving their customers a generous share of the benefits thus derived. The business was founded by Mr. E. N. Thorn who was succeeded by the present firm in 1889. The firm is composed of H. M. Hoyt and Mrs. N. F. Wallace, both of whom are natives of Rochester, their store is of the dimensions of 65 × 20 feet and a fine stock of imported and domestic dry and fancy goods is carried, and also ladies' furnishings. Four competent and reliable assistants are constantly employed, and prompt and courteous service is the rule of the house, and our advice to those who wish good articles and do not care to pay fancy prices is to give this establishment an early call.

J. H. Meserve & Co., manufacturers of and dealers in Mouldings, Window Frames, Doors, Brackets, Stair Rails and Boxes, Planing, Sawing, Turning, Scroll Sawing, etc., Lumber, Shingles, Clapboards, Glazed Windows, and Builders' Finish, Autumn Street, Rochester, N. H.— Messrs. J. H. Meserve & Co. have an extended reputation for furnishing mouldings, window frames, doors, brackets, stair rails and other house finish, lumber, shingles, clapboards, etc , of standard quality in quanties to suit at positively the lowest market rates, and not only is this reputation thoroughly well-deserved but it is the natural and inevitable consequence of the facilities enjoyed and the methods pursued by the firm, these facilities and methods enabling all honorable competition to be easily met. The business was founded in 1876 by Mr. J. H. Meserve, the present firm name being adopted in 1888. Mr. Meserve is native of Rochester and is associated with Mr. George H. McDuffee a native of Minnesota. The firm buy and clear timber land and are very extensively engaged in the manufacture of mouldings, window frames, doors, brackets, stair rails, and boxes, besides doing planing, sawing, turning, scroll sawing, etc., to order. The premises made use of are located on Autumn street, and comprise a two-story mill measuring 50 × 100 feet, besides several commodious storehouses. The plant of machinery in use is of the most improved type and is very complete, enabling an immense amount of work to be turned out and reducing the expenses of production to a minimum. Power is furnished by one fifty and one forty-horse engine and employment is given to from fifteen to thirty assistants. A large stock of lumber, shingles, clapboards, glazed windows and builders' finish is constantly carried and orders can be filled without delay, the very lowest market prices being quoted to both wholesale and retail buyers.

R. Frank Tibbets, dealer in Watches, Jewelry, Silver and Plated Ware, Spectacles, etc., Fine Watch Repairing and Engraving, No 16 Main Street, Wentworth Block, Rochester, N. H.—Among the best known and most reliable establishments of the kind in Rochester is that now conducted by Mr. R. Frank Tibbets at No. 16 Main street, Wentworth Block. This enterprise was started by W. J. Lewis, who was succeeded by the present proprietor in 1882, since which date it has gained a well earned reputation for the excellence of its wares, and the fidelity with which orders entrusted to it are filled, hence its business is prosperous and steadily increasing. With the advancement of any community in wealth, intelligence and culture, the fine arts of decoration and adornment prosper, and the skill and taste of the jeweler is brought more constantly and generally into requisition. Twenty years ago it would have been impossible to have found customers for that class of goods, which are now really in the greatest demand. The premises utilized by Mr. Tibbets are of the dimensions of 10 × 20 feet, and the stock carried comprises the finest grades of watches, and a beautiful selection of jewelry, also silver and plated ware, spectacles, etc. Fine watch repairing and engraving is done here in the most thorough manner, and at very reasonable prices A competent assistant is employed, while the proprietor gives his personal attention to the business; he is a man of judgment and sound business principles and of superior taste in the selection of his stock.

J. G. Morrill & Co., Groceries and Grain, Nos. 63 and 65 Main Street, Odd Fellows' Block, Rochester, N. H.—By a careful examination of the commercial facilities enjoyed by the merchants of Rochester, we are led to make special reference to the house of Messrs. J. G. Morrill & Co. as a representative one in the line of groceries and grain. Its rank has been secured by enterprise, energy and reliable business methods. It is located at Nos. 63 and 65 Main street, in Odd Fellows' Block, and was opened to the public by this firm in 1884. The premises occupied comprise a double store and basement, 60×60 feet each, with an L 15×90 feet, and a storehouse 22×60 feet, giving ample accommodations for the large stock that is constantly carried, and for the prosecution of the business upon an extensive scale. Even the most casual observer, upon visiting this house, cannot fail to be impressed with the extent, system and completeness of the establishment, and it may be safely asserted that in quantity, quality, freshness and variety the stock carried here has no superior in this section. In the line of family groceries the firm deal in the finest teas, the purest coffees and spices, the leading brands of flour, sugars, syrups and molasses, canned goods in great variety, preserves, sauces and table delicacies of the most desirable kind. The stock of grain is always large, choice and complete, received direct from the hands of the producer, and sold, both at wholesale and retail, at the lowest market prices. Goods are promptly delivered, and customers are assured complete satisfaction, not only in the character of the goods, but in manifest advantages in terms and prices. The firm is composed of Messrs. J. G. Morrill, a native of Maine, C. F. Cliverly and J. L. Swain, both natives of Rochester, and well and favorably known in this community.

A. V. Sanborn, Furniture, Undertaker, Floral Designs, Hanson Street, Rochester, N. H.—The business conducted by Mr. A. V. Sanborn on Hanson street is one of the best managed of its kind in Rochester. Operations were begun here by the present proprietor in 1878. He is a native of Great Falls, N. H., and is one of the best known and most highly esteemed of all our resident business men. The premises made use of comprise a store 25 × 60 feet in dimensions, and three floors above, each measuring 50×60 feet. Mr. Sanborn is an undertaker and dealer in furniture, general goods and floral designs, he carrying a heavy stock, and being in a position to fill orders at very short notice, and the stock on hand is so arranged as to make examination very easy. Coffins, caskets, etc., will be supplied at very moderate rates, and the assortment is sufficiently varied to allow all tastes and circumstances to be suited. Three assistants are employed, and they are thoroughly experienced and reliable. The entire charge of funerals will be undertaken if desired, and every commission will be promptly, faithfully and intelligently executed.

Cascade House, A. A. Hayes, Proprietor, Rochester, N. H.—The Cascade House is just such an establishment as the majority of travellers like to come across for its proprietor pays more attention to comfort than to style, and the consequence is that his guests obtain most satisfactory accommodations at most reasonable figures. Of course it is hard to define just what is meant by "style," for what may seem very stylish to one man may appear quite the opposite to another, but generally speaking, the most "stylish" hotels are those that charge the highest rates for the least satisfactory service. Mr. A. A. Hayes' house has become known as a most excellent place to get a good substantial meal and a comfortable room for very little money, and there is not a similar establishment in this section deserving a more liberal patronage. The bill of fare is always extensive, and at all times of year the supply of substantials and delicacies is sufficiently abundant and varied to allow of all tastes being suited. The premises are located on Railroad avenue, and are well fitted up, and sufficient help is employed to promptly attend to the wants of all patrons.

Geo. W. Sayward, Dining Rooms, Hanson Street, Rochester, N. H.—It might seem at first thought easy enough to manage a restaurant, but there is no man who has had much occasion to patronize these places but what will say that the really good ones are a small minority. Why, it is not for us to state; we have our own theories on the subject, but our readers want facts rather than theories, and are naturally more interested in learning of one good dining-room than in hearing the reasons why a half-dozen are not good. Therefore we will hasten to call their attention to the dining-rooms, conducted by Mr. Geo. W. Sayward and located on Hanson street, for this gentleman is one of the few who know how things should be done and spares no pains to attain satisfactory results. Mr. Sayward was born in Maine, and opened his present place of business in 1886. The premises can accommodate twenty guests and are nicely fitted up with all the necessary facilities. But after all the main point to be considered in an establishment of this kind is the food, and here Mr. Sayward comes out strong, for he supplies his customers with the best the market affords, and takes measures to see that it is properly cooked and promptly and courteously served. Ice cream is served at all hours either by plate or quantity. Employment is given to from two to four assistants. The prices here are very moderate, and a trial of the accommodations will result in another call.

Mrs. M. A. Richardson, dealer in Millinery, Hair and Fancy Goods; Hair Work of every description made to order; No. 2 McDuffee Block, Rochester.—There is one establishment in particular which the ladies of Rochester and vicinity speak very highly of, and that is the one conducted by Mrs. M. A. Richardson at No. 2 McDuffee Block. This enterprise was inaugurated in 1871 by the present proprietress, and has been under her skillful management since that date. The premises occupied consist of half a store and are well fitted up the stock on hand being displayed to excellent advantage. It comprises millinery of every description and also hair and fancy goods, and bears evidence of careful selection in every department. Mrs. Richardson is a native of Maine, and has a large circle of friends and patrons in Rochester. She displays excellent taste both as a milliner and hair worker. She manufactures hair goods of every description, and the general appreciation of the results she attains is shown by the large patronage enjoyed. Seven assistants are employed on an average and all commissions are promptly executed, and uniformly moderate charges made. Every thing offered for sale here is guaranteed to prove strictly as represented in every instance and the service is prompt and courteous at all times.

E. F. Sleeper, Meat, Vegetables, and Canned Goods, Odd Fellows' Block, Rochester, N. H.—An accommodating spirit and a determination to do the fair thing in every transaction are powerful aids to success in every business enterprise, and they have not failed to exercise their usual effect in the case of Mr. E. F. Sleeper, who carries on business in Odd Fellows' Block, Rochester. Business was started here by Mr. J. S. Gilman, who was succeeded by Mr. J. N. Varney, who gave place to the present proprietor during the current year. This gentleman is a native of Barnstead, N. H., and is well known in this community as an enterprising and reputable merchant, who neglects no honorable means to extend his business operations. Mr. Sleeper's store is of the dimensions of 22 × 50 feet, and he claims to have one of the best stocks of meat, vegetables and canned goods in Rochester, and certainly the assortment he exhibits of these goods is admirable, not only for its completeness, but also for the standard character of the articles composing it. A competent assistant is given employment, and everything is so arranged as to permit of the prompt and accurate filling of orders, and those who want superior meat, etc., at low prices should certainly patronize the establishment conducted by Mr. E. F. Sleeper, in Odd Fellows' Block.

J. E McDuffee, Teacher of Instrumental Music, No. 9 McDuffee Block, Rochester, N. H.—That a person may be a most execrable musician and at the same time an excellent teacher of music, may seem to be a paradox to such of our readers as have never given the matter special thought ; but it is as true in the teaching of music as in that of arithmetic or language, that personal mastery of the subject does not necessarily involve the capacity to make its details plain to others. Of late years this fact has come to be generally appreciated, and the result is that teaching has been elevated to the dignity of a profession, being no longer considered merely a mechanical occupation which might be successfully followed by any one having the necessary technical knowledge. The born teacher never loses interest in even the primary principles of the art he or she may teach, and it is this exhibition of interest—this ever free enthusiasm—which inspires the most unresponsive pupils to exert themselves, and which wins complete success in many a case which would otherwise have resulted in utter failure. Those who are at all conversant with the methods followed by Mr. J. E. McDuffee need not be reminded how noticeable is the interest which he takes in the progress of each of his pupils, and it is hardly necessary to add that this genuine personal interest has much to do with the success this gentleman has met with. He is considered by good authority to be one of the best teachers of instrumental music in New Hampshire, and the record he has made here proves that judgment to be well founded. His rooms are located at No. 9 McDuffee Block, where full information concerning hours of tuition, terms, etc , will be given upon application.

Edwin W. Standley, dealer in Choice Groceries, Tea, Coffee and Spices, Rochester, N. H.—Such of our readers as are seeking for an establishment where there may always be found a large and complete stock of groceries, where the service is prompt and courteous, the goods reliable and the prices low, may very profitably visit the store conducted by Mr. Edwin W. Standley on Elm street, for here is just the combination they are looking for. Doubtless many who read these lines will not need to be told of the fact stated, for Mr. Standley's establishment is already well and favorably known throughout this vicinity, and the extent to which it is patronized, affords the best possible proof that the inducements offered are appreciated. The proprietor is a native of Falmouth, N. H. He began operations here in 1883 as successor to Mr. Walter Standley who established the business here in 1878. The store occupied is 50 × 70 feet in dimensions, and the stock carried is a very well-selected one, comprising choice family groceries, teas, coffees, spices, etc., flour and grain, and quite an assortment of crockery is also offered. Employment is given to four assistants, and the promptness and accuracy displayed in the filling of orders might be profitably imitated by many establishments less extensively patronized, for two order and delivery teams are constantly employed in this work Mr. Standley is in a position to quote bottom prices, and does so every time. A very large exchange trade is carried on in farmer's produce of every description.

Holt & Morrison, Machinists and Pipers. Particular attention paid to Job Work. (Connected with Soule's Iron and Brass Foundry.) Opposite Union Depot, Rochestee, N. H.—The firm of Holt & Morrison was formed in 1890, but the business is not of such late origin as this would indicate for it was founded in 1888 by Messrs. Barry & Morrison, Mr. Barry being succeeded by Mr. J. H. Holt, who is a native of Biddeford, Me., Mr. W. N. Morrison being a native of Wolfboro, N. H. Both these gentlemen are thorough mechanics and have an excellent idea of the needs of steam users and manufacturers in general, so the service they offer is both intelligent and comprehensive and is a distinct benefit to the manufacturing interests of this section. The firm are machinists and pipers and constantly carry a good stock of shafting, hangers, pulleys, pipe and fittings, engines, boilers, pumps and blowers; thus being in a position to fill orders at very short notice. Pumps and blowers are specialties with this concern and will be furnished in any desired size at the very lowest market rates. Particular attention is paid to job work, and as the shop is very thoroughly fitted up and is connected with Soule's iron and brass foundry, almost any work of their kind can be successfully undertaken, and carried out with very little delay, employment being given to six competent assistants. The shop is conveniently located, opposite the Union Depot, and has an area of between 1500 and 2000 square feet.

Joseph Fleury, Drugs and Medicines, Grange Block, Rochester, N H.—It may seem a strange assertion to make to say that the carrying on of a large number of drug stores argue well for the public health, but there is ground for the statement for the simple reason that many drugs depend greatly upon their freshness for their effect, and the existence of a large number of drug stores has the result of causing each dealer to carry but a comparatively small stock of any one article, the consequence being that physicians can depend upon having their prescriptions filled by the use of ingredients much fresher than would otherwise be possible—a fact which we commend to the consideration of the few who think that now as formerly every doctor should compound his own medicines. Mr. Howe who conducts this store is prominently known throughout this vicinity, having been the postmaster here for about five years. The premises are 75×22 feet in dimensions, and contain a fine assortment of all that is usually to be found in a first-class drug store. Three assistants are employed, and great care and attention is given to the compounding of physicians' prescriptions. Mr, Fleury is a native of Suncook, N. H., and opened his store here in 1889. He is a well known business man and the proprietor of a fine clothing establishment in his native town. Many residents of Rochester can testify to the merits of his pharmacy, and a careful examination of the methods pursued will convince any one of the value of such an establishment.

Rochester Shoe Co., Rochester, N. H.—There is every reason to believe that shoe manufacturing is destined to become one of the most important of New Hampshire industries, for many extensive establishments have been opened in this State of late years and the results attained have been so favorable as to have attracted the attention of shoe manufacturers throughout the East. The Rochester Shoe Company began operations in 1884, the proprietor, Mr. F. W. Breed, being a resident of Lynn, one of the best known manufacturers in that " City of Shoes." He also carries on a factory at Athol and another at Marblehead, Mass., and his productions are shipped to all parts of the country and held in high favor by both consumers and the trade. The Rochester factory is three stories and an attic in height and 46×150 feet in dimensions, and is fitted up throughout with the most improved machinery ; employment being given to from 250 to 300 assistants, and the capacity per day being about 2500 pairs of ladies' and misses' shoes in medium and cheap grades. The Boston office is at No. 286 Devonshire street, and the facilities are such that the heaviest orders can be filled at comparatively short notice and at the lowest market rates. Mr. T. L. Witherell is superintendent of the Rochester and Athol factories, and to his close and skillful supervision the uniformity of merit so noticeable in the several grades produced at these establishments is to a great extent due. Some idea of the importance of Mr. Breed's plants for shoe manufacturing may be gained from the fact that his three factories have a combined capacity of 125 sixty-pair cases per day. Mr. Breed is very prominently known in New England, being one of the World's Fair commissioners for Massachusetts for the Chicago Fair, under appointment from President Harrison.

Wilder B. Neal, proprietor "The Globe" Crockery and Variety Store, Market Street, Rochester, N. H.—Among the establishments to which general consent has accorded the leadership in their special line is that conducted by Mr. Wilder B. Neal on Market street, and "The Globe" variety store, as it called, has no reason to avoid comparison with any similar enterprise in Rochester. We make this assertion advisedly, and after a careful review of the subject may add without egotism that we have had exceptional opportunities to form an adequate opinion regarding the comparative standing of any establishment o the sort mentioned. The enterprise was established in 1884 by the present proprietor who has shown from the first that he would not be content with any second place in his line of business. Mr. Neal is a native of Farmington, Me., and is widely known and highly esteemed in this community, because of his honorable business methods and the enterprise at his popular store. The premises used are 19×80 feet in dimensions. Crockery, tinware and toys of all descriptions are largely dealt in. A very fine and large assortment of crockery and glassware is carried from which to select, and we need not inform those who have patronized this store that all goods are sold at the very lowest rates, but to those who have not we will say no greater bargains are to be found in Rochester, and certainly no such stock of goods from which to select. A specialty is made of picture framing, which is done to order at short notice and at very reasonable rates.

———

F. L. Chesley, Hatter, Market Street, Rochester, N. H.—Among those doing business in Rochester none is better known than Mr. F. L. Chesley, who is town clerk and has a large circle of friends, by no means confined to any particular section The establishment now conducted by Mr. Chesley was founded by Mr. James Smith, who was succeeded by F. H. Orr, who gave place to C. H. Chase about 1878, the present proprietor assuming control of the business in 1883. The premises utilized are located on Central square, and are about 500 square feet in size, where a fine stock of all the latest styles of gents' hats is constantly kept on hand as well as a very complete line of gents' furnishings. Mr. Chesley's goods are perfectly reliable, and are, in fact guaranteed to prove as represented. So that no fears need be entertained that anything bought of him will not prove satisfactory, and the purchaser can well feel sure that all he buys will be sold at prices as low as the lowest. The services of a courteous and well informed assistant are employed, and customers are assured polite treatment and honorable dealings.

———

S. H. Burnham's Ladies' and Gents' Oyster and Dining Rooms; Charles W. Hoyt, Clerk; Cigars and Tobacco; Oysters constantly on hand; 9 Hanson Street, Rochester, N. H —Considering that Mr. S. H. Burnham has been engaged in feeding the public for about twenty years it would be strange if he didn't understand the business by this time, and as a matter of fact we believe he *does* know about all there is to be known about it, for his establishment at No. 9 Hanson street, is as satisfactory a place for a hungry man (or woman either, for that matter) to visit as we have ever had the good fortune to find. Meals may be had at all hours, and we are sure that even the most fastidious will find no reasonable cause for complaint at the food, the cooking or the service, for all are first-class, and quantity is looked after as well as quality. Accommodations can be made to seat fifty guests, and six competent assistants are employed. Oysters are constantly kept on hand and can be served in any desired form; cigars and tobacco are also carried, and every thing is sold at very moderate prices. Mr. Burnham is a native of Farmington, N. H.; he began operations here in 1864. In connection with his oyster and dining-rooms, he also carries on a bakery, and is prepared to cater to parties, etc., at short notice and very reasonable terms. Mr. Chas. W. Hoyt acts as clerk for the restaurant, for which position he is indeed, well adapted.

———

Mansion House, N. F. Ham, Proprietor. Reduced Rates to the Dramatic Profession; First-class Sample Room Connected; Heated by Steam; Electric Bells. Main Street, Rochester, N. H.—The Mansion House was originally opened by Mr. L. H. Wentworth in 1867. Several changes were made in the management, when Messrs. Cotton & Ham took the management of it in 1887. During the year Mr. Cotton retired, and Mr. N. F. Ham assumed sole control of the house, and the Mansion House has never been more skillfully and liberally conducted than has been the case since Mr. Ham became its proprietor. He is a native of New Durham, N. H., and is one of the few men who have a "natural gift" for hotel keeping, for it is only such men that are able to so manage as to make their guests feel perfectly at home and at ease. While at the same time maintaining that order and propriety essential to the conduct of a really first class house. The house is located on Main street. It is heated by steam and is fitted throughout with electric bells. The beds and other furnishings are strictly first class in every particular. Employment is given to from eight to ten competent assistants, and the service, at the table and elsewhere, is prompt, intelligent and courteous. The house has accommodation for sixty guests. Mr. Ham gives special attention to the *cuisine,* and the bill of fare is varied enough to suit all tastes, while the best the market affords is placed before the guests at all seasons of the year. There is a finely equipped sample room connected with the hotel. The terms to all are very moderate, while reduced rates are given to the dramatic profession, and all strangers visiting Rochester may avoid much annoyance by putting up at the house. A good livery stable is connected with the hotel, where first class livery accommodations can be had at moderate charges.•

———

Wm. Bell, Dry Goods and Groceries, River Street, Rochester, N. H.—Generally speaking, it is safe to say that it always pays for a business man to keep faith with his customers, and, although there are some who believe differently, and think that "sharp practice" is profitable and "smart," the success they generally meet with is not pronounced enough to prove their position. The enviable reputation held by the establishment conducted by Mr. Wm. Bell on River street could never have been built up by questionable methods, and the proprietor may well take pride in maintaining an enterprise which has so good a name in the community. Mr. Bell opened his present store in 1879, since which date his business has increased to such proportions as to require the enlargement of his store—in connection with which he uses a roomy storehouse. He carries a large stock of staple and fancy groceries, and also dry goods, which have been carefully selected and are of a quality which renders them acceptable to the most fastidious. The prices on all goods are below the average. Only capable assistants are employed. Orders are promptly and carefully filled, and every caller is assured immediate attention and courteous treatment.

ized by him in carrying on his business is of the dimensions of 60 × 25 feet—in which a fine stock is to be seen, consisting of stoves, furnaces and ranges, and tin, iron, glass and wooden ware is handled in great variety. Mr. Cooper is prepared to quote the lowest market rates on all goods dealt in, and to guarantee everything to be exactly as represented in every instance. From one to three experienced assistants are employed who are courteous and prompt in all respects. Roofing and furnace work is given special attention, and repairing of all descriptions is done in a most thorough manner and at small prices, the facilities for doing such work being first-class. Mr. Cooper gives all work his own personal supervision.

Rochester Steam Laundry, George F. Willey, Jr., proprietor. All Goods C. O. D. Corner Main and Arrow Streets, Rochester, N. H.—We sometimes hear people say they can't afford to send their clothes to a public laundry, but in the majority of such cases if the matter were accurately figured out it would be found that as a matter of fact, they can't afford to have their washing done at home, if they did but know it. Everybody knows how "washday" upsets the average family, making a vast amount of extra work, causing everybody to feel uncomfortable and filling the house with steam and bad odors, and many know that physicians trace many a case of serious sickness to this "economical" practice, which thus saves laundry bills and gives the doctor a chance to make a dollar. Those who patronize a laundry have one solid satisfaction at all events, they know just what this washing is costing them, and that is much more than can be said of those who consume fuel, hire help and expose their families to sickness, and after all don't attain half such satisfactory results as are assured to all sending their goods to a first-class public establishment, as, for instance, the Rochester Steam Laundry, located on the corner of Main and Arrow streets. The proprietor of this popular enterprise, Mr. George F. Willey, Jr., is a native of this town, and has carried on business here since 1885, and has built up an extensive and desirable patronage, which is steadily increasing. The business has increased to such proportions that the old quarters occupied recently on Central Square could not accommodate it and the proprietor was forced to provide new quarters with greatly increased facilities for doing the work, both in room and improved machinery, hence the present site, formerly known as Cole's estate, was obtained, and a new two-story building, 60×40 feet, was built, with a fine basement under the whole. This building has been fitted up and new machinery added to the plant before in use at an expense of about $7000. It includes a steam dry room of ten racks, and as family washing is to be a specialty, a mangle for that purpose has been put in. Agencies in nearly every town in the State are being established, the capacity being sufficient for any amount of work, and everything is reduced to a system, so that errors are thus obviated. With these increased facilities in room and latest improved machinery, Mr. Willey is enabled to do first class work and quote very low prices. All work is guaranteed, to the satisfaction of customers. Employment is given to from twelve to fifteen assistants, and the largest orders can be filled at the shortest notice. The office is in front of the brick block opening on Main street.

TILTON & RICHARDS, SOLE AGENTS.

Tilton & Richards, Watchmakers and Jewelers, No. 2 McDuffee Block, Rochester, N. H.—The establishment located at No 2 McDuffee Block, occupies a prominent position among similar houses in this town. It is one of the most complete and attractive stores of its kind in Rochester, and carries a reliable stock of goods embracing a fine variety of watches, clocks, jewelry and optical goods. The store (or rather the half store, as part of it is devoted to the sale of fancy goods, etc.) is 20 × 80 feet in dimensions. The proprietors, Messrs. G. H. Tilton and F. I. Richards are both natives of Rochester, and are very well known and highly esteemed gentlemen. They began operations here in 1888 as successors to Mr. M. H. Osgood, who had then carried on the business for about twelve years. The firm conduct their business on a high plan of honor with fair representation of all goods, and one price, that the very lowest. They have always tried to carry on business to the satisfaction of their patrons, and from the amount of patronage now enjoyed it is fair to presume they have succeeded. Special attention is paid to the repairing of watches, jewelry, etc., and the most intricate job will be satisfactorily performed in a workmanlike manner at exceedingly moderate rates. Special attention given to fitting glasses and spectacles to impaired vision. A good line of optical goods in stock.

Leroy G. Cooper, Stoves, Furnaces, Ranges, Repairing of all kinds done to order. Roofing and Furnace work, Tin, Iron, Glass, Japan and Wooden Ware, 41 Market Street, Rochester, N. H.—The establishment conducted by Mr. Leroy G. Cooper at No. 41 Market street, has only been in operation a short time, but during that time has proved entirely successful—as is only natural as the proprietor has spared no pains to completely satisfy all those who have given him their custom. The gentleman in question is a native of Parsonsfield, Me. The store util-

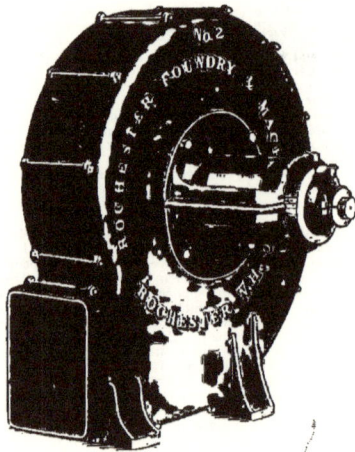

Rochester Foundry and Machine Co. (successors to Chas. E. Clark,) manufacturers and dealers in Engines, Boilers, Feed Pumps, Shafting, Hangers, Pulleys, Shaving Exhausters, Mill Machinery, etc., Mechanic Square, Rochester, N. H.—The Rochester Foundry and Machine Company was organized in 1887 to continue the business founded by Mr. Charles E. Clark in 1880, the proprietors being Messrs. C. E. Clark and J. C. Furnald, the former a

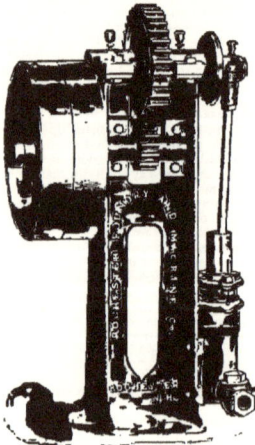

native of Dover and the latter of Exeter. The company are manufacturers of and dealers in engines, boilers, feed pumps, shafting, hangers, pulleys, shaving exhausters, mill machinery, etc., being prepared to furnish these and kindred commodities at short notice and at moderate

figures. This concern has a well-earned reputation for furnishing machinery that fully bears out all claims made concerning it, and manufacturers throughout this section naturally appreciate such a policy and place a large proportion of their orders with Messrs. Clark & Furnald. The company give particular attention to repairing, and are in a position to guarantee satisfaction in this important department of their business, not only as regards the quality of the work and the charges made but also in connection with the promptness with which orders are filled, as the facilities available are such as to obviate all unnecessary delay. The premises made use of are located in Mechanic Square and comprise a machine shop occupying two floors of the dimensions of 30×60 feet, together with a spacious foundry. Employment is given to from six to twelve experienced assistants. All sizes of pipe and fittings are constantly on hand and will be furnished in any desired quantities at the lowest market rates.

Hofmann & Wolf, Ladies' Furnishing Goods, Kid Gloves, etc., next to Post-Office, Rochester, N. H.—The most successful buyer is the one who discriminates the most successfully between "goods cheap" and "cheap goods," and it is just such a buyer who will find the most to admire in the assortment of ladies' furnishing goods, fancy goods, small wares, etc., offered by Messrs. Hofmann & Wolf, for these gentlemen carry on business on the "quick sales and small profits" system, and both the goods and prices combine to form a powerful argument in favor of patronizing this store. The residents of Rochester are too intelligent not to perceive the force of an argument of this kind, and the natural result is that this store is becoming a popular resort, and is gaining in favor daily. The firm in question is made up of Max Hofmann and Benny Wolf, they began their present business here in 1889. The premises in use are located on Hanson street, next door to the post-office. The firm give personal attention to the business and as a result, all customers are sure of being promptly and politely served. The goods dealt in are guaranteed to be strictly as represented.

J. M. Humphrey, Watches, Clocks, Jewelry and Repairing and Telephone Exchange, Rochester, N. H.—Everybody ought to have a reliable watch for time is money nowadays and no one can afford to waste his own or anybody else's time, in business hours at all events, and one of the first things to do if you would avoid such waste is to get a watch that can be entirely depended upon. Don't say you can't afford it, for dependable watches are sold at such low figures at the present time that they are within the means of all. If you doubt this fact call at the establishment conducted by Mr. J. M. Humphrey, on Main street. He can show you a full line of reliable watches in gold and silver cases, and is prepared to name prices that will compare favorably with those quoted by any other dealer. Clocks are also largely dealt in, and so is jewelry, silver plated ware and optical goods, and Mr. Humphrey names low prices on all the goods he handles. The premises occupied are about 350 square feet in size, and two reliable assistants are employed. Particular attention is given to repairing, the work being done in a skillful and painstaking manner, and orders being filled at short notice at moderate rates. Mr. Humphrey is a native of Boston, Mass., and began his present business during the current year. He has also a telephone exchange located in his store.

BIRD'S EYE VIEW OF FARMINGTON.

HISTORICAL SKETCH OF FARMINGTON

AND ITS POINTS OF INTEREST.

THE history of Farmington is quite devoid of those romantic and exciting features which figure so prominently in the story of the settlement and development of Dover, Portsmouth and other early settled towns, for Farmington was not incorporated until very near the opening of the present century, long after all Indian troubles had ceased and nearly a score of years after the colonies had fought for and won their independence. Thus the annals of the town record peaceful progress rather than "hair breadth 'scapes 'mid flood and field," and those who are interested only in accounts of war and adventure must turn to the history of Rochester to find such tales relating to Farmington's territory, for the town was originally a part of Rochester and during the years from 1745 to 1749 was overrun by the hostile Indians who terrorized that settlement.

The first recorded division of what is now Farmington territory was decided upon April 20, 1730, when the Rochester proprietors voted to cut up that portion of their grant of land which had not previously been disposed of, into lots of not less than two hundred and forty acres each. The lots were drawn December 17, 1730, the territory affected comprising the greater part of that now included in Milton and Farmington. The first settler came to Rochester in December, 1728, and it was not until seventy years afterward that that portion of the township which is now Farmington had a sufficient number of inhabitants to warrant its being set off from the parent town, Farmington being incorporated December 1, 1798. The first town meeting was held March 11, 1799, and Aaron Wingate was chosen moderator; Jonas C. March, town clerk; and Ichabod Hayes, Ephraim Kimball, and David Roberts were chosen as selectmen. At that time the office of constable was considered very desirable, and hence with true Yankee shrewdness the townspeople voted "that the privilege of being a constable in said town of Farmington the present year shall be sold at vendue to the highest bidder, and the purchaser to give bonds to the satisfaction of the selectmen for the faithful performance of his duty." It is evident that our forefathers did not hold to the modern maxim, "the office should seek the man." Ensign Samuel Knowles bought the position of constable for $21.25. He was granted a tavern license the same year, and so were four others ; and licenses to retail foreign distilled spiritu- ous liquors were granted to Joseph Holmes, Lakeman & Marsh, Benjamin Rundels, and Elezear Pearl.

The first settlement in Farmington's territory was made about 1770 near the point now known as Merrill's Corners, and that was the center of what little business there was, among those settling there from 1770 to 1783 being Benjamin Furber, Samuel Furber, Richard Furber, Samuel Jones, Benjamin Chesley and Paul Demeritt. Other settlers in various parts of the town were : Joseph Leighton, Levi Leighton, Moses Horne, Caleb Varney, and Judge Wingate. The first school-house was built about 1791 and was located at Merrill's Corners ; the first meeting-house was erected on Robert's Hill, about two miles south of Farmington village, near the birth-place of Henry Wilson.

As its name indicates, Farmington was long a distinctively agricultural community, and, indeed, farming is still extensively and successfully carried on, for much of the town is fertile although its surface is very hilly and in parts mountainous. In the southwestern portion is located Blue Job

MAIN STREET, FARMINGTON, N. H., LOOKING SOUTH.

Mountain, so called because it was once owned by Job Allard and is one of the Blue Hill range. There is a wide-spread and beautiful view from its summit, ranging from the White Mountains to the ocean, ships off Portsmouth harbor being plainly visible to the naked eye. The town is well watered, the principal streams being the Cocheco, Mad, Ela, and Waldron rivers. The Cocheco River rises in New Durham and enters Farmington near the northern corner of the township, flowing southeast across its entire width. Farmington village is situated on this stream, between it and the Ela River, which also rises in New Durham and empties into the Cocheco just below the village. West Farm- ington is located in the northwestern part of the town and Merrill's Corners in the southwestern part.

Mad River is well named, for it is a typical mountain stream, and when swelled by heavy rains or the effects of a sudden thaw, dashes turbulently along, overflows its banks and seems possessed by a mad desire to sweep everything before it. Sometimes a storm lasting but two or three hours will cause it to rise many feet, move boulders weighing thousands of pounds and destroy everything in its path.

The other rivers are much more reliable and there are some valuable water powers in town. The outlines of Farmington are very regular, in that respect resembling those of the adjoining town of Strafford and forming a decided contrast to the "crazy patchwork" shapes of New Durham, Middleton and Milton, which bound Farmington on the north and east. Rochester bounds it on the east and south, and Strafford on the south and west, New Durham also forming a part of its western boundary.

The business of the town is principally centered at Farmington village, the site of which is situated on what was known in bye-gone days as the "old John Ham farm." The first frame house to be built at this point was erected in 1781 by John Roberts. The village is on the line of the Dover & Winnipesaukee Railroad, a branch of the great Boston & Maine system, and as the adjoining town of Rochester is a great railroad center, direct communication with all parts of the country is enjoyed by Farmington business men. The completion of the Lake Shore Railroad, extending from the terminus of the Dover and Winnipesaukee Railroad at Alton Bay to Lake Village, gives direct connection with the Concord & Montreal Railroad, and adds very materially to Farmington's transportation facilities. Shoe manufacturing is the principal industry of the village and has given rise to various tributary industries, the most important of which is the manufacture of wooden and paper boxes. Shoe making, or rather the production of what was then known as "Natick sale work," was begun in Farmington in 1836 by Elijah H. Badger. The product was called Natick sale work from the fact that it consisted entirely of brogans, and the town of Natick, Mass., at that time led the country in brogan manufacturing. Mr. Badger failed to make his enterprise profitable and in about a year left town; but the shoe industry was not abandoned, Martin L. Hayes, a native of Farmington, beginning it about this time on a very small scale. His business steadily grew and he became the largest shoe manufacturer in New Hampshire. Mr. Hayes was no believer in that "dog in the manger" policy which seems to actuate some men, on the contrary he used his best endeavors to get other manufacturers to come to Farmington, and did not hesitate to give substantial aid to such enterprises as seemed calculated to advance the interests of the community as a whole. Nor did his public spirit stop here. He manifested it in many different ways, and to him more than to any other one man, is the existence of the many beautiful shade trees which add so much to the attractiveness of the village due, for he not only persuaded his fellow townsmen to plant trees, but set them the example by placing many shade and fruit trees on his own grounds. Some of Farmington's present business men are noted for their public spirit, and who can say how much they have been encouraged in their good works by the memory which Martin L. Hayes left behind him? It is true that "the evil that men do lives after them," but it is not true that "the good is oft interred with their bones." Good is more nearly immortal than evil and the effects of good deeds remain, although doubtless in many cases the doer of them is forgotten.

Shortly after Mr. Hayes began operations, George M. Hening came from Natick to Farmington and engaged in the same line of business. He also was a man who lived for others as well as for himself, and worked hard and efficiently to promote the best interests of the community. The success attained here in shoe manufacturing soon began to attract outside capital. From small beginnings the trade has grown to its present magnitude.

The first wax-thread sewing machine ever used for shoe work in New Hampshire, was brought to Farmington by Mr. Cloutman about the year 1855. He is now superintendent and manager of the factory of Wallace, Elliott & Co., in this village; the establishment being devoted to the production of ladies', misses', and children's fine boots, and affording employment to between three and four hundred hands. Altogether there are five large shoe factories in Farmington and one heel factory, and this industry affords employment to about one thousand two hundred operatives of both sexes.

Many of the early Farmington shoe manufacturers learned the business in Natick, being drawn to that town by the fact that the late Vice-President Henry Wilson, a native of Farmington, went to Natick in 1833, commenced business for himself in 1838, and soon became a prominent manufacturer there. Some of the young men from Farmington lived with his family part of the time they stayed in Natick, among them being Martin L. Hayes, whom we have before had occasion to mention. He was a life-long friend of Henry Wilson, and deeded to the town of Farmington the latter's birth-place, marking the spot on which the house had stood by a great boulder weighing about twelve tons and inscribed: "Henry Wilson, vice-president U. S. A., born here February 12, 1812."

Like all other prosperous manufacturing villages of large population, Farmington contains many well-stocked stores and a very extensive retail trade is carried on at all times. Some of the stores are very spacious and are handsomely fitted up, presenting a very attractive appearance, especially in the evening, for the more enterprising store-keepers make liberal use of the gas furnished by a local company, which was incorporated in 1886 with a capital of $60,000. This gas is made from naphtha and is of a very superior quality; the bright, white light it gives at once attracting the attention of one accustomed to the dingy yellow flame, characteristic of gas made in the ordinary way. The service thus far has given excellent satisfaction and the facilities offered by the company are being very generally availed of. Hon. J. F. Cloutman is president; Hon. C. W. Talpey, treasurer; and Hon. E. T. Wilson, manager.

There are two banks in town: the Farmington Savings Bank, chartered June, 1868, and the Farmington National Bank, organized, July, 1872, with a capital of $100,000. Many representative business men are identified with one or both of these institutions, and as a natural consequence both

CENTRAL SQUARE, FARMINGTON, N. H.

are well managed and enjoy the entire confidence of the public. An idea of the standing of the Savings Bank and the opportunity offered for remunerative employment in Farmington may be gained from the following: May 1, 1882, the deposits amounted to $212,552.83; September, 1890, they amounted to $646,628.44—a gain of some 300 per cent. in about eight years.

Since March 14, 1879, local interests have been looked after by the *Farmington News*, published by J. E. Fernald & Son. This is a handsome and well-edited weekly, has a circulation of about 1,500 and a good advertising patronage, and is a credit to the town and to its managers.

Farmington has had its ups and downs the same as every live community has; its prosperity has been checked by fire, by national business depression, and by other causes from the effects of which no town is exempt, but on the whole progress has been steady and at times rapid; and, considering the advantages of location, the ability and resources of local manufacturers and merchants, and their high confidence in the future of the community, there seems good reason to believe that confidence justified not only from a sentimental but also from a sternly practical standpoint.

LEADING BUSINESS MEN OF FARMINGTON.

Sanitine Remedy Company, Proprietors of Blake's Vegetable Remedy for Constipation, Blake's Cough Balsam, etc., Albert Garland, Secretary and Manager, Farmington, N. H.—There are two ways of estimating the value of a remedy, the first is to see if the claims made concerning its mode of action and efficacy are in accordance with common sense and known physiological truths; the second is by investigation of the results attending its practical use By a combination of these methods the actual status of any remedy may be readily and accurately determined. Let us apply them then to a preparation in which the residents of Farmington have reason to be particularly interested for it is manufactured here by a company with which are identified some of the most prominent business men of this section of the State. We refer to Blake's Vegetable Remedy, formerly known as Blake's Sanitine, and supplied to the trade by the Sanitine Remedy Company, the sole proprietors. The full name of this medicine is "Blake's Vegetable Remedy for Constipation," and the claim is made that it will cure constipation, whether recent or chronic, and that it is therefore of great value in the treatment of dyspepsia, kidney and liver diseases, piles and headache, and will remove moth patches and pimples on the face and do away with "that tired feeling," which is so common, especially among the gentler sex. No well-informed person, and particularly no experienced physician, will deny that constipation or costiveness is the cause of a host of diseases and hence if Blake's remedy can cure constipation its great value in the treatment of many serious disorders must be admitted. But can it? Read the following testimonials and judge for yourself:

LYNN, Mass.
SANITINE REMEDY Co —I have been troubled with constipation all my life. I was advised to take Blake's Remedy, and it has cured me.
MRS. W. K. EATON.

SOUTH BERWICK, ME.
SANITINE REMEDY CO.—For three years I have suffered the tortures of obstinate constipation; have used every known remedy, and have failed to find relief or even benefit until I took your valuable constipation cure—Blake's Remedy. I have taken three bottles previous to March, '84, and consider myself cured, having taken nothing since that time. I cannot speak too highly of it, and earnestly recommend it. It is truly wonderful. JAMES G. WHITEHOUSE.

Certainly there is no mistaking the meaning of these letters; but perhaps some of our readers may desire direct proof that Blake's Remedy can cure some of the specific diseases we have mentioned. Here it is:

FARMINGTON, N. H.
Gents—For ten years I have suffered from malarial poisoning and the most obstinate constipation. The disease progressed so rapidly that my kidneys were diseased. I consulted many physicians of repute, among them my old army surgeon of New Jersey. I took almost everything, but the disease gained upon me, and I was obliged to give up my business to my sons. I have taken Blake's Remedy four months, and I feel like a new man. I feel justified in saying that it is the most wonderful remedy I ever saw. I would most earnestly recommend it to my comrades who are suffering from malaria, or anybody else who is suffering from diseased liver or kidneys. ALONZO NUTE.

DERRY DEPOT, N. H.
I have been troubled with sick headache and bad feelings in my stomach I have taken Blake's Remedy and it has cured me.
MRS. GEO. HOLDEN.

CAPE ELIZABETH, ME.
SANITINE REMEDY Co.—I have been troubled with bloody piles for forty years and have tried almost every kind of medicine without receiving any help until I took Blake's Remedy, which has entirely cured me, and I cannot say too much to its praise. Yours truly,
MRS. SARAH R. GOULD.

A well-known lady of Wolfboro, N. H., writes:

I have tried almost everything for moth patches that have troubled me for a long time, but nothing seemed to do any good. My face was literally covered, and I felt ashamed to go into company. While riding one morning, I noticed your advertisement—"Blake's Remedy clears the complexion"—and bought a bottle. Since then I have taken six bottles, and my skin is clear and smooth.

The Sanitine Remedy Co. have received several thousand just such testimonials as these and to print them all would require an entire book the size of this one, but "a word to the wise is sufficient," and we will only add that these testimonials are not signed by people living on the other side of the continent but come from points near at home, and that the company will forward the original of any testimonial we have presented to any person doubting its authenticity. If additional evidence of the company's good faith be wanted it may be found in the standing of the men identified with it, the officers and directors being as follows: president, John F. Cloutman; vice president, Jared P. Tibbetts; secretary and treasurer, Albert Garland; directors, Chas. W. Talpey, John F. Cloutman, James B. Edgerly, Asa A. Hall, Dwight E. Edgerly, Albert Garland, Jared P. Tibbetts. Mr. Cloutman has served as State senator, Mr. Garland is one of the Farmington selectmen and is a first lieutenant in the State militia, Mr. Talpey has been State senator and is treasurer of the Farmington Savings Bank, Mr. James B. Edgerly is cashier of the Farmington National Bank, Mr. Hall has been deputy sheriff and postmaster, and Mr. Dwight E. Edgerly has been representative and is county commissioner. The company was formed in 1888, but Blake's Remedy has been on the market four years and is kept in stock by all the Boston and Portland wholesale druggists and by retail druggists throughout the country who sell it for $1.00 per bottle or six bottles for $5.00, and report a very extensive and rapidly growing demand for it. The company are also proprietors of Blake's Cough Balsam, which is warranted equal to any in the market. It is agreeable to take and is perfectly safe besides being economical to use: for the dose is small, the bottle large, and the price is but 25 cents. The balsam is sold by all druggists and is steadily gaining in popularity as it quickly cures coughs, colds, bronchitis and all diseases peculiar to the throat and lungs. All correspondence should be addressed to *Sanitine Remedy Co.*, Farmington, N. H.

A. F. & H. C. Waldron, manufacturers of Wooden and Paper boxes, and dealers in Lumber, Farmington, N. H.—It is, of course, important for the manufacturers of any article to be prepared to fill orders promptly and accurately and at the lowest market rates, but this is particularly the case with those engaged in the production of boxes, for the competition in this branch of industry is so close and keen that only the providing of an exceptionally efficient service will ensure success in it. It is evident that Messrs. A. F. & H. C. Waldron thoroughly appreciate this condition of affairs, for although they have long been successfully engaged in the manufacture of boxes they have recently materially improved their facilities and hence can now fill their steadily increasing orders even more satisfactorily and promptly than ever before. Both wooden and paper boxes are manufactured, a specialty being made of those adapted to the wants of the shoe trade, and they are prepared to furnish shoe cases and cartons of superior quality at bottom prices, and to fill the most extensive orders at very short notice, for they utilize an elaborate plant of the latest improved machinery, including a machine for which they own the right within a radius of twenty miles of Farmington, and can furnish its product to customers within that territory. This machine turns out a carton made without scoring and with double heads, it being not only much stronger than any previously offered but also neat in appearance, while it can be furnished at a figure considerably below that quoted on cartons made in the ordinary manner. The box factory is run by both water and steam power so that orders can be filled without undue delay at any season of the year. The entire plant covers more than an acre and comprises, in addition to the box factory, a large lumber mill in which whole logs are sawed out and lumber and builders' materials of all kinds are manufactured, spacious storage sheds, offices and a commodious yard. A large force of assistants is employed, and every department of the business is so thoroughly systemized that the expense of production is reduced to a minimum and all orders can be filled promptly, accurately and at the lowest market rates.

Carleton & Bennett, Merchant Tailors, dealers in Ready-made Clothing, Hats, Caps and Gents' Furnishings, Farmington, N. H.—It is difficult to see what greater inducements could be offered to those in need of clothing, etc., than are extended by the firm of Carleton & Bennett, for these gentlemen are not only first-class merchant tailors, but are also large dealers in ready-made clothing, hats, caps and gentlemen's furnishings, so they are admirably prepared to cater to all classes of trade, and well deserve the extensive patronage their enterprise receives. It was inaugurated in 1877 by Mr. F. C. Tilton, he being succeeded in 1884 by Messrs. Tilton & Furber, and the present firm assuming control in 1885. The partners are Messrs. E. E. Carleton and J. P. Bennett, the former being a native of Farmington and the latter of Northwood, N. H. Mr. Bennett is the present representative of Farmington in the legislature, and is prominently identified with local business interests, he being a trustee of the Savings Bank and a director of the Gas Company in addition to his connection with the enterprise now under consideration. The firm utilize good-sized and conveniently fitted-up premises and carry a large and complete assortment of foreign and domestic fabrics for gentlemen's wear besides a fine stock of ready-made clothing, hats and furnishings. The facilities for the doing of custom work in a superior manner at short notice are excellent, employment being given to from five to eight experienced assistants and the business being so systemized that every order is assured immediate and painstaking attention. The charges made are as low as is consistent with the use of suitable materials and the employment of skilled labor, and this applies to the ready-made as well as to the custom department, for the firm handle no goods made only "to sell," their policy being to deal only in such articles as can safely be guaranteed to prove as represented, and to furnish them at prices in strict accordance with the lowest market rates.

George W. Bailey, manufacturer of and dealer in Hardware, Stoves, Tinware, Woodenware, Paints, Oils, Varnishes, etc., Steam, Gas and Water Piping and Plumbing, 14 Central Street, Farmington, N. H.—One of the most truly representative establishments of the kind to be found in this section is that conducted by Mr. George W. Bailey, at No. 14 Central street, for this is a recognized headquarters for hardware, stoves, tin-ware, wooden-ware, etc., and is also very widely and favorably known in connection with the doing of steam, gas and water piping and plumbing, and the handling of paints, oils, varnishes and kindred goods. The proprietor is a native of Manchester, N. H., and has been identified with it since 1887, it having been founded a number of years previous to that date. Under the present management the business has largely increased and as the available facilities have increased correspondingly Mr. Bailey is better prepared than ever to fill orders promptly, accurately and at bottom rates. The premises have an area of 5000 square feet and contain improved tools and machinery for the manufacture of tin-ware of all kinds to order, and for the doing of steam, water and gas-fitting, plumbing, etc. A specialty is made of tin-roofing, the best of material being used, skilled help employed and satisfaction confidently guaranteed. The stock of hardware, stoves, tin-ware, etc., is large and complete and includes cooking and heating stoves of the latest design, made by leading manufacturers. Reliable paints, oils, varnishes, etc., are sold here at bottom figures, and in fact whatever is bought from Mr. Bailey will be found to prove just as represented and will be furnished at the lowest market rates.

DR. ALBERT GARLAND,

Fellow of the N. H. Dental Society.

Member of the N. E. Dental Association.

FARMINGTON, N. H.

Blake's Pharmacy, Central Street, Farmington, N. H. —Although one may not be prepared to assert that every dispensing chemist should also be a practical physician, it still remains a fact that no man making a business of the handling of drugs and chemicals can know too much about them and about their effects upon the human system, and as this is the popular conviction it is not surprising that the public should manifest a preference for such pharmacies as are carried on by a medical practitioner. What is popularly known as "Blake's Pharmacy" is an excellent example of an establishment of this kind, it being a well-stocked drug store conducted by W. P. Blake, M. D., a prominent practicing physician. The premises are located on Central street, and we need hardly say are fitted up with all necessary apparatus, etc., for the accurate and prompt compounding of prescriptions, such orders being filled at the lowest rates consistent with the use of the best obtainable ingredients. Fancy and toilet articles, druggists' sundries, etc., are well represented in the stock, and sufficient assistance is employed to ensure prompt attention to every caller. Dr. Blake is a native of Barnstead, N. H., and has carried on this store since 1886. Dr. Blake is assisted by his wife, who is a registered pharmacist, and the only lady registered in the State. Special attention is given to the compounding of prescriptions, and the service is maintained at the highest standard of reliability and efficiency.

D. E. Edgerly, Dry and Fancy Goods, Groceries and Provisions, Flour and Grain of all kinds, Shoe Tools and Findings, 16 Main Street, Farmington, N. H.—"A representative enterprise conducted by a representative man" is about as short a description as can be given of the undertaking with which Mr D. E. Edgerly is identified, but despite its brevity no one acquainted with the facts will question its correctness, for certainly a business which has been honorably and successfully conducted for thirty-five years in one community is entitled to be called representative, and certainly the same title may properly be applied to one who has been and is so prominent in business and public life as the gentleman in question. Mr. Edgerly is a native of Gilmanton, N. H., and has carried on his present business since 1880, it having been founded by Mr. Charles W. Wingate a quarter of a century before that date. The present proprietor has served two years as State representative, and now occupies the position of county commissioner. The premises made use of have an area of about 1800 square feet, and are located at No. 16 Main street. They contain a large and very varied stock, for it includes not only a complete assortment of dry and fancy goods, etc., but also a full line of staple and fancy groceries, provisions and flour and grain of all kinds, together with shoe tools and findings. An extensive business is done but as employment is given to two efficient assistants all orders are assured immediate as well as careful attention. Mr. Edgerly quotes the lowest market rates on all the commodities he handles, and we need hardly say that articles bought at this representative store will prove just what they are claimed to be in every respect.

F. J. Hanson, manufacturer of Boot and Shoe Heels, Central Street, Farmington, N. H.—The great industry of boot and shoe manufacturing in New England has developed other very important enterprises which are tributary to that business. An important example of this is found at the factory of Mr. F. J Hanson, where he manufactures boot and shoe heels on a very extensive scale. Mr. Hanson has had long experience in this business but started this factory in 1885, and has developed a prominent industry in Farmington The factory is a three-story structure 30×60 feet, and is furnished with steam power, and is equipped with a good plant of machinery adapted to the manufacture of heels for boots and shoes, and employment is given to from forty to fifty hands. A ready market is found for the product among the numerous boot and shoe factories of New England, as the standard quality of the work turned out is not excelled by any manufacturer.

J. M. Berry & Co., manufacturers of Men's and Boys' Shoes, in Kangaroo, Dongola, Calf, Grain, Buff and Veal, Farmington, N. H. Sample Room, 57 Lincoln Street, Boston, Mass. At Sample Room Wednesdays and Saturdays.—Every ordinarily well-informed person knows that shoe manufacturing has become one of the most important of New Hampshire's industries, and there is every reason to believe that it is destined to rapidly develop far beyond its present proportions, for the conditions are favorable to bring about that result and the progress made during the past decade shows what may reasonably be expected in the decade to come. Among our New Hampshire shoe factories are some that will compare favorably as regards equipment and the quality of the goods turned out with any in New England, and it is not necessary to go outside of Farmington to find proof of this statement, as any competent and unprejudiced judge will admit after inspecting the establishment and the product of Messrs. J. M. Berry & Co., who manufacture full lines of men's and boys' shoes, in kangaroo, dongola, calf, grain, buff and veal. This firm is constituted of Messrs. J. M. and Arthur R. Berry, both of whom are natives of Farmington and have had long and varied experience in shoe manufacturing. They founded their present business in 1888 with a capital of only $5000, and sold their goods to only one house, but since have enlarged operations, having a capital of $20,000, and now sell direct to the jobbing trade; they have an intimate acquaintance with the wants of consumers and the trade, and as a natural consequence they have fitted up their factory with the latest improved machinery throughout and are prepared to furnish footwear that will hold its own, in comparison with any of similar grade in the market, in every detail of material, style, fit and workmanship. The factory is a four-story structure, having a total floor space of nearly 18,000 square feet, and as the plant of machinery is correspondingly extensive and employment is given to 100 experienced assistants the capacity of the establishment is sufficiently great to ensure the prompt filling of all orders, especially as the business is so carefully systematized and supervised as to obviate all confusion or unnecessary delay. Messrs. J. M. Berry & Co., wholesale directly to the jobbing trade and are in a position to quote bottom prices on all their various styles. They maintain a sample room in Boston, at No. 57 Lincoln street, where a full line of their productions may always be seen. A member of the firm is at the sample room every Wednesday and Saturday and dealers who wish to handle shoes that will sell on their merits, yield a fair profit and build up a permanent trade would do well to call and investigate

J. F. Safford, Watches and Jewelry, Silver Ware, etc. Fine Watch and Jewelry Repairing a Specialty. Barker's Block, Farmington, N. H.—If the average resident of Farmington were asked to point out a thoroughly reliable jewelry store, the chances are all in favor of his directing the inquirer to that conducted by Mr. J. F. Safford, in Barker's Block, for this business was established in 1867, and has been so managed as to be well and favorably known to practically every resident of this section. The proprietor is a native of Rockland, Me., and served three years in the army during the Rebellion. Probably not one of our local business men is more generally known and hence extended personal mention would be quite superfluous, but for the benefit of strangers in Farmington we may say that Mr. Safford's business policy is as simple as it is admirable, it being to give honest value for cash received every time. A good stock of watches, jewelry, silver ware, optical goods, etc., is constantly carried, the productions of the leading manufacturers being represented and many late and attractive novelties being shown. Particular attention is given to the repairing of fine watches, jewelry and optical goods, and optical work and the furnishing of scientifically made optical goods are leading specialties, so that those wanting anything in the line of eye-glasses, spectacles, etc., would do well to give Mr. Safford a call. All his work is fully guaranteed and uniformly moderate charges are made.

J. E. Fernald & Son, Publishers and Proprietors of the *Farmington News*. Weekly; established 1879. Corner Main and Central Streets, Farmington, N. H.—There is little or nothing to be gained by enlarging upon the benefits bestowed upon a community by a well-conducted local newspaper for these benefits are so obvious that those who are incapable of appreciating them of their own free will and by the exercise of their own judgment would probably not be convinced by any reasoning even if it were supported by many practical examples. But happily but very few of our Farmington readers belong to this class, and in proof of this assertion we need refer only to the general support given to the *Farmington News* since its establishment, in 1879, for this handsome weekly is a welcome visitor in many homes, it having a circulation of 1400 copies. It also has quite a large advertising patronage and this is not to be wondered at, for the business men of this section have a well earned reputation for enterprise and shrewdness and hence can readily see the advantages of advertising in a paper which circulates among the very people they wish to reach. The *News* is owned and published by Messrs. J. E. Fernald & Son, and as we have said was established in 1879, but the enterprise of which it may be said to be the outcome was inaugurated a score of years before that date, Mr. J. E. Fernald beginning operations as a job printer in 1859. The firm carry on a finely-equipped steam job printing office in connection with the *News*, and are prepared to undertake the finest work in that line and to guarantee satisfaction, not only as regards the quality of the work and the lowness of the prices, but also the promptness with which even the largest orders can be filled. The partners are Messrs. J. E. and G. W. Fernald, the former a native of Sanford, Me., and the latter of this town. Mr. J. E. Fernald is one of the oldest and best-known business men in town. Close attention is given to their printing and publishing enterprise and they propose not only to fully maintain but to heighten if possible the high reputation gained by eleven years of faithful and intelligent work. Mr. G. W. Fernald is also a civil engineer and surveyor and was recently engaged in the survey for York Beach Extension by the Boston & Maine Railroad Company.

H. W. Roberts & Co., Steam Grist-Mill, 70 Central Street, Farmington, N. H.—It is unnecessary to dwell upon the importance of being able to purchase grain, flour, feed, etc., in any desired quantities at the lowest market rates, for the advantages derived from an enterprise which has for its object the furnishing of an abundant and dependable supply of these staple commodities at bottom prices are so obvious as to be understood by every member of the community. Therefore it goes without saying that the establishment conducted by Messrs. H. W. Roberts & Co., is popular throughout this vicinity, for this is a finely equipped steam grist-mill and the proprietors are in a position to meet all honorable competition in their line of business; filling the most extensive orders at short notice and always quoting prices strictly in accord ance with the lowest market rates. The mill is a two-story structure of the dimensions of 30 × 40 feet, and is fitted up with improved machinery driven by a twenty-five horse power steam engine, the boiler-room being an annex 17 × 35 feet, thus orders can be filled with equal facility at all times of year. It is conveniently located at No. 70 Central street, and employment is given to two efficient assistants. Mr. Roberts is a native of Rochester, N. H., and has been connected with his present enterprise since 1889, during which time he has built up an extensive patronage which is still steadily increasing.

A. E. Carter & Co., Furniture Dealers, Curtains, Carpets and Bedding. Upholstering a Specialty. Roberts Building, Main Street, opposite Opera House, Farmington, N. H.—The experienced and wise buyer of furniture, carpets and other household goods does not seek so much for the cheapest as he does for a house which he feels he can thoroughly depend upon, but of course if he can find a concern that combines fair dealing with bottom prices, so much the better for him—and that is just the kind of a concern we introduce to our readers when we call attention to the establishment conducted by Messrs. A. E. Carter & Co. Doubtless many of them know this already, for the enterprise to which we have reference was inaugurated in 1881 and has held a leading position almost from the beginning. It was founded by Mr. A. E. Carter, a native of Maine, who in 1890 became associated with Mr. H. O. Mooney, a native of New Hampshire, thus forming the existing firm. The premises utilized are located in Roberts Building, on Main street, opposite the Opera House, and comprise four floors, each of which measures 23×48 feet, and every available inch of space is occupied by the heavy stock of furniture, carpets, curtains, bedding and other house furnishing goods that is constantly carried. We don't propose to describe this stock in detail—first, because we haven't the room and second, because it is so frequently renewed that before the description would reach our readers it would be out of date, but the stock is always complete, always contains the latest fashionable novelties and is always made up of goods made for use and not simply to sell and guaranteed to prove precisely as represented. Callers are assured prompt and polite attention, and the prices quoted by this well-equipped concern are as low as can be named on goods of equal merit.

J. P. Tibbitts, Furnishing Undertaker, Carriage and Sleigh Manufacturer. Job Work, Varnishing, Painting and Repairing, Farmington, N. H.—Such of our readers as are natives of Farmington or vicinity, or have lived for any length of time in that section, will not need introduction to Mr. J. P. Tibbitts, for he was born in this town and has carried on the business with which he is now identified for a full score of years, beginning operations in 1870. He is a furnishing undertaker and also a carriage and sleigh manufacturer and repairer, being prepared to do job work, varnishing, painting, etc., in a superior manner at short notice. Mr Tibbitts furnishes a large proportion of the coffins, caskets and other funeral goods used in this vicinity, it being generally understood that he is in a position to fill orders very promptly and to quote the lowest market rates on articles of this kind. The premises utilized by him comprise two floors of the dimensions of 20×60 feet, and are fitted up with all necessary tools and other facilities to carry on the several departments of the business to the best advantage. The carriages and sleighs made at this shop have a well earned reputation for strength and durability, for Mr. Tibbitts uses selected material in the doing of custom work and also in repairing, and the workmanship is always equal to the best in every respect.

Thomas Pride & Son, Granite Works, Farmington, N. H.—There is no question but that granite is by far the best material for cemetery work, especially in our New England climate with its great and sudden changes of temperature, and other characteristics which have a most distinctive effect upon marble and other soft stones. Granite cemetery work is not only more durable but also more handsome than that made from any other material and indeed its advantages are so many and so pronounced that it now leads all other kinds in the favor of the public. A Farmington concern which has a high and well deserved reputation for the production of artistic and thoroughly first-class cemetery work at moderate rates is that of Thomas Pride & Son, who began operations here in 1885. Both members of the firm are Maine men by birth, and they not only know what the public want but spare no pains to supply that want and to thoroughly satisfy every customer. They have an almost endless variety of designs for monuments, tablets, headstones, etc., embracing all grades of work from the most simple to the most elaborate, and suited to all tastes and purses. Employment is given to three assistants, and orders will be filled at very short notice, and at prices as low as the lowest in every instance.

C. H. Pitman, Book, Card and Job Printer. Office over Breen & Berry's, Central Square, Farmington, N. H.—It is safe to say that practically everybody in Farmington and many who are not residents of the town know Mr. C. H. Pitman, or "Pit, the printer," as he is familiarly called, for he is not only active and successful as a business man but also holds the position of town clerk and has done so for several terms, while he is as prominent in social circles as he is in business life. Mr. Pitman is a native of Barnstead, N. H., and has carried on operations in Farmington for about ten years. He is agent for some of the leading life and accident insurance companies, and is prepared to furnish such insurance to practically any desired amount on the most favorable terms, and to give prompt and careful attention to every commission placed in his hands. But this does not explain why he is called "Pit, the printer," and those who wish satisfactory information on that point should place an order with him for job printing of any sort, for he is prepared to furnish posters, flyers, dodgers, bill heads, letter heads, note heads, statements, envelopes, receipts, tax bills, milk bills, business cards, address cards, wedding cards, and in fact anything in the job printing line at short notice and at very low prices. Work will be done in black, colors or gilt and it will be well done too, for Mr. Pitman has the experience, facilities, skill and disposition to attain results equal to the best. His office is over Breen & Berry's, Central Square, and every order is assured immediate and painstaking attention.

Wallace, Elliott & Co., manufacturers of Ladies' Misses' and Children's Fine Boots ; J. F. Cloutman, Superintendent ; Central Street, Farmington, N. H.—Those who are aware how extensively the shoe manufacturing industry is carried on in Farmington will readily believe that the firm who carry on the largest shoe factory in town must operate a very elaborate and extensive plant and such is in fact the case, the establishment in question being one of the largest and best equipped of the kind in the State. But large as it is it by no means comprises all the firm's resources, for the proprietors, Messrs. Wallace, Elliott & Co., also operate factories at Haverhill and Stoughton, Mass., each of which turns out distinctive lines of goods, so that the firm are exceptionally well prepared to cater to all classes of trade and it is not surprising that their business extends to every State in the Union and their products are accepted as the standard wherever introduced. The Farmington factory is located on Central street, and is made up of two thoroughly made brick buildings connected by an arch. One of these is five stories in height and 165 × 40 feet in dimensions, and the other measures 115 × 70 feet. The plant of machinery in use is of the most improved type and includes an engine of thirty-horse power with boiler sixty horse. As employment is given to from 300 to 400 assistants it is obvious that the annual output must be very large in amount, and it is very great in value from the fact that it is made up in a large degree of fine goods. This factory has been devoted to the production of ladies', misses' and children's fine boots exclusively until during the current year they have added men's, boys' and youths' calf, buff, splits and dongola goods. A full line of each is manufactured, including the latest fashionable novelties, and among the leading specialties are bright dongola, kid and French kid. From the selection of the material to the completion of the last process incidental to manufacture no trouble is spared to attain the best possible results as regards all the essentials of shapeliness, style, ease and durability, and as the best obtainable mechanical facilities are provided, skilled labor employed and careful supervision exercised nothing is wanting to ensure the production of goods that will sell on their merits everywhere and give the best of satisfaction to both consumers and dealers. Messrs. Wallace, Elliott & Co., began business something more than a score of years ago, and for more than eighteen years they have employed Hon. J. F. Cloutman as superintendent and manager. His exceptional fitness for those positions is so conclusively proved by the results attained that no eulogy of his ability is necessary, but it is but just to state that no one identified with this great enterprise has worked harder to develop it to its present magnitude.

George W. Lane, Jeweler, No. 6 Main Street, Farmington, N. H.—Among Farmington's business men are found a good many examples of financial success won by the energetic pursuit of honorable industry and honorable business methods, and they afford a valuable object lesson to encourage young men starting in business life at the foot of the ladder, for some of those above referred to commenced under most discouraging circumstances and surroundings. Among the young business men of Farmington who are making the creditable effort to build up a successful business and gain an honorable livelihood upon the merits of their work and enterprise, mention should be made of Mr. George W. Lane, whose place of business is located at No. 6 Main street, where he is prepared to do all kinds of watch and clock repairing and cleaning in first-class shape, and all work is guaranteed to give entire satisfaction. He also deals in clocks, and is prepared to give his patrons the benefit of very low prices. All kinds of repairing and engraving of jewelry will be done at short notice in a workmanlike manner. Umbrellas and parasols will be repaired, and keys made and fitted promptly when ordered. Mr. Lane solicits a share of the patronage of the public with the determination to render a service in return that shall be favorably appreciated by every patron. Mr. Lane commenced business during the current year, and is a native of Lewiston, Maine.

Wilson House, E. T. Cotton, Proprietor; H. S. Cotton, Clerk and Manager; Farmington, N. H. —It is said that "experience is the best teacher," and no doubt such is the case in the sense that those who are so taught have reason to remember their lesson, but the teachings of experience are sometimes pretty hard to endure so the wise man profits by the experience of others and thus saves himself much unnecessary discomfort. For instance, one way to learn what hotel in any given place offers the best accommodations is to put up at all of them, one after the other, but such a course is manifestly foolish, the sensible mode of procedure being to patronize that one which is highest recommended, and those who would do this in Farmington would go at once to the Wilson House,—and they would never have reason to regret doing so either. This hotel is owned by Mr. E. T. Cotton, who is also proprietor of the Langdon House in Portsmouth. He is a native of Bromfield, Me., and so is Mr. H. S. Cotton, who officiates as clerk and manager of the Wilson House, and deserves no small share of the credit for its popularity, for he spares no pains to secure the comfort of guests and maintains the service at a high standard of efficiency in every department. The building is pleasantly located and commodious, it comprising three stories and a French roof, and containing thirty-two comfortable beds and other accommodations in proportion. The dining-room has seating capacity for seventy-five, and employment is given to nine assistants, so that even when the house is full the service is prompt and satisfactory. The building is heated by steam, being thoroughly comfortable in the coldest weather. An abundant variety of excellent food is provided at all seasons, and the cooking will compare favorably with that done in many pretentious city hotels at which the terms are much higher than those of the Wilson House, for the prices quoted here are very reasonable, special inducements being held out for regular boarders, although transient trade is also accommodated at very low rates.

Amasa W. Shackford, Photographer, Shackford Block, Central Street, Farmington, N. H. —If improved apparatus and reliable chemicals and unbounded self-confidence were all that is necessary to make a first-class photographer the country would be full of such, for about every tenth man you see nowadays practices photography for fun or for money and can talk to you by the hour about "negatives," and "exposures," and "developing," and many other things of which you know little or nothing, but when it comes to putting theories into practice the average photographer, amateur or professional, cannot seem to make a very excellent showing. The fact is, long experience and considerable natural ability are absolutely essential to the attainment of thoroughly satisfactory results in photography and an illustration of this may be had by comparing the work turned out by Mr. Amasa W. Shackford with that produced by other photographers who might be mentioned, for Mr. Shackford has been in the business for more than thirty years and of course is thoroughly familiar with it in every detail. He was born in Barnstead, N. H., and considering his long and honorable business career it is hardly necessary to state is very favorably and also universally known throughout this section. His rooms are located on the third floor of Shackford's Block, Central street, and are heated by steam and very thoroughly fitted up in every way. Photography in all its branches is carried on, orders being filled at short notice and at uniformly moderate rates, while the results attained are such that it is perfectly safe to fully guarantee satisfaction to all who may place orders at this popular studio.

Farmington Savings Bank, Farmington, N. H. —Of all the many institutions which the progress of civilization has developed there is not one more admirable than the savings bank, for the operations of this are distinctly and entirely beneficial in their effects upon individuals, upon communities and upon the nation itself. The most valuable feature of such a bank is that it helps the people by giving them the means to help themselves, and as this assistance is not at all of a charitable nature, but is a purely business transaction, the proudest have no reason to refuse it, while those who are too willing too depend upon others are not injured by it in the least. Those who avail themselves of the help of such a bank are encouraged to form industrious and frugal habits ; they are encouraged to deny themselves the gratification of injurious and expensive tastes ; they are encouraged to provide for the future by making the best possible use of present advantages, and in short, their character is strengthened and improved in many ways and they profit morally, mentally and physically by their connection with the institution. Of course, we have reference to a savings bank which is soundly established and ably managed, and the residents of Farmington and vicinity need not go away from home to find an institution of this kind, for the record the Farmington savings bank has made since it was chartered, in 1868, entitles it to a leading position among the most sound and progressive savings banks of the State. And we are happy to say that the facilities it offers for the safe and profitable investment of small sums are generally appreciated and largely availed of, a late statement showing deposits of $646,628.44. The same statement showed that there was a surplus of $32,789.48 and a guaranty fund of $24,000, so it will be seen that the bank is conservatively managed, but an even more satisfactory proof that the interests of depositors will be ably and faithfully guarded is that afforded by the standing of those identified with the institution, as the following list of officers will show : president, H. B. Edgerly ; vice president, Levi Pearl ; treasurer, Charles W. Talpey. Trustees : Charles W. Wingate, John H. Barker, Charles W. Talpey, Jonathan R. Hayes, James B Edgerly, E. T. Willson, G. A. Jones, Alonzo Nute, Levi Pearl, George N. Eastman, J. F. Cloutman, H. B. Edgerly, E. P. Nute, D. E. Edgerly, J. P. Bennett, B. P. Chesley.

Roberts & Peavey, Druggists and Stationers. Wall Paper, Paints and Oils, Artists' Materials, Weekly and Daily Newspapers and Periodicals, 21 Main Street, Farmington, N. H. —The firm of Roberts & Peavey was formed in 1889, but the enterprise carried on by this concern is of much earlier origin, its inception dating back some twenty years as operations were begun about 1872 by Mr. A. C. Newell. This gentleman was succeeded in 1879 by Messrs. Emerson & Garland, they giving place in 1885 to Messrs. E. W. Emerson & Co., who were succeeded by Messrs. Roberts & Avery in 1887, the present firm assuming control two years later. The partners are Messrs. W. W. Roberts and W. L. Peavey, both of whom are natives of Farmington, and are too well known here to need extended personal mention. Their store is located at No. 21 Main street, and has an area of 1500 square feet, affording ample room for the carrying of a heavy and exceptionally varied stock which comprises not only a full line of pure drugs, medicines and chemicals, but such other articles as are usually found in a first-class drug store, but also an attractive assortment of wall papers, paints and oils, artists' materials, fashionable and business stationery, weekly and daily papers, periodicals, etc. Employment is given to two assistants and callers may depend upon receiving prompt and courteous attention at all times, while the prices quoted are always in strict accordance with the lowest market rates. The drugs and medicines handled are of the best quality obtainable, and as great care is exercised to ensure the nicest accuracy in the compounding of prescriptions it is natural that an extensive trade should be done in this important department.

John H. Barker & Co., dealers in General Merchandise, Main Street, Farmington, N. H.—Among those old-established and representative enterprises which are known to everyone at all acquainted with Farmington and its resources, that conducted by the firm of John H. Barker & Co., deserves prominent and favorable mention, for this has been carried on for fully thirty years, and is to day one of the best managed and most reliable and popular general stores in this section of the State. Operations were begun in 1860 by Mr. John Barker, father of the present proprietor, in company with his son, Mr. J. H. Barker, who has been sole owner since his father retired, in 1880. Mr. J. H. Barker is a native of Wolfboro, and, of course, is widely known in business and social circles in Farmington and vicinity. The premises utilized comprise one floor and a basement, each 25 × 50 feet in dimensions, and they contain about as varied a stock as it is possible to conceive of, for this is a "general store" in the full sense of the term and includes everything to be found in a first class country store. The assortment is as carefully selected as it is varied, and every article in it is guaranteed to prove as represented, while the prices quoted will bear the severest comparison with those of other dealers in goods of equal quality.

L. S. Flanders & Son, manufacturers of Lasts and Sole Patterns, Farmington, N. H.—As the manufacture of boots and shoes has long been the industry in which New England is more largely engaged than any other section of the Union, we would naturally expect to find in the New England States many of those enterprises which are tributary to this great branch of manufacture, such, for instance, as that conducted by Messrs. L S. Flanders & Son, manufacturers of lasts and sole patterns. This concern are well and favorably known in business circles, for the undertaking they carry on was founded nearly twenty years ago and has developed to a point where they wholesale to manufacturers throughout New England. Operations were begun in 1873, by Messrs. Haynes & Flanders, the present firm being formed in 1885 and consisting of Messrs. L. S. and A. W. Flanders, both of whom are natives of Concord, N. H. Mr. L. S. Flanders served as representative in 1877-8 and has long been one of the most prominent of our local business men. The concern utilize spacious and well equipped premises, employ experienced assistants and are prepared to furnish lasts and sole patterns and upper patterns of all kinds, in any desired quantities, at the lowest market rates, all orders being assured immediate and painstaking attention.

E. T. Willson, dealer in Groceries, Flour, Grain, Crockery, Paints and Oils, Shoe Findings and Hardware, 8, 10 and 12 South Main Street (Talpey's Block), Farmington, N. H. —The establishment conducted by Mr E T Willson at Nos. 8, 10 and 12 South Main street, Talpey's Block, is a thoroughly representative one, for not only is the enterprise itself a leader in its special line but the proprietor is a representative business man, he having done much to advance the interests of this town and now holding the position of State senator. Mr Willson is a native of York, Me., and has carried on his present business since 1882, it having been founded in 1870 by Mr. C. W. Talpey. The premises occupied are very spacious and contain a heavy and carefully chosen stock comprising staple and fancy groceries, flour and grain, crockery and hardware, paints and oils, shoe findings, sporting goods, including guns, rifles ammunition, fishing tackle, etc., the assortment as a whole being one of the most complete and desirable in the country. Both a wholesale and retail business is done and every order, large or small, is assured immediate and careful attention, for employment is given to four competent assistants and every facility is provided to enable commissions to be promptly and accurately executed. Under these circumstances it goes without saying that Mr. Willson is in a position to meet all honorable competition by quoting the lowest market rates on goods of standard and dependable quality.

A. Nute & Sons, manufacturers of Mens' Shoes, Farmington, N. H.—There is no establishment in town more clearly entitled to be classed as representative in the full sense of that much abused word than that conducted by Messrs. A. Nute & Sons, and its claim to such a title is based not only on a long and honorable record, on a very high present standing and on prospects of the brightest description, but also on the powerful influence the enterprise has exerted in developing the interests of this town and section, and on the standing in the business and social world of the men identified with it. This undertaking was founded many years ago, at a time when shoe manufacturing on a large scale in New Hampshire was a new and somewhat hazardous experiment, and the success it met with had much to do with the present standing of Farmington as a shoe manufacturing centre. Many and radical have been the changes in machinery and in methods since this enterprise was inaugurated but the management of it has been steadily progressive, and to-day the establishment is a fine example of a modern shoe factory, both as regards its equipment and the quality of the work produced. The main structure is four stories in height and 110 × 32 feet in dimensions, and there is a two story addition measuring 75 × 32 feet, and another one story in height and 100 × 40 feet in size. Power is furnished by a fifty-horse engine, and employment is given to 250 assistants. The annual product is very large in amount and consists of men's shoes, these being manufactured for Messrs. Potter, White & Bailey of Boston. The firm is constituted of Mr. Alonzo Nute and his sons, Messrs. E P. and A. I. Nute. The prominence of these gentlemen deserves more than a mere mention of their names in this consideration. The senior member of the firm, Hon. Alonzo Nute, began his connection with the boot and shoe business when sixteen years of age, going to Natick, Mass., for this purpose where he remained for six years, about two of which he was in the employ of Vice-President Henry Wilson and lived in his family. Returning to Farmington he began the manufacture of boots and shoes which has developed into its present large proportions and become one of the most important plants in the town. When the war of the Rebellion came in 1861 he went out as quartermaster of the Sixth N. H. Regt., and later was placed on the staff of Genl. R. C Hawkins of the Ninth N. J. Zouaves. He is the present congressman from this district, having long been prominent in public life. He is vice-president of the Farmington National Bank and is a trustee of the Savings Bank, as is also Mr. E. P. Nute, who at one time represented Farmington in the legislature. Mr. A. I. Nute holds the office of bank commissioner. But although men of affairs as well as of business the members of the firm give the enterprise in the management of which they are associated close personal supervision, and steadily maintain the enviable reputation it has held so long.

Mrs. L. A. Small, Millinery and Fancy Goods, Central Street, Farmington, N. H.—Although by no means every lady has that combination of taste and skill which is essential to the attainment of satisfactory results in millinery work, there is no reason why every lady should not know where to place orders for such work in the full assurance that they will be satisfactorily filled, and many residents of Farmington and vicinity have found by experience that Mrs. L. A. Small is admirably qualified to meet all demands made upon her for fine custom millinery work at all times of year. Mrs. Small was born in Alton, N. H., and has been identified with her present business since 1868, so we need hardly add that she is thoroughly familiar with it in every detail. She carries a large and well-selected stock of ribbons, laces, velvets, feathers, flowers, trimmed and untrimmed hats and bonnets, besides some fancy goods, but particular attention is given to order work, and as Mrs. Small attains results equal to the best, is moderate in her charges, and is prepared to execute commissions at short notice, it is natural that her establishment should be a pronounced favorite with ladies throughout this section.

Dr. J. E. Nichols, Dentist, Barker's Block, Farmington, N. H.—Americans have the unenviable reputation of possessing the poorest teeth of any nation in the world, and whether this reputation be deserved or not it is certainly a fact that in this country poor teeth are the rule and perfect ones the rare exception. Just why this is the case has never been satisfactorily explained, although numberless explanations have been offered, most of which were much more remarkable for their ingenuity than for their conclusiveness. The blame has been laid on our climate, on our food, on our nervous temperament as a people, and on our mode of living, as well as on many other things too numerous to mention, but no one of these has been demonstrated to be the prevailing cause although doubtless most if not all of them have their effect in bringing about the present condition of things. The truth is, individual cases of defective teeth are the result of individual causes, that is to say, each of us can by observation and the exercise of common sense learn how to keep his own teeth in good order although none of us may be able to assign just cause for the national characteristic. But it is necessary to "start fair," in the first place and the only way to do this for those whose teeth are not perfect is to visit a competent dentist and have them put in order,—after which intelligent care will preserve them in that condition. Of course there is no lack of competent dentists in a country which is conceded to lead the world in dental science, and among those located in this vicinity, Dr. J. E. Nichols is entitled to prominent mention, for he is a thoroughly skillful and very gentle operator and has all necessary mechanical facilities for the practice of his profession in accordance with the most approved methods. Dr. Nichols is a native of Ashby, Mass., and located in Farmington in 1889, his office being at the corner of Central and Main streets, in Barker's Block. He has already built up an extensive practice, and as his work is always thoroughly and durably done and his charges uniformly moderate, it is not surprising that his service should be in steadily increasing demand.

Frank E. Farwell, Market, Central and Main Streets, Farmington, N. H.—No review of the mercantile enterprises of Farmington which omitted to make prominent mention of the leading meat markets could be regarded as complete, for not only are these important in and of themselves but also because of the fact that they make the town much more desirable as a place of residence than would otherwise be possible, insomuch as they tend to reduce the expense and increase the enjoyment of living by furnishing nourishing and palatable food at the very lowest rates. Not one of these establishments is more worthy of commendation and patronage than that of which Mr. Frank E. Farwell is proprietor, for he caters successfully to all classes of trade and has an unsurpassed reputation for giving full value for money received. He was born in this State, and succeeded Mr. W. I. Nutter in the ownership of the enterprise to which this notice refers in 1888. The store is located at the corner of Central and Main streets, and is sufficiently spacious to accommodate a complete assortment of fresh, salted and corned meats and such other commodities as are usually found in a first-class market. Mr. Farwell employs two assistants, and spares no pains to ensure prompt and courteous attention to every caller, small and large buyers being treated with equal consideration and all goods being sold strictly on their merits, so that complete satisfaction can be safely guaranteed.

E. E. Downing, wholesale and retail Baker, and dealer in Groceries, 28 Central Street, Farmington, N. H.—The enterprise carried on by Mr. E. E. Downing certainly deserves prominent mention in a review of Farmington's most valuable and popular business undertakings, for no establishment in this town or vicinity is more favorably known in connection with the sale of family food supplies. Mr. Downing is a wholesale and retail baker and dealer in groceries and is prepared to furnish bread, cake and pastry of the best quality in quantities to suit at bottom prices. Staple and fancy groceries are also largely dealt in, a heavy and varied stock being carried and no pains being spared to supply goods that will give uniform satisfaction at prices as low as can be named on articles of similar grade. Mr. Downing is a native of this town and is very widely known here in both business and social circles. He was formerly a member of the firm of Downing & Schlenker but for some time has been sole proprietor of the business with which he is now identified. Spacious and well-equipped premises located at No. 28 Central street, are utilized, and employment is given to four assistants. Callers are assured prompt and polite attention, and all orders, large or small, will be carefully and accurately filled at short notice and at the lowest market rates.

Strafford House, Frank H. McAlpine, Proprietor; Good Livery and Boarding Stable connected; Farmington, N. H.—It is by no means an agreeable task to recommend a hotel to a man unless you know what his tastes are, for some individuals go in for "style" alone and will put up with comforless accommodations and poor service as long as they know they are in a "high-toned" house, while others put comfort before style and don't care how exclusive and aristocratic a house is as long as it is home like and respectable. But in recommending the Strafford House to our readers we will avoid all possible misunderstanding by saying at the outset that this hotel is run on the assumption that the public want pleasant rooms, comfortable beds, an abundance of good, substantial food and prompt and polite attendance, and that they don't want to pay fancy prices but are willing to pay a fair amount for homelike accommodations. The Strafford was furnished new throughout in 1889 and consequently the beds are of modern style, comfortable and roomy, and the toilet facilities, etc., are convenient and complete. The dining room will seat thirty-six guests, and the table is bountifully supplied at all seasons of the year, while the cooking and service are excellent. The proprietor of the house is Mr. Frank H. McAlpine. This gentleman does all in his power to secure the comfort of guests and is very popular among the patrons of the house, who speak in the highest terms of his readiness to furnish any desired information and to make things as easy and pleasant as possible for strangers in town. There is a good livery and boarding stable connected with this hotel, and those desiring teams for business or pleasure purposes can obtain them without delay and at very reasonable figures.

Frank Pearl, dealer in Choice Family Groceries, Dry and Fancy Goods, Farmington, N. H.—If any of our readers who have "kept house" for any length of time have never experienced difficulty in getting dependable groceries at fair prices, they have been far more fortunate than the majority of us are, or else have exercised unusual discrimination in the placing of orders, for it is unquestionably an easy matter to obtain first-class groceries at moderate rates provided you know what establishment to patronize; while it would be absurd and unjust to claim that that carried on by Mr. Frank Pearl is the only one in this vicinity at which such goods may be had, it may still be truthfully asserted that the inducements he offers are unsurpassed, and hence those dissatisfied with their present service would best serve their own interests by favoring him with a trial order. Mr. Pearl is a native of Farmington and has conducted his present business since succeeding Mr. C. W. Wingate in 1887. He occupies one floor and a basement, measuring 30 × 35 feet, and his stock includes not only a full line of choice family groceries but also dry and fancy goods, etc. All orders are assured prompt and careful attention, and although low prices are quoted, no trouble is spared to furnish goods that will give the best of satisfaction to every reasonable customer.

J. Wesley Locke, Livery and Sale Stable. Dealer in Carriages and Harnesses, Crowley Street, Farmington, N. H.—The establishment conducted by Mr. J. Wesley Locke is of interest both to those who wish to hire and those who wish to buy horses and carriages for Mr. Locke not only carries on a first-class livery stable but also deals largely in horses, carriages and harnesses, and is prepared to give big value for money received every time. Some of our readers who have never had dealings with him may think this latter statement somewhat exaggerated, but let them remember that "the proof of the pudding is in the eating," and not definitely make up their minds on the matter until they have given Mr. Locke a call and found out for themselves what he is in a position to do, and we have no fear but what they will then agree that our assertion is correct. Mr. Locke is a native of Dover, N. H., and opened his present establishment in 1889. Spacious premises located on Crowley street, are utilized, and from eighteen to twenty horses are always on hand, together with a number of stylish and easy riding vehicles, so that livery teams of excellent quality can be furnished without delay, and as the charges are moderate the public make extensive use of the facilities provided. Lack of space forbids our making extended mention of the sale business but suffice it to say that Mr. Locke is always in a position to sell you a good horse at a fair price and that when you buy of him you can safely depend upon getting an animal that will prove as represented, while he can furnish carriages and harnesses at as low prices (quality considered) as any dealer in the State.

I. Hayes & Sons, Shoe Manufacturers, Farmington, N. H.—Not the least among the marvels of the present day is the almost nominal price at which a pair of boots or shoes honestly made from good material can be bought, and it is, in one sense of the word, an industrial paradox, that the more complete and costly the plant employed in manufacturing operations, the less is the expense of production. The factory conducted by Messrs. I. Hayes & Sons on Grove street in this town, is a three-story building, most convenient in construction and equipment. It having the form of a hollow square affords light and well-ventilated rooms, and is heated by steam which also furnishes the power for the machinery, which is of the most approved pattern. Employment is given to from 200 to 250 hands. The product reaches quite large proportions, and is composed of full lines of men's, boys' and youths' fine calf, P calf, veal calf and A calf shoes. The goods are distributed in the market through Messrs. John S. Fogg & Co., of Boston, and are sold mostly in the Southern and Western States. The business was established about 1878 and has from the first been attended with phenomenal success, in that it has had a continued and healthy growth and development, and has acquired an excellent reputation for its manufactured goods. The firm is composed of Mr. Israel Hayes and his son, E. W. Hayes, while F. C. Hayes, another son, is clerk. Each of these gentlemen are too well and favorably known in business and social circles to require any extended notice in this review. Mr. Israel Hayes had valuable experience in the shoe manufacturing business in Natick, Mass., as did also a number of Farmington manufacturers, returning to Farmington to establish this enterprise.

Mrs. E. H. York & Co., Millinery and Ladies' Furnishing Goods, Farmington, N. H.—There is really but one way in which to estimate the comparative standing of such an enterprise as is conducted by Mrs. E. H. York & Co., and that is to make a personal canvass of such members of the community as would naturally be in a position to offer a competent and an unprejudiced opinion of it, and the result of such a canvass would be to give this undertaking the leading position it deserves, for there is not one of a similar nature in this section more thoroughly popular or more generally known. It was established in 1880, and has been so efficiently managed that for some years this establishment has been regarded as the headquarters for the doing of fine millinery work ; particular attention being given to such orders, although millinery and ladies' furnishing goods are quite largely dealt in and the latest novelties in these lines are constantly in stock. But custom work is made a specialty of and such care and skill are shown in adapting means and methods to individual cases that those who have experienced difficulty in obtaining millinery suited to their needs should by all means make trial of the service here offered. Orders are promptly filled, and moderate charges are made in every instance.

W. F. Thayer, dealer in Stoves, Tinware, Pumps, Sheet Lead, Pipe, Kitchen Furnishing Goods, etc., Farmington, N. H.—The difference in price between a stove that embodies all the latest improvements and one that contains but few or none of them is but small, comparatively speaking, but even if it were ten times as much as it is it would still be true economy to pay it, for a strictly first-class modern stove is so economical of fuel and is so easy to manage and so certain in its operation that it will soon pay for itself when it displaces a stove made in accordance with old ideas. Of course, in order to be sure of getting the best possible stove for the least possible money you must deal with the right party, but the residents of this vicinity need have no difficulty on that score for Mr. W. F. Thayer is prepared to furnish the latest types of cooking and heating stoves at positively bottom prices, and to guarantee that they will do all that is claimed for them if used in accordance with directions. Mr. Thayer is a native of Gray Corner, Me., and needs no introduction to our Farmington readers, he having carried on his present business here for ten years and being chief engineer of the fire department. He utilizes very spacious premises, comprising one floor of the dimensions of 134 × 22 feet, and another measuring 60 × 22 feet, and carries a heavy and varied stock of stoves, tinware, pumps, sheet lead, pipe, kitchen furnishings, etc. Every facility is at hand for the doing of job work in tin, brass and sheet-iron, and special attention is given to tin roofing, such work being promptly, skilfully and durably done at moderate rates. In fact, all orders of whatever nature are assured immediate and careful attention, for employment is given to six competent assistants and no trouble is spared to fully maintain the enviable reputation so long associated with this representative enterprise.

J. E. Fernald, dealer in Groceries, Hardware, Shoe Findings, Paints, Oils, Glass, Books, Stationery, etc., etc.; Steam Job Printing Office connected with the Store; Farmington, N. H.—Mr. J. E. Fernald is a native of Sanford, Me., but is certainly a Farmington man by adoption at least, for he has carried on business here for a third of a century, and has been and is very active and successful in promoting the best interests of this town and section. He served on the board of selectmen, for the past eleven years has held his present position of town treasurer, while at one time he officinted as postmaster. In company with Mr. George W. Fernald, his son, he owns and publishes the *Farmington News,* and also carries on a thoroughly equipped steam job printing office. Mr. Fernald deals in groceries, hardware, shoe findings, paints, oils, glass, books, stationery, etc., carrying a large and complete stock and utilizing premises of the dimensions of 46½ × 32½ feet. He founded this business in 1857 and it has since become so generally known to the purchasing public throughout this vicinity as to render extended mention of it quite superfluous. The people know that the goods bought at this store will prove just as represented ; they know that the stock is varied enough to allow all tastes and purses to be suited ; they know that the lowest market rates are quoted on all the commodities dealt in, and they know that all orders, large or small, are assured prompt and careful attention, and knowing these things it would be strange if they did not give the enterprise hearty and continuous support, which, as a matter of fact, they do.

F. E. Mooney, dealer in Coal and Wood, Pressed Hay and Straw. No. 35 North Main Street, Farmington, N. H. —Mr. F. E. Mooney is very generally and favorably known in Farmington and vicinity, for not only is he a native of that town and has a large circle of friends there, but he carries on one of the most popular of the local establishments, he being extensively engaged in the sale of coal and wood, pressed hay and straw, clapboards, shingles, lath, lime, cement, hair and brick, besides conducting a first-class livery stable. And this stable *is* first class in the full sense of that often misused word, for Mr. Mooney maintains eight good horses, has some stylish and easy riding vehicles and in fact can furnish you with a rig that will give the best of satisfaction and appear well in any company. Teams may be had at very short notice and the charges are moderate every time. Orders for coal and wood, pressed hay and straw are also assured immediate and painstaking attention, for ample shed room for storage purposes is available and a large stock is constantly carried, while employment is given to three assistants, and the facilities for prompt and accurate delivery are excellent. The lowest market rates are quoted and equal care is given to the filling of large and small orders.

Charles H. Berry, Fruit, Confectionery, Ice Cream, etc., Main Street, Farmington.—The business carried on by Mr. Charles H Berry was established for some years and passed through the hands of several proprietors before it came into his possession, in 1885, but it is only fair to say that it was never so well managed and popular before as it has been and is under the present management. Mr. Berry is a native of Strafford, N. H., and has a large circle of friends in Farmington and vicinity, many of whom he has made by his straightforward business methods and the accommodating spirit he shows in the carrying on of his enterprise. The premises utilized by him are located on Main street, and contain a soda fountain and other facilities for the carrying on of the extensive trade in soda and ice cream which is enjoyed during the proper season. A good stock of seasonable fruits is also always on hand to select from, together with choice confectionery, cigars, tobacco, etc. These goods are carefully chosen and will suit the most critical, but the prices are uniformly moderate, being in fact as low as can be named on articles of equal merit.

G. A. Jones & Co., Furniture, Carpets and Room Paper, No. 12 Central Street, Farmington, N. H —Those wishing to purchase anything in the line of furniture, carpets or wall paper, if they have had much experience in the buying of such goods, will seek a house that carries a large and varied stock, that caters intelligently to all classes of trade, and that has a well-earned reputation for sound integrity. Such houses are to be found in every business centre, and one of them right here in Farmington is that of G. A. Jones & Co , carrying on operations at No. 12 Central street, where premises having an area of 4500 square feet are utilized. The business has been conducted by the present concern since 1887, succeeding Mr. E. B. Small who had conducted the business for over a score of years. The management of this house for enterprise and fair dealing is not surpassed by that of any house in the country. Mr. Jones is a native of Farmington, and is so well known here in both business and social circles as to make extended personal mention quite unnecessary. He has striven from the first to build up the enterprise on the sound basis of perfectly and permanently satisfied patrons, and that he has succeeded, the present standing of the undertaking fully proves. The very latest fashionable novelties in furniture, carpets and roompaper are constantly on hand to select from, and all tastes and purses can be suited from the stock, as it is kept complete in every department. The prices are as low as the lowest, quality of course considered, and sufficient assistance is employed to ensure prompt and painstaking attention to every caller.

P. M. Frost, Dry and Fancy Goods, Cloutman Block, Farmington, N. H.—In these days of sudden and frequent changes in fashion and sharp and intelligent competition it is no easy matter to carry on a really first-class dry and fancy goods store, for the stock of such an establishment must of necessity be large and varied, must be so frequently renewed as always to include the latest fashionable novelties, and the goods of which it is composed must be sold at a narrow margin of profit in order to be disposed of as rapidly as is necessary. Consequently first-class stores of this kind are not common, and as that of which Mr. P. M Frost is proprietor is thoroughly first-class it naturally follows that it enjoys a very large share of the patronage of residents of this section. This business was founded in 1878 and is under the direct management of Mr. F. B. Frost, son of the owner. The premises utilized have an area of 1200 square feet and contain as full and desirable a stock of dry and fancy goods as can be found in this section of the State, but we don't propose to attempt to describe it for the simple reason that it is replenished so frequently and largely that any description of it would soon be "out of date." Suffice it to say that it comprises full lines of staple articles as well as many of the latest and most attractive novelties, and that the goods are in every instance guaranteed to prove as represented and are sold at positively bottom figures. Callers are assured prompt and courteous attention, employment being given to four experienced assistants.

W. A. Elliott, Ice Cream, Fruit, Cigars, etc., Central Street, Farmington, N. H.—It is no easy task to successfully carry on such a business as is conducted by Mr. W. A. Elliott, for nearly all the articles dealt in by him are of a nature that renders it necessary to continually renew the stock if it is to be kept in an attractive condition, and to exercise great care in the choice of the goods he offers the public. That he has succeeded in accomplishing this task so far is proved by the popularity of his establishment, and this popularity is evidently destined to steadily increase, for he spares no pains to continually improve the service rendered, and has considerably extended the business since assuming control of it in 1889. Mr. Elliott carries on a large ice cream trade during the warmer months, his store, which is located on Central street, being conveniently fitted-up as an ice cream saloon, and the service being very prompt and satisfactory, while the cream is strictly first-class and the prices are moderate. Confectionery, fruits, tonic beer and other light drinks, cigars, tobacco. etc., are also dealt in, a well chosen stock being carried and all callers being assured immediate and courteous attention.

M. W. Small, dealer in Groceries, Grain, Crockery, Glass-ware and Farming Tools, 10 Central Street, Farmington, N. H.—It is a very heavy and varied stock that is offered by Mr. M. W. Small, and as he deals in such indispensable commodities as groceries, grain, glass-ware, crockery, farming tools, etc., it is natural that a very extensive business should be done, especially as the goods uniformly prove as represented and are sold at the lowest market rates. Mr. Small was born in Raymond, Me., and has been identified with his present establishment since 1877, during which time it has become one of the most generally and favorably known stores of the kind in this town and vicinity. The premises made use of comprise one floor of the dimensions of 20 × 70 feet, and a basement having an area of 3000 square feet, the latter being specially devoted to the handling of grain, feed, flour, etc., as this is one of the most important departments of the business. The service at this popular store is remarkably prompt and efficient, much more so than that offered at many establishments doing a much smaller business, for employment is given to four competent assistants and no trouble is spared to ensure immediate and careful attention to every caller, orders being accurately delivered at short notice.

H. P. Fall & Co., Druggists and Stationers, 37 Main Street, Farmington, N. H.—The business conducted by Messrs. H. P. Fall & Co., would be worthy of prominent mention on account of its age alone, even if it had no other thing to recommend it to notice, for this is one of the oldest established enterprises of the kind in the State, it having been inaugurated in 1837 by Dr. D. T. Parker. But its claims to notice, far from resting entirely on its antiquity, is based very largely on its present standing, for under the management of the existing firm, who began operations in 1880, this enterprise is one of the most reliable and useful of the kind of all those carried on in this vicinity. The proprietors are Mr. H. P. Fall and Dr. H. P. Wheatley, the former being a native of Farmington, while the latter was born in Brookfield, Vt. Both give close personal attention to the details of the business, and the advantages gained by having a physician connected with a pharmacy are certainly too obvious to require mention. The firm are druggists and stationers and carry a very large and complete stock requiring the occupancy of two floors, each of which measures 18 × 50 feet. The assortment of drugs, medicines and chemicals is not only extensive but is made up of goods selected from the most reliable sources, which fact, combined with the facilities for handling provided and the thoroughness of the system employed, commends this store to all wishing to have prescriptions compounded,—especially as the charges made are uniformly moderate. Toilet and fancy goods are well represented in the stock, many attractive novelties being offered, together with trusses of the most approved make, and a full line of fashionable and business stationery; pocket cutlery is also dealt in to a considerable extent, and all the articles handled are guaranteed to prove as represented and are offered at the lowest market rates. This establishment has made itself known throughout this region as manufacturing chemists. Star Synteretic, Star cough balsam, Star liniment, Star cordial and Star pills, being among the best known of their productions.

C. W. Jenness, manufacturer of Wood and Paper Boxes; Job Sawing, Planing, and Mill Work of all kinds; Timber, Boards, Sheathing, Moulding, etc., kept on hand; Lumber sawed by portable mills; Farmington, N. H.— The manufacture of wood and paper boxes is one of the important industries of this section and it is also one of the most promising for the demand for boxes is steadily and rapidly increasing and some of our local manufacturers show great enterprise in catering to this demand, the natural result being that Farmington is becoming a prominent centre for supplies of this kind. One of the most enterprising and successful of those engaged in wood and paper box making is Mr. C. W. Jenness, who is a native of Rochester, N. H., and began operations in this town in 1878. The premises utilized by him have an area of 5,000 square feet and are fitted up with improved machinery, driven by two steam engines of forty and fifteen horse-power respectively. Every facility is provided for the manufacture of wood and paper boxes and the largest orders can be filled at short notice and at low rates, but the business is by no means confined to this, it also including the doing of job sawing, planing and mill work of all kinds, and the sale of timber, boards, sheathing, moulding, etc., a large stock of which is constantly carried. Mr. Jenness operates two portable mills, and in short is thoroughly well prepared to do business on a large scale and to successfully meet all honorable competition, as is shown by the steady development of his enterprise during the past twelve years.

THE CONCORD HARNESS,

MADE ONLY BY

JAMES R. HILL & CO.,

CONCORD, N. H.

ESTABLISHED 1840.

James R. Hill & Co., the only makers of the "Concord Harness" and collars, are probably as well and favorably known as any other house in this country as makers of the celebrated and world-renowned "Concord Harness," and the firm's business forms no small portion of the manufacturing industry of the capital city. The founder of the house, Mr. James R. Hill, commenced business, in a small way, in 1840, and by his indomitable energy and perseverance, attending strictly to business and making good work, soon gained for him a good reputation throughout the State. And as the railroads pushed out into the far West, necessitating connecting lines by staging, those who had used his harness in the East, wanted them in their new enterprises, and so as time rolled on, the business was increased. In 1851, the present senior partner of the firm, George H. Emery, entered the employ of Mr. Hill as an apprentice, commencing at the very foot of the ladder, learning all the details of every part of the trade, and, in 1859, was placed in charge of the manufacturing department, and, in 1865, was admitted to equal partnership with Mr. Hill and J. E. Dwight, the son-in-law of Mr. Hill, and since that time, the practical management has rested on his shoulders. On the decease of Mr. Hill, in 1884, Mr. Emery and Mr. Dwight purchased the heirs' interest, and the business has since been managed under the same firm-name ; in 1888, a stock company was formed continuing the same name, Mr. Emery becoming president and general manager and Mr. Dwight treasurer. A word in regard to the workshops which are very extensive, although the stranger passing by on Main street would not see the immense workshops in the rear. The building located on North Main street, comprises a three-story building and basement, 40 × 125 feet, with a three-story and basement building connected in the rear, 40 × 160, and a collar shop building, two stories in height, 25 × 60 feet. The company has recently opened a store in Boston at 30 Sudbury street, 61–63 Portland street. Employment is given to from 100 to 150 skilled workmen, according to the season. The company does an extensive wholesale business, the largest probably of the kind in New England. No concern in the country gives more genuine value for every dollar received. The quality of the work manufactured by this concern stands unrivalled, being acknowledged not only to be the best to be had, but

the Standard Harness of America. The trade of this house extends to every part of the inhabited globe where American or English enterprise has gained a foothold. The firm took the highest award at the Centennial in 1876, special awards at Sidney in 1879, and was the only party receiving two awards at the Melbourne exhibition of 1880. Their harness also took the first prize again at Melbourne in 1888, and have always taken the highest awards when placed in competition. Barnum & Bailey are heavy patrons of this company's productions, and are using a complete outfit in all their departments of harness made by this firm. While express and coach harness are a prominent feature, yet a specialty of the house is the making of fine harness, including fine carriage harness, coupé, rockaway, gentlemen's light driving and business harness of all sorts and descriptions. The customer can have his taste gratified in every respect, and, in point of style, they are surpassed by none.

The following editorial article, taken from the *Coach and Saddlery Journal*, published in New York City, shows how the trade look upon the goods manufactured by this firm : "George H. Emery, senior member of the firm of James R. Hill & Co., Concord, N. H., paid a flying visit to this city last week for the purpose of buying stock for the firm, whose business is steadily increasing, notwithstanding their factory is located in a city that of itself offers little inducement to business visitors. The value of a good reputation, honorable and square dealing, was never made more apparent than it is with the house of 'The Concord Harness,' their trade mark being an imperturbable barrier to rival houses, and especially to that class who have not the ability to invent new styles themselves, and can only copy and imitate others. There are such houses in the trade, and their reputations in this respect are well known. This house is among the pioneers and in the advance ground in getting up new styles, and probably there has been more copying from 'The Concord Harness' than all others in the country, as it seems to be the *ne plus ultra* of some harness manufacturers of the class we have mentioned to say they can make as good a harness as the 'Concord Harness,' made by James R. Hill & Co. It was Mr. Emery who first conceived the idea of making a standard harness, and obtained for his house their trade mark, which consists of the words 'The Concord Harness,' and also, at a later date, another in which music is made to appear, the significance of which has been a puzzle to many, as it was to us, to know what music had to do with a harness. We asked Mr. Emery for the meaning, who said : 'Why, what is music but harmony, and what is harmony but a concord of sounds ? And in our harness we combine harmony in their proportions, one strap with another ; hence they are 'Concord Harness.' There is no danger of the good name of the house being sacrificed under its present management, as both members of the firm have had a long and practical experience, the senior from 1851, and the junior from 1865. Knowing how and what to buy is an attainment reached by comparatively few, but Mr. Emery is prominent among that few. He is looked upon by the New York harness leather manufacturers as one of the most competent judges of harness-leather that visits this city. When David Moffat, the acknowledged leader in the manufacture of harness leather, says, as he did to the editor, of Mr. Emery : 'He is a thorough and critical judge of harness leather ; he knows all about it. He knows good leather at sight, and, in buying, selects only the best ; it is useless to offer him anything else. He buys close, but he buys good stock only.' It speaks volumes in praise of the buyer, and gives assurance to those who buy 'The Concord Harness' that they will get harness made of good stock and in a workmanlike manner."

No higher endorsement can be had. The use of the firm's trade mark, "The Concord Harness," is not limited to any one style of harness, but is and always has been applied and used by them for every description of harness of superior quality of stock and workmanship, meaning that the purchaser should become accustomed to rely upon the quality of any harness sold him under this name, and while the motto, which is original with this house, (although it has been copied by others) "Not how cheap, but how good," when applied to the quality of "The Concord Harness," is wholly true : yet, if a cheap harness is wanted, it can be obtained of them in any style desired, at prices lower than the lowest. Aside from the manufacturing of harness, the firm carry a line of all kinds of goods belonging to the trade ; carriage and stable furnishings, horse clothing, trunks, travelling valises, and all sorts of saddlery hardware generally. On seeing the firm's trade mark, where the music is made to appear, the poet has furnished the following verses, which state the facts very clearly :

TUNE, AMERICA.

I.
Come, drivers, let us sing,
Make all the welkin ring
With songs of praise.
Praise for the harness fine,
Made in the best design,
Beauty in every line,
Strong in all ways.

II.
" Not how cheap, but how good,"
Long has our motto stood
Before all men.
Surpassed by none e'er made,
No matter what the grade,
Of no fair test afraid,
By draft or pen.

III.
In Afric's sunny clime,
Australia's land sublime,
O'er Europe's plains,
O'er Asia's boundless ground—
In fact the world around,
Is " Concord Harness " found,
Where men draw reins.

IV.
So, with harmonious voice,
Proclaim the people's choice,
From near and far,
Shout, to the heavens blue !
Shout, men of every hue !
Shout, for the " Concord " true
Concordia !

ORGANIZED 1845

New York Life

INSURANCE Co.

WILLIAM H. BEERS, PRESIDENT.

CROWELL & McKELLAR GEN'L AGENTS .

CHASE'S BLOCK 15 NO. MAIN ST. CONCORD, N.H

What the lawyers call the " burden of proof," is now thrown on the man who is not insured, for such a revolution has occurred in public sentiment within a decade or so, that a man who can be insured but neglects to take out a policy, is regarded as careless and selfish unless he can prove the contrary to be the fact. Really the only question for a sensible man to consider is where he can place his insurance to the best advantage, and we can aid powerfully in an entirely satisfactory solution of that by directing our readers' attention to the facilities offered by the New York Life Insurance Company, whose State agency for New Hampshire is in Room No. 4, Chase's Block, 15 No. Main St., Concord. Here may be found Messrs. Crowell & McKellar, who are the general agents for New Hampshire, and control sub agents throughout the State. They established their agency in April, 1889, and have already written a great many policies, for they are in a position to furnish the highest type of insurance at the lowest market rates. The New York Life is one of the strongest and most extensive life companies in the world, and the magnitude of its operation is most significantly shown by the record of a single year (1889) :

INCOME ACCOUNT.

From policy-holders......................	$24,585,921.10
" interest, rentals, etc..............	4,577,345.14
Total income........................	29,163,266.24

DISBURSEMENT ACCOUNT.

Death-claims and endowments...........	$6,252,095.50
Dividends, annuities and purchased insurance..................................	5,869,026.16
Total paid policy-holders.............	12,121,121.66

These figures are impressive and would be even more so were it not for their magnitude, which prevents their being entirely comprehended. For instance the total income for the year of 1889, over twenty-nine millions of

dollars, is too huge to be appreciated, but its significance becomes evident when it is learned that it amounts to nearly one-fifth of the total income of all the life companies. Look for a moment at the summary for the 45 years' business. Received from policy-holders in premiums, $207,679,689.43 ; premiums for annuities, $15,846,595.06 ; Total from policy holders, $223,526,284.49 Payments to policy-holders and their representatives with assets now held as security for policies in force exceeds the amount received from policy-holders, $10,871,375.31. Interest, rentals, etc., $52,868,009.94 ; death-losses paid, $50,040,257.60 ; interest and rents exceed death losses paid, $2,827,-812.34. Assets, $105,053,000.96 ; surplus, $15,600,000.00. Wm. H. Beers, the president, has been connected with the Co. from its infancy, advancing step by step from clerk to cashier, actuary, vice-president, to his present position. First vice-president, Henry Tuck : second vice president, A. H. Welch ; and actuary Rufus W. Weeks, have all reached their present positions by advancement step by step. With such an administrative staff of officers, the company have and are always advancing the interests of its policy-holders and when we consider the fact, that the amount of its endowment and annuity policies is larger by more than forty millions of dollars, its forms of policies and the results more satisfactory than any other company, it speaks volumes for the executive ability of its officers. The New England Branch, located at Boston, Mass., comprising the New England States, excepting Vermont, is under the supervision of Major Ben. S. Calef, one of the oldest and most prominent life underwriters of Massachusetts, with Hon. D. P. Kingsley—late insurance commissioner of Colorado—as inspector of agencies. Messrs. Crowell & McKellar will be happy to give full and detailed information upon application, and will gladly furnish the actual results of policies which have matured and been settled in 1889, and mail communications will be promptly and carefully attended to.

Popular Loans

are loans to avoid — there is always a better **use** for money.

A short crisp sentence may not have the whole of the truth in it; but it is likely to carry more of the truth to the reader's mind than a circumstantial statement.

Competition for loans in the west results in lending too much, and lending too much—we all know what that leads to.

The typical Western spirit is one of great cheerfulness. There is no such word as "fail" in the local vocabulary. The Westerner promises anything, mortgages everything. Rate per cent has no terrors for him, if only you lend him money enough.

When a dozen lenders bid for his loan the one that bids most is the one that gets it—perhaps that loan is a good one. Keep out of the dozen.

How? By looking ahead instead of behind; by seeing the present condition of things at least; by using your eyes instead of your ears. The majority, even of lenders, lean on others. The current opinion, even of lenders, is always late.

But this is for us, not you.

For you there is this one maxim: Choose a lender you can trust; and trust him.

We have a primer designed to meet the wants, the real wants, not the whims, of a man or woman with money to lend—no matter how little or much. Shall we send it?

THE KANSAS CITY INVESTMENT COMPANY.

EDWARD E. HOLMES, President, Treasurer, and Western Manager, Kansas City.
WILLIS G. MYERS, Vice-President and Eastern Manager, Portsmouth.

Kansas City, Missouri.   Hartford, Conn.   Omaha, Nebraska.   Beloit, Kansas.
Portsmouth, New Hampshire.   Office John Jeffries & Sons, Boston.   Toledo, Ohio.   Dallas, Texas.

www.ingramcontent.com/pod-product-compliance
Lightning Source LLC
Chambersburg PA
CBHW021424090426
42742CB00009B/1240